*GROWTH OF
AN AMERICAN
INVENTION*

Recent Titles in
Contributions to the Study of Education

GROWTH OF AN AMERICAN INVENTION

A DOCUMENTARY HISTORY
OF THE JUNIOR
AND COMMUNITY
COLLEGE MOVEMENT

THOMAS DIENER

CONTRIBUTIONS TO THE STUDY OF EDUCATION, NUMBER 16

GREENWOOD PRESS
NEW YORK • WESTPORT, CONNECTICUT • LONDON

Library of Congress Cataloging in Publication Data

Diener, Thomas.
  Growth of an American invention.

  (Contributions to the study of education,
ISSN 0196-707X ; no. 16)
  Bibliography: p.
  Includes index.
  1. Junior colleges—United States—History.
2. Community colleges—United States—History.
I. Title. II. Series.
LB2327.D53 1986   378'.1543   85-9832
ISBN 0-313-24993-8 (lib. bdg. : alk. paper)

Library of Congress Catalog Card Number: 85-9832
ISBN: 0-313-24993-8
ISSN: 0196-707X

First published in 1986

Greenwood Press, Inc.
88 Post Road West, Westport, Connecticut 06881

Printed in the United States of America

The paper used in this book complies with the
Permanent Paper Standard issued by the National
Information Standards Organization (Z39.48-1984).

10 9 8 7 6 5 4 3 2 1

Copyright Acknowledgments

To

Carolyn

CONTENTS

FOREWORD

> Think as the few, and speak as the many....
> It is the talent of the great to agree with
> the great: a veritable wonder of nature both
> because of its mystery and because of its
> usefulness.
>
> Baltasar Gracian (1653)

One of the really wonderful experiences in learning to
understand democratic values and principles is to
revisit the original documents. Each of us who has had
the experience of reading "When in the course of human
events......" as displayed with original signatures in
its case in Washington, D.C., comes away with a sharper
understanding of why We the People in this nation have
remained dedicated to the expanding values of
democratic government longer than any other nation in
the world today. We can also gain perspective of our
relationships with the other great democracies of the
planet Earth. We can understand the heritage from
whence we came.

It is disturbing to hear educated members of the
legal profession who have been selected to serve in a
political capacity demonstrate that they either have
forgotten that heritage or somehow never really
understood it. One wishes for them an opportunity to
"touch base" with the documents as mentioned above and
to relive vicariously some of the experiences our
predecessors knew in order to reaffirm their faith in a
principle of freedom that was accepted long ago.

This volume performs some of those same services for
those who need to become inspired once again with the
desire to equalize the educational opportunity for all
citizens and to make certain that it happens. It is
disturbing to see presidents of community colleges,

deans of community colleges, or other members of the educational profession who either have forgotten or never knew the background and the commitments that made the community college a necessary and logical addition to the system of higher education that has developed in the United States.

Diener has pulled together into a single volume some of the outstanding documents that are representative of the historical development of the American Community College. As one reviews the growth of higher education in this country one can come to only one logical observation: a major goal, both expressed and unexpressed, but emphasized repeatedly, has been increasing access to higher education and to continuing or lifelong education. The mission of the American college has been to develop leadership for the nation: political leadership, economic leadership, social leadership, religious leadership, and community leadership. This same mission was a major emphasis in the newly developing universities during the nineteenth century. With the democratic emphasis on opening avenues to leadership roles and the need to increase access in order to keep those avenues open to the whole structure of American society, there had to be an ever increasing number of alternative roads to higher and continuing education. The statements of the university presidents of that period emphasize this need and demonstrate that they were concerned.

It is reassuring to read that Henry Tappan of the University of Michigan pointed out that a way of attaining quality in the developing universities was to expand the ability of the colleges to prepare individuals to enter specializations at subsequent university levels and it must naturally follow that clear institutional roles were essential to provide a total system of higher education. A similar concern and related solution was suggested by little known but apparently knowledgeable William Mitchell of Georgia, illustrating that concern for access and quality was not limited to one or two individuals.

Diener could have included quotations from Thomas Jefferson and Pierre du Pont de Nemours in their volume of letters referred to as "National Education in the United States" to illustrate these points even further; he has selected appropriate quotations from the events of the late eighteen hundreds, however, to illustrate the time when the junior college was first being developed. In chronological order the contributions of California and cogent observations of Alexis Lange are examined within a framework of the early development in Chicago and Indiana, resulting in an argument that still permeates the junior/community college field: whether this level of education is secondary or higher

education. Selections from the pioneer researchers in
the field, L.V. Koos, W. C. Eells, and F. M. McDowell,
further support the authenticity of the origins as well
as the value systems of the junior/community colleges.
  The documentation of the kind of support received
from the professional leadership in the federal
government, specifically the Bureau of Education/Office
of Education as reflected in the Truman Commission
report, provides an opportunity to reexamine the
leadership role that such individuals may play. Diener
has selected appropriate documentation for this purpose
as well.
  No single volume can be expected to cover all
possibilities and all areas. Diener has thoughtfully
omitted several important areas for another volume.
The shift to increased state responsibility for
education has affected higher education as well as
elementary and secondary education during the period
since 1945.   The growth of state planning for higher
education in particular has been a major factor in the
rapid growth of the community colleges. A part of that
growth has been the evolvement of a variety of programs
for financing these colleges.   The public community
college has far outstripped those founded, operated,
and supported by private and church-related sources.
Federal concerns as expressed through the congressional
discussions as well as the statutes of the 1950's and
the 1960's need to be documented too. One can see that
a high regard for what Diener has accomplished in this
volume causes plans for the next to be a given. I am
certain we will all look forward to that one as well as
appreciate the value of this one.

June, 1985   James L. Wattenbarger
Gainesville, Florida   Director
                                  Institute of Higher
                                     Education
                                  University of Florida

PREFACE

The design and construction of a book of writings does not proceed smoothly. Whereas one's own thoughts can readily establish the framework for discussion, finding the thoughts of others and fitting them into a coherent whole requires more than a little mental agility.

Half the task is producing a conceptual frame, a structure by which the reader can note ideas and themes appearing, growing, changing, and perhaps disappearing.

The other half is identifying those writings which will most clearly illustrate those ideas or trends under consideration--the work of a sleuth!

Appreciation is given to all who assisted with this enterprise. Some, like Dr. Walter Sindlinger of Teachers College, Columbia University, scarcely knew of their influence. Others, like many graduate students in classes at the University of Georgia and the University of Alabama, were of assistance in choosing issues and reviewing materials directly applicable to this book.

To all those who supported and stimulated this work, may they rejoice in its benefits. For errors or omissions, I accept full responsibility.

Thomas Diener

INTRODUCTION

The purpose of this volume is to present carefully selected and important materials about the junior and community college movement in this country--materials long ago forgotten, or rarely known, or difficult for the present-day scholar to find.

The book's design is primarily chronological. Those first initiatives which today we view as the beginning of the junior and community college movement were then hazy, tentative ideas or activities, a part of the continuing efforts at renewal and reform of American education in the 19th century. Especially after the Civil War, the enlargement of the public sector of education, the creation of the high school and the modern American university, the press of serving newly urbanized students, the increasing fragmentation of the job structure in the United States--all these and more stimulated a range of internal changes in American schools and higher education institutions.

Part I addresses itself to that exciting and rather rambunctious period when high schools pushed up, colleges pushed down, universities tried to separate themselves from general education, and new, often technical institutes or schools of science appeared. All these developed in an effort to better serve the American public and its growing thirst for knowledge.

In Part II, organizations calling themselves junior colleges are recognized. From about 1900 until the 1920's, sufficient numbers of institutions were formed and students served that accrediting agencies and state departments of education took notice. A national study was conducted of this phenomenon, and by 1920 a national meeting was held of junior college leaders. A new chapter of American education was being written.

Part III of this volume picks up the story of junior

college development in the 1930's.   In this part are
highlights of the effects of the depression, post-World
War II federal interest, and emergence of a new concept
and form of the junior college--the community college.
Recurring issues comprise Part IV.   These include
questions of access to higher education, programs for a
diversity of students, and concerns about quality,
opportunity, ideology, and mission.

This is not just a textbook on the junior and
community college. First, it is a documentary history,
limited to those relatively few and unique written
statements which can be found which help complete a
panoramic view of the growth of junior and community
colleges in this country.   Second,   there are themes--
like curriculum, governance, finance, instruction,
services to students and community, technical or career
education--any one of which might alone command the
attention of a book the size of this one and all of
which are valuable to study.   These themes can only be
highlighted here.

The junior and community college movement is now, in
the late 20th century, so vast, so complex, no one
volume can completely capture all its dimensions.
These materials aim to illumine selected and essential
elements of the present and future by looking at the
past.   Those themes mentioned earlier existed at the
beginning of the junior and community college movement;
they will continue to exist through its life. Brought
together here is evidence about certain of these trends
and the beliefs, thoughts, and motives of those
laboring to, first, improve American education and,
second, create a new educational entity.   It brings
into one place hard-to-locate materials important to a
realistic understanding of the growth of junior and
community colleges in this country.   It furnishes, in
its totality, a comprehensive view of this remarkable
American social invention.

GROWTH OF
AN AMERICAN
INVENTION

GROWTH OF AN AMERICAN INVENTION: FROM JUNIOR TO COMMUNITY COLLEGE

The Age of the College--from the founding of Harvard through the Civil War.

The Age of the University--from the 1870's through World War II.

The Age of the Junior and Community College--from the 1960's through the last decades of the 20th century . . . and beyond?

Is this an accurate way to categorize American higher education? Does it help us understand some fundamental changes in the structure and mission of higher education in the United States? In broad strokes, this schema delineates major emphases in American higher education and points to underlying social transformations crucial to the development of our nation. In the beginnings of our country, men of learning, wealth, and power pushed for the creation of colleges and universities to serve private and public purposes. For the private good, they yearned for a college education which would mold the character of young men and give them the classical learnings then thought to be so essential to a cultivated and elegant gentleman. For the public good, this prescribed classical curriculum served very well to prepare the young male citizen for responsible leadership in government and the professions of law, medicine, and the ministry.

These early colleges, designed primarily on the basis of European and English progenitors, wore familiar garb: a prescribed and classical curriculum generally of four years in length. They served familiar faces: those of young men often from the families of the elite and affluent. They served a familiar purpose: to transmit the body of knowledge and values deemed important in those days to the potential leaders of the

oncoming generation. The popularity of these colleges
was extremely high. Their presence served an emerging
society in important ways. They meant leadership for
these shores could be educated here. They stood for
the growing strength of the colonies. And, these seats
of learning, spurred by the spirit of the Revolution,
became important symbols for new peoples creating a new
land. At one and the same time they stood for the
creation of a new political entity, a new nation
(unity), and for the diverse religious and social
values so vital to immigrants to these shores
(pluralism).

Rumblings of change, however, were reverberating
throughout the world. Discoveries in the natural
sciences, the forces of industrialization,
urbanization, and immigration, rising equalitarianism,
the increasing secularization of society--all these and
many more forces were producing a new nation with
special opportunities for personal advancement. The
United States of the late 19th century was moving
toward a more cohesive and centralized society. The
ties of the railroad, the lines of the telegraph, the
advent of the airplane and automobile were more than
man-made creations. They symbolized the shift of this
country from a collection of hunters, pioneers, and
small farmers into a more interdependent and urban
society; they stood for an era of large industrial and
business enterprises . . . and a nation preparing to
step into the 20th century and the dawning of the
technological age.

It was time for a change in colleges, too. The
fervent boosterism of earlier days had produced a
plethora of tiny, often isolated higher education
institutions, many of which were hardly worthy of the
lustrous names they gave themselves. Some critics of
the day looked to other shores, looked to the roots of
the new American society and its educational
enterprises, seeking enlightenment for reform in the
United States. Especially attractive was the German
university (indeed, the whole of the German educational
system pleased many, too!) with its emphasis on
scholarship, faculty specialization, and research.
Here was an educational enterprise fit for the
times--an enterprise of knowledge production, not
just knowledge transmittal. The spirit of the
scientific approach which urged delving into all
corners and dimensions of our world, the belief
that rational inquiry could and would not only
drive out ignorance but provide new ways to solve
human and social problems, this mental set toward
human manipulation and domination of the environment
fit hand in glove with the argument advanced
by many that a university, German style, should

be built atop many colleges spread about the
nation.

The view from abroad was not the only alternative.
Another version of what American higher education might
become sprang from efforts to mechanize, indeed
industrialize, not only our cities but our farms. For
example, passage in 1862 of the Morrill Act, calling
for the establishment in each state of higher education
institutions dedicated to instruction in agriculture
and the mechanic arts, helped crack the monopoly the
Middle Ages-based classical curriculum held on American
higher education. True, this act did not completely
transform the curriculum in an instant, nor did it
totally obliterate the traditional and classical
courses. But the seeds of change were planted with
vigor. And they grew rapidly.

From it eventually came new kinds of faculty with
vocational interests, with research interests, with
interests in reaching out to the people of their states
and regions and helping individuals and groups work on
problems and issues affecting their work and their
communities. From it eventually came new courses in
the social sciences, in natural science, in
agriculture, engineering, and business. These courses
tended toward the practical, presenting learning which
might be applied in emerging vocations, which met
immediate needs of the society. From it eventually
came new structures for learning. Graduate and
professional schools were initiated, experiment
stations created. Schools of science were launched,
often to be incorporated into developing university
structures, sometimes to become independent, free-
standing universities of science and technology.

The land-grant movement was not the sole instigator
of collegiate change. Other forces, in and out
of higher education, were also prompting the
transition from College Era to University Era.
Professionalization of the faculty with an emphasis on
knowledge production, development of an elective system
by which undergraduates could exercise more control
over their programs of study, the development of
business and industry-allied professions and,
concomitantly, programs of education for these
professions, the emerging public junior high school and
high school, increased emphasis on vocational training
and engineering education, the creation of complex
business and industrial enterprises, some spanning the
nation in their influence and organization, increasing
currents of power flowing to the federal government
with its consequences for national intervention in
education--these several trends illustrate the broad
scope and complex nature of the changes in the social
fabric of our nation and its educational agencies.

Thus, the Age of the University drew its strength from both the transformation of American society and the international as well as national concepts of what higher education might be.

The Age of the University in the United States produced (as supporters of the German university concept had so hoped) a grand array of scientific investigations.   Scholarship and inquiry advanced in the natural sciences, in medicine, in the social sciences, in the humanities, in agriculture, engineering, and business and commerce; scarcely a field of human endeavor was exempt from the analytical review of the university researcher-teacher.   The knowledge explosion of the 20th century was aided mightily by the American university with its rapidly expanding force of highly trained specialists, its laboratories and experiment stations, and its sophisticated means for designing and managing complex research efforts.   Indeed, World War II and, in its wake, the rebuilding of Europe and Japan, along with the requirements of the developing nations of the world, further accelerated the dramatic growth and influence of higher education in the United States, especially the research-oriented university.

In view of this scenario, is it presumptuous to now speak of an Age of the Junior and Community College? One which might follow the Age of the University? One which might mark a major new era of educational development in this country?   Let us examine this unique development in the United States.

The configuration of the first junior colleges is not known precisely.   Courses taught, faculty characteristics, organizational structure, and many other features remain largely a part of a hazy, time-dimmed past.   Yet, as one reviews carefully the actual and proposed changes in American education, by very late in the 19th century one can discern certain fundamental issues emerging which would constitute characteristics or themes of the junior college: the debate over the definition, nature, and scope of secondary education; the promulgation of the associate degree; university efforts to separate general from specialized learning.   For example, in view of the earlier growth of numerous small, usually private, colleges on the American scene, by the late 19th century the recently established U.S. Office of Education and its Commissioner of Education saw the plight of many of these institutions and began to call for reorganization of American higher education and for stronger evidence of quality collegiate-level instruction.   By the early years of the 20th century, the U.S. Office of Education even dared identify a few

standards which a "real" college must meet. Attempts
to publish a list of these "real" colleges were quickly
quashed by strong political as well as educational
forces.
   By the second decade of the 20th century, colleges
were dropping some of their years of instruction (often
for lack of students in the upper classes rather than
as any genuine attempt to be educational pioneers),
high schools were adding 13th and 14th years to their
curricula, technical or vocational schools were also
attempting some collegiate-level instruction, and a few
major universities had redesigned their undergraduate
programs to draw distinctions (at least on paper)
between the "junior college," or first two years, and
the "senior college," or last two years of a four-year
liberal arts baccalaureate program.   Regional
accrediting agencies had begun the tedious task of
sorting out collegiate from precollegiate, secondary
from higher education. Later years brought even more
diversity to the "junior college" ranks--university
two-year extension centers, temporary federally
supported emergency colleges activated during the
depression of the 1930's, two-year finishing schools
primarily for young women, federally established
colleges (e.g., in the Canal Zone and, much later, the
Community College of the Air Force), normal schools for
teachers, privately owned two-year colleges, and, of
course, the comprehensive community colleges.
   One reason the junior college in the United States
has been difficult to understand is that it has taken
on so many forms of sponsorship and control. Is the
junior college a high school and a part of secondary
education? Is it collegiate and a part of higher
education? Is it a unique educational enterprise
standing apart from both of these worlds yet, at the
same time, able to link them in new and constructive
ways? Answers, at times cool and rational, at times
rendered with some passion, have been offered in the
affirmative to all three of these questions. While
debates over definition and organizational form have
waxed and waned, leaving not a few educators and
probably most citizens perplexed (if concerned at all
with these issues), a core of functions began to
emerge, a core which, in the main, helped determine the
essence of a junior college.
   Certainly early on, the concept of the junior college
as a shortened version of a regular or four-year
liberal arts college held great attraction. Thus, the
two-year college offering the freshman and sophomore
courses seemed most advantageous. The courses were a
known commodity, they served a good purpose in
supplying young citizens with what many educators
regarded as the basic general liberal education, and,

best of all, with careful monitoring, students could transfer these course credits to a senior college or university, at which point they would begin their specialized or professional studies. To a lesser extent, the provision of a general education useful to many citizens was an early junior college function; to a greater extent, the intent to provide a college transfer program--one which provided the two-year general education component of a four-year liberal arts program--was a legitimate, indeed laudable, function. To this day these first two functions continue as important parts of junior and community college work.

Another function, guidance and counseling of students, also has a long history in the junior college. If students were enrolled in these institutions but expected to actually complete their work elsewhere, the college had responsibilities to help those students succeed at the junior college and move smoothly to the university. So, directly related to the early instructional program was a complementary noninstructional activity, that of student guidance.

As the junior colleges of the United States grew in number and importance another basic function emerged. This one had to do with the emerging employment needs of our nation. As the country became more heavily industrialized, as business and commerce expanded, the need for trained technicians, accountants, and clerical personnel increased rapidly. Even women who might spend their time as homemakers needed, some felt, to have education beyond the high school, education in the domestic and homemaking arts. Some early junior colleges began their work as technical and vocational colleges. More likely an institution beginning as a junior college would add vocational programs to its existing transfer programs. The vocational or job training function became, especially by the 1930's, an important portion of the mission of many junior colleges.

Following World War II the junior college expanded still further its basic set of functions. Beyond the general education, transfer, guidance, and vocational education functions, society was demanding greater access for all citizens to higher education, greater opportunity for technical and job skill learning, greater availability of programs and services for adults, not just the youth of our nation, and institutions which not only were locally controlled but drew their inspiration, their spirit for being, from their clientele. The clientele, as the century progressed, tended more and more to be "the public"-- thus public schools and school districts, public colleges, and even specially created public junior college districts were established.

Services to adults in the community did not mean sacrificing those original and more traditional functions; it meant adding a new range of services. It also meant opening the collegiate door to more women, to blacks, hispanics, and other minority members, to working men and women who needed to upgrade their job skills or broaden their avocational interests, to retirees and those making mid-life career changes, to citizens interested in the economic or cultural or political development of their community.

The other wing of this new function--community service--might include some of the aspects of adult education named above, but it also meant more. It was a way by which the junior college, a product of the community, became a means for the community to examine itself, its strengths and weaknesses, its aspirations. So the college engaged in community surveys, formed education-community or education-work councils, and initiated other means by which the local community analyzed its political, economic, educational, or cultural needs. In turn, the junior college also became a central figure in community discussions on how to create a new future, how to solve some of its problems. This attitude of participation in community life and development, this proactive stance toward not only individual learning but community reformation, left outmoded the name and concept of the junior college.

Finally, the junior college became known for the development and provision of remedial or compensatory education. Given the post-World War II "open door" philosophy of admissions to education, two-year institutions attracted a wide range of human talent--including many students who aspired to higher education but did not have the requisite academic preparation (oftentimes despite the award of a high school diploma). Older adults as well as younger students saw the junior-becoming-community college as a ready point of access to higher learning. The colleges, in turn, found themselves struggling to take virtually all learners, regardless of educational level or competence, and prepare them for advanced study.

Difficult task that it was, the fast-changing junior college ventured into these rarely charted educational waters. These new community colleges abandoned the traditional notion in higher education that quality was defined by the high numbers of persons denied admission or the high rate of academic failure among those admitted. The concept of adding value--taking the learner where he or she is and promoting tangible academic success--became a mission, a hallmark, of the two-year community college movement.

The public, two-year, comprehensive community college

(called by a variety of names, including technical
college and junior community college) became the
dominant model, the mid-20th-century model, of the
junior college. A number of private junior colleges
survive today.   So do large numbers of institutions
whose primary focus is on career training.   But the
predominant modern form of the junior college is the
public community college, regardless of name, whose
mission embraces all of the functions just described.
That is the institution most often found in our large
urban centers, most often serving the first-time and
minority college student, most often the major two-
year-college supplier of educational services to
persons and communities in the late 20th century. The
impact of the community college by the 1980's is
dramatic and massive: it enrolls over one of every
three students in American higher education and over
half of all entering freshmen.

     What forces supported and nourished this growth of
the junior and, later, the community college? First,
much of American education in the 19th and early 20th
centuries was enamored with ideas coming from the
rising tide of industrialization and free enterprise.
The United States, land of opportunity, gave public and
private entrepreneurs alike the chance to succeed.
Faith in the efficacy of education was a leading light
in the building of the nation.   So colleges and
universities sprang up, especially in the 19th century,
very quickly and very frequently.   A kind of social
Darwinism was at work, prompting one and all to have a
go at starting a college.   Americans responded with
vigor and pride. Those institutions which met the
challenge survived.   Survival was the measure of
quality.
     At the same time, the movement toward efficiency in
business and industry was making its inroads in
education, too. Many of the reformers in higher
education saw the excesses a policy of complete
laissez-faire would bring--a breakdown in adherence to
standards of excellence and an extreme and deleterious
dedication to growth and expansion.   Whether from a
desire to espouse quality education or efforts to shut
off competition (or both), early university reformers
of higher education like William Rainey Harper of
Chicago, David Starr Jordan at Stanford, and Alexis
Lange at California urged reorganization to bring about
efficiency and eliminate waste.   Their efforts helped
promote the junior college as a social and educational
device prompting efficiency and order.   Efforts to
reshape and restyle the American university were
important in creating a climate, and indeed a form, for
the junior college. The undergraduate college in some

cases was divided in half to create a junior college and senior college. While more active as an idea than in actual practice, this concept had powerful repercussions in giving credibility to the notion of junior (general) versus senior (specialized) education.

The weakening and demise of many of the four-year colleges launched in the 19th century also added strength to the call for higher education reform. Many colleges were struggling for existence, had limited facilities and faculties, and, often, scarcely any students in the junior and senior classes. Regular colleges were, in fact, often junior colleges. The more efficient use of resources prompted educational leaders such as Philander Priestly Claxton, U.S. Commissioner of Education in the second decade of the 20th century, to urge weak senior colleges to become stronger institutions by shedding the last two years of course offerings and becoming authentic junior colleges.

The public high school was another force supporting the growth of the junior college. The Kalamazoo case of 1874 established the principle of supporting public education with public monies. The rapid increase in public high schools laid the foundation for further expansion of educational opportunities. Pride in their communities and their high schools motivated educators to look for additional ways to serve their eager new constituencies. The lure of university leaders eager to push onto and into the secondary school curricula the so-called general education of the freshman and sophomore years of college was hard to resist. Particularly in California and throughout the Midwest, the early 20th century saw numerous examples of high schools pointing proudly to their new plans and programs which offered the 13th and 14th grades to qualified students.

Hand in hand with this rise of the secondary school was a change in the structure of employment opportunities. Early in the 20th century technological developments adopted by American business and industry created fewer jobs for unskilled youth. Machines were displacing workers in large numbers. These changing job requirements demanding more highly skilled workers gave impetus to the work of the junior college. Many youths enrolled in vocational courses in high school. But this training was often insufficient or outmoded; prospective workers needed more adequate preparation for the new jobs being created in business and industry. The training needs of the U.S. economy provided a strong push for the establishment of technical junior colleges and the inclusion of technical and business programs in the curricula of existing junior colleges.

National and regional agencies and procedures were still another force guiding the emergence of the junior college. The U.S. Office of Education was never an accreditation agency, but its reporting standards, with rare exception, helped frame definitions of junior colleges as institutions of higher education, not secondary education. So, too, did the early efforts of the American Association of Junior Colleges. More powerful in their effects were the efforts of regional and state accrediting agencies charged with the responsibility of insuring some semblance of quality in educational institutions. The regional agencies--in particular, educators attempting to police their own institutions and offerings--viewed the emerging junior college movement as just that--primarily a college-level course of study and not a high school. Although often housed in high school buildings, early policies of regional accreditation agencies were quite explicit in outlining how junior college programs were to be separate and distinct from secondary school programs.

Lastly, a major drive in the United States--the extension of educational access to more and more citizens--was of special import for the development of the junior (by now becoming a community) college. A movement in American higher education has been from the notion of college-as-fortress to one of college-as-service-provider. What has transpired in the development of common schools and the secondary schools, the provision of increasingly diverse programs and services for an increasingly diverse student body, has been mirrored in higher education. The junior college, at first a copy of a portion of the elitist university, began to widen its course offerings. It expanded in its types of students served. The inclusion of vocational programs and daughters as well as sons of blue-collar workers began the transformation of the junior college to the community college.

The great surge of transformation, however, awaited the consequences of the cataclysm of World War II (and resultant education boom energized by the GI Bill) and the pricking of the national conscience in such events as Brown vs. Board of Education, the civil rights movement of the 1960's, and the leadership of Martin Luther King, Jr. The political pull for expanded educational opportunities for the poor, the disadvantaged, and minorities came strongly and principally from many federal sources: legislation, executive orders, and federal task forces, all urging the expansion of American higher education to serve new clientele. The community college was proposed as a major entry point for the growing masses of American citizens who wished advanced education beyond the high school. The push for expanded educational opportunity came as women, minority groups, the handicapped, those with little or no prior experience with higher education, those seeking middle management and technical jobs surged forward in search of higher education credentials. Thus, the concept of the open door college, or democracy's college, became the means by which access to educational opportunity was established for all Americans. The two-year community college was the chief vehicle by which this was accomplished. The open door college was committed to all graduates of the American high school, to offering a wide variety of educational programs, and to serving the fast growing numbers of a diverse student body.

Was the coming of the community college an unblemished achievement? Was its influence all for the good? Were there no flaws in its concepts and execution of its programs? Some critics maintain that the community college tried to be all things to all people. In good economic times perhaps society could afford to offer something of everything to everyone. When economic hard times strike, what must give way? Would the traditionally free or low tuition fees remain free or low, thus serving the poor? Would adult programs or community services not carrying traditional academic credit be eliminated? Would the community college become simply a technical school?

What of academic standards? Is it a service to provide an open door for the admission of virtually all who would seek entrance to higher education only to have that open door become a revolving door--easy in, easy out? Has easy access and the attempt to provide educational opportunity actually been a ruse by which academics have been able to lower their expectations for student performance? Or inflated their grades to make higher education not only accessible but painless and failure proof? And if lowered standards have prevailed, what does this mean for businesses and industries and our nation as a whole, which rely on increasing levels of job expertise and citizen skills?

Are the community colleges simply educational systems for the further manipulation of the poor, the minorities of our society, our lower socioeconomic class citizens? Are they a hoax appearing to offer access and opportunity when in fact offering mediocre training for dead-end jobs? Are they a pacifier to divert the attention of the poor and disadvantaged from their lot in life and prepare them to labor contentedly in the lower echelons of a technological world? Materials toward the end of Part IV of this book raise serious concerns about the capability of these institutions to extend quality educational opportunity and cast doubt on their future directions and vitality.

The evidence is mixed. The scholar must be cautious in framing a response to these troublesome questions. Perhaps some builders of the junior and community college movement saw it more as a way of keeping unsullied the halls of the university (that is, of excluding the poor, minority persons, and women) than as a democratic device for the uplifting of large sectors of our population. Some community colleges have promised more than they could deliver; misleading statements of intent have damaged sincere attempts to work with disadvantaged learners. Academic standards of quality have at times been diluted and grades inflated as a way of coping with the flood of new students in community colleges.
Upon long reflection, however, and after careful review of all the evidence (collected here as well as that found in many other places), I believe the two-year college movement stands for more victories than defeats, more successes than failures. The junior and community college is an important American invention which, despite imperfections, was and is remarkably effective. While all of American higher education has broadened its vision of who should be taught what and how, the community college has been the principal way by which the United States, in the post-World War II era, has in fact offered valid and expanding educational opportunities to increasing portions of our citizenry.

What trends have been evident in the 20th century development of the junior and community college?
Certainly the locus of control has swung sharply from private to public control. The early junior colleges usually were private, and they remained the dominant model of organization really until World War II (although the public sector enrolled the majority of two-year college students by the 1920's). This had many implications for the two-year college movement, first, by helping establish junior colleges as part of higher education rather than as part of secondary education. Secondly, though, it meant the early planning and perpetuation of a more traditional and standard collegiate curriculum. The emergence of the public two-year college signaled a greater sensitivity to a greater diversity of students and the need for a more comprehensive curriculum.
Another trend was the enlargement of the curriculum from an early reliance on the standard freshman and sophomore or general education college offerings to an increase in vocational and career-oriented courses and programs. American societal and business needs were changing rapidly; the two-year colleges began to offer more and more opportunities for job training and

retraining. Increasingly, learners were workers first, students second.

Coincident with this change in American job structure and requirements was a rising expectation on behalf of civic education. Being a good citizen, and trying to define what that entailed, was a priority matter for the early 20th century in the United States. Public schools were struggling with this concept, and the junior college was seen as a part of the educational apparatus by which active citizenship was defined, instilled, and inspired. The role of the community college in the Americanization of post-Vietnam War immigrants indicates this is still an important function.

The trend first toward local establishment and control of the junior college and more recently toward more state-wide coordination and control is of great importance. The early literature of the junior college makes almost sacred the theme of local control. And, indeed, part of the genius of the movement was that it sprang from a variety of environments and was dedicated to meeting those particular local needs. That theme is still strong today. Late in the 20th century, however, the move toward centralization in many areas of our society is also strong. The economics of recession forces states to look very closely at the use of scarce resources and plan for greater coordination and, in many places, control. State-wide systems of community colleges have tempered the educational individualism and localism of an earlier day.

Along with the rest of the nation, junior and community colleges have moved to town. Urbanization has directly affected two-year institutions. The mid-century decades have seen not only the development of state systems of colleges but a rapid increase in massive, metropolitan, multi-campus systems. Like the colleges and universities ahead of them, junior colleges tended to begin in rural and small-town settings. By the late 20th century, the people and, therefore, large community college enrollments were in the large urban and suburban areas of the United States.

The community college movement has made a distinct turn from single purpose institutions to colleges with a range of purposes and programs. The first junior colleges saw the transfer function as their sole purpose--serve the university and serve it well by careful preparation of students for study in the junior and senior years. That noble purpose was useful but limited. As the junior college concept matured so did its view of its mission (to educate persons for jobs, to serve adults, to enroll part-time students, to provide community services, to be a "second chance" college, to offer guidance and counseling services, to be a point of educational access for women and minorities). Consequently, the junior college has become a multi-purpose institution.

Along with this expansion in purposes has emerged a change in student clientele and campus climate. Even today remnants remain of some early junior college notions of elitism. Small enclaves still exist where a classical curriculum is taught to a carefully screened and selected group of students. By and large, however, the drive toward egalitarianism in American society has produced a wide variety in students and their learning environments. The community college and its faculty serve the widest range of student ages, abilities, and interests of any institution in American higher education. It represents the American-built opportunity for a greater variety of individuals to develop and cultivate their talents and skills more fully than any other educational institution. It is the setting in which part-time, low-income, and working citizens enjoy equal educational opportunity with their full-time, middle-class, and affluent counterparts. The community college is truly the "people's college" for it serves young and old, educated or illiterate, U.S. citizen, immigrant, refugee, or international student, Ph.D. holder or seeker of a G.E.D. (high school equivalency certificate). And it serves all these clientele by design.

Lastly, the modern community college faces issues of accountability not dreamed of by its pioneers. Little was done to hold early American colleges accountable for their programs and services. Governing boards, presidents, and faculties went about their business secure in the knowledge that they, especially the faculty, knew what was important to be taught. Even the lay board, a distinctive feature of American higher education, did little to determine educational programs and courses. The college, in the person of the faculty, held sway.

Then came the business and industrial revolution of the late 19th century, the surge of public education in the early 20th century. Employers, students, farmers, minority groups, women, workers, unions, civic organizations, and others pressed higher education more closely for relevant and practical and technological programs. As the public paid more of the educational bills, had more sons and daughters enrolled, became more and more vocal and concerned about educational services, the cry for accountability grew louder.

Consumer groups, accrediting agencies, federal bureaus, civil rights activists, and modern concepts of goal-oriented management helped create an aura in which the public community college not only could but should reveal its means of organization, program development, financing, and control.   Beyond that, accountability meant actively pursuing and using a range of citizen, employer, and student representatives to help develop institutional policies and service.

Perhaps this is the most American feature of this American invention: that the community college is of the people, by the people, and for the people.   It arises from the aspirations and faith of the people of a locale or state; it holds itself open to rapid change; it adapts and reshapes its organization and offerings in response to changing societal needs.

Is consideration of an Age of the Junior and Community College useful in a study of the history of American higher education? I believe it is.   The American college, as a model, is still lively; so is the American university.   Together their members constitute major segments of a higher education enterprise admired and imitated around the world.   But the transformation of American secondary and higher education in the last 100 years has produced a new institution--the junior and community college.   The American college and university have been joined by a third major type of institution, enlarging and expanding the mission and scope of American education beyond the high school.   I believe we see now that the advent of the Age of the Junior and Community College signaled the opening of another and distinctive chapter in the evolutionary development of American higher education.

PART I.
CHALLENGING THE
EDUCATIONAL STATUS QUO

Nineteenth-century higher education saw the seeds of change sown
and cultivated for reform of American education. The colonial
colleges of the 1600's and 1700's, antedating the very founding of
a United States of America, were New World re-creations of
European and English models. Their curricula and style mimicked
their transatlantic origins as faithfully as possible. But not
for long. European models themselves were changing. The
influence of the great American continent, immigrant populations,
the rise of science and technology, of individualism all served to
jar existing and traditional notions about who should be
educated . . . and how . . . and about what.

Henry Tappan's insightful treatise of 1851 speaks not so much
to the virtues of the old but the needs of the new. He sees the
German university, with its emphasis on graduate and specialized
studies, as a desirable future direction for American higher
education. The American college, copied from the English,
provides preparatory studies for young students (as does the
German gymnasium). These colleges are necessary in that they
serve to identify, screen, and prepare young men to undertake the
rigors of a university education. What the country needs in mid-
century and the years ahead, Tappan argues, is a series of
universities (pinnacles of perfection, he feels, in the hierarchy
of education) so that the spirit of scholarship may inspire men to
make themselves "learned and wise" and ready to perform "every
great and good work" in service, religion, or government. In
essence, then, let the college prepare youngsters for the
university--where mature men may achieve the apex of learning!

We see this same attitude displayed even more sharply, and
indeed put into practice, in succeeding events. For example, the
University of Georgia, before the Civil War, makes an attempt to
separate "the men from the boys," to establish a university life-
style quite distinctive from college studies. Henry Barnard, U.S.
Commissioner of Education, is asked by the Congress to recommend
changes for education in the District of Columbia. His ideas

foretell of junior college work in his concept of "superior" or extended secondary education.

By the 1880's, John Burgess, dean of Columbia College in New York City, bemoans the overloading of collegiate education with university specializations. He argues for adding two or three years of academic work to the high schools, with graduates of those institutions then well prepared to move immediately to the university. Burgess also saw sharp differences between the curriculum of the gymnasium (or extended high school education) and that of the university.

The material on Lewis Institute, allegedly one of the first junior colleges, illustrates the search to provide practical education to help young men and women prepare for work in an increasingly mechanized society (the dream of its founder, Allen Lewis). At the same time, students should have "literary work" to prepare them as citizens and to enter advanced studies at a university (the dream of the Institute's first director, George Carman).

Thus, the seeds of junior college education are sown. They are not planted primarily in an effort to increase educational opportunity for American citizens, to provide new career training options, or even to "meet the needs of students"--all firmly established goals in our society in the 20th century. They are sown because of discontent with inflexible classical higher education forms imported into this country. These forms of education are not adjusting to the changes needed by a growing and dynamic United States of America. Among many efforts at reform, a particularly strong feeling of some leading educators is that the German concept of a university should be the capstone for American higher education. Extant colleges should not attempt to be both college (or pre-university training school) and university.

As we shall see shortly, university advocates often felt small colleges and high schools should become preparatory schools for the universities. Among high school leaders, evidence is strong that some, at least, welcomed this challenge and took steps to offer pre-university courses of study. The Goshen, Indiana, "junior college" noted in Part II is a prime example.

Particularly helpful background materials for both Parts I and II of this volume are edited by Richard Hofstadter and Wilson Smith in American Higher Education: A Documentary History, 2 vols., Chicago, Ill.: University of Chicago Press, 1961. The documents and the commentaries in this series are sources important to a full understanding of the growth and expansion of higher education in the United States.

John Brubacher and Willis Rudy in Higher Education in Transition, 3rd ed., New York: Harper and Row, 1976, provide a comprehensive general history of higher education in the United States with extensive references to source materials and detailed analyses of the forces prompting reform of postsecondary education.

Finally, a book by John Corson, Governance of Colleges and Universities, New York: McGraw-Hill, 1960, identifies sources *dealing with administration, governance, and institutional characteristics. Especially useful is Appendix B, "Comments on Selected Readings," pp. 187-202, which notes publications dealing with the educational plans of many college and university presidents, some of whom such as William Rainey Harper at the University of Chicago or David Starr Jordan at Stanford University play important roles in the early stages of junior college development.*

1. TAPPAN ON UNIVERSITY EDUCATION

Henry Philip Tappan, named president of the University of Michigan in 1852, much admired the German system of education. In this treatise he envisioned a full-fledged university as a capstone to a state educational system. He drew great distinctions between college and university work. True universities are institutions of research and inquiry; they have the materials, buildings, laboratories, libraries, and faculty required to engage in scholarship. Colleges are institutions of teaching. They focus their efforts on the general education required of all literate persons. Colleges are preparatory to the specialized studies which ought to take place in a university.

The United States, Tappan felt, had many colleges--and not one university as he defined it. Colleges are necessary and useful. They lay the foundations for university study. The United States needs to develop a university which will provide the highest of inquiry and study and provide a fitting capstone to the overall structure of education.

Tappan (b. 1805 in New York; d. 1881) was a teacher, minister, and author. Under his leadership the University of Michigan became a model for later state universities.

Henry Tappan, University Education, New York: G.P. Putnam, 1851 reprinted in New York by Arno Press and The New York Times (1969) as part of a series, American Education: Its Men, Ideas, and Institutions, pp. 43-51. See also Richard Hofstadter and Wilson Smith, American Higher Education: A Documentary History, Vol. II, Chicago, Ill.: The University of Chicago Press, 1961, pp. 488-511, 515-545.

We have spoken of the German Universities as model institutions. Their excellence consists in two things: first, they are purely Universities, without any admixture of collegial tuition. Secondly, they are complete as universities, providing libraries and all other material of learning, and having professors of eminence to lecture on theology, law, and medicine, the philosophical, mathematical, natural, philological, and political sciences, on history and geography, on the history and principles of Art, in fine, upon every branch of human knowledge. The professors are so numerous that a proper division of labor takes place, and every subject is thoroughly discussed. At the University every student selects the courses he is to attend. He is thrown upon his own responsibility and diligence. He is left free to pursue his studies; but, if he wishes to become a clergyman, a physician, a lawyer, a statesman, a professor, or a teacher in any superior school, he must go through the most rigid examinations, both oral and written.

Collegial tuition in the German Universities does not exist, because wholly unnecessary, the student being fully prepared at the Gymnasium before he is permitted to enter the University. Without the Gymnasium the University would be little worth. The course at the Gymnasium embraces a very thorough study of the Latin and Greek languages, a knowledge of the mathematics below the Differential and Integral Calculus, general history, and one or two modern languages besides the German, and Hebrew if the student design to study theology. The examinations are full and severe, the graduations of merit are accurately marked, and no one below the second grade is permitted to enter the University.

The Gymnasia thus guard the entrance of the Universities. Besides, the University course would not be available to him who had not prepared himself for it. It presumes certain attainments, and passes by the elements of the sciences. It is true, indeed, that a student may neglect his opportunities in the University, but then he throws away all hopes of professional life, and of employment in the State.

The Educational System of Germany, and particularly in Prussia, is certainly a very noble one. We cannot well be extravagant in its praise. Thorough in all its parts, consistent with itself, and vigorously sustained, it furnishes every department of life with educated men, and keeps up at the Universities themselves, in every branch of knowledge, a supply of erudite and elegant scholars and authors, for the benefit and glory of their country, and the good of mankind.

In comparing the University system of Germany with

that of England, it is worthy of remark that Germany
has also admirable common-school systems for popular
education, while England is strikingly deficient in
this respect. In the one case properly-developed
University system has reached its natural result of
invigorating general education; in the other the
priestly privilege of a cloistered learning is still
maintained.

The Colleges of America are plainly copied from the
Colleges of the English Universities. The course of
studies, the President and Tutors, the number of years
occupied by the course, are all copied from the English
model. We have seen that in the English Institutions,
the name of University alone remained, while the
collegial or tutorial system absorbed all the
educational functions. In America, while Colleges were
professedly established, they soon assumed a mixed
character. Professors were appointed, but they
discharged only the duty of tutors in the higher grades
of study; so that the tutors were really assistant
professors, or the professors only tutors of the first
rank. Our Colleges alsc have from the beginning
conferred degrees in all the faculties, which in
England belongs only to the University. By
establishing the faculties of Theology, Law, and
Medicine, some of our colleges have approached still
more nearly to the forms and functions of a university.
By assuming the title of University and College
indifferently, as we are prone to do, we seem to
intimate that we have some characteristics belonging to
both, and that we deem it in our power to become
Universities whenever we please. Sometimes the only
advance made to the higher position, is by establishing
a medical school; which, however, has little other
connection with the college than its dependence upon it
for conferring the degree of Doctor of Medicine.

If we understand aright the distinction between a
College and a University, the latter is not necessarily
constituted by collecting together schools under the
different faculties. These may be merely collegial
schools. A University course presumes a preparatory
tutorial course, by which the students have acquired
elementary knowledge, and formed habits of study and
investigation, to an extent sufficient to enable them
to hear the lectures of professors with advantage, to
consult libraries with facility and profit, and to
carry on for themselves researches in the different
departments of literature and science. A University
course may be indefinitely extended at the pleasure of
the student. He may here undertake the fullest
philosophical education possible--passing from one
branch of study to another, and selecting courses of
lectures according to the state of his knowledge, and

the intellectual discipline which he requires; or, having accomplished a satisfactory general education of his powers, he may next, either enter upon professional studies, or devote himself to some particular branch of science as the occupation of his life. In the German Universities any one, whether he designs to give himself wholly to a student's life, or to fit himself for a professor's chair, may, after undergoing the requisite examination, obtain from the faculty to which he belongs, permission to teach, without receiving any compensation, and only as a form of education. The professors extraordinary are selected from these licentiates, and receive a small salary. From these again the professors of the different faculties are usually selected. Every person of these three classes may lecture upon any subject he pleases: but professors are obliged, besides, to lecture on the branches particularly contemplated in their appointment. In this way at a University alone can the intellectual life be varied and enlarged. A University is literally a Cyclopaedia where are collected books on every subject of human knowledge, cabinets and apparatus of every description that can aid learned investigation and philosophical experiment, and amply qualified professors and teachers to assist the student in his studies, by rules and directions gathered from long experience, and by lectures which treat of every subject with the freshness of thought not yet taking its final repose in authorship, and which often present discoveries and views in advance of what has yet been given to the world. In fine, a University is designed to give to him who would study every help that he needs or desires.

A College in distinction from a University is an elementary and a preparatory school. A College may be directly connected with the University, or it may not. Its original connection with the University was partly accidental, and partly necessary. It was necessary to provide convenient habitations for students who flocked to hear the lectures of the doctor or professor. Many of these students might require private tuition, in relation both to preparatory and additional studies, and thus the Colleges would become places of separate study, under masters appointed for that purpose. This must especially have been demanded in the early period of the Universities, when preparatory schools were not common.

In Germany the Gymnasia are really the Colleges. The education which they furnish is more thorough, we believe, than what is obtained at the Colleges of either England or of our own country. In England, schools like that of Rugby, under the late Dr. Arnold, and those of Eton and Westminister; and in America,

those schools commonly called *Academies*, and indeed
other classical schools, are of the nature of a
college, only of a still lower grade, and more
elementary. In passing from the classical school to
the college the studies are not essentially changed,
nor is the kind of discipline. Hence, a student in our
country can prepare at the academy for the second,
third, and even fourth year of collegial study. In
college there are generally greater advantages. What
gives college, however, its chief distinction, is the
power of conferring academical degrees. We may say,
therefore, the academy prepares for the college, and
the college prepares for a degree. In England the
colleges are directly connected with the University.
But, it appears the University has fallen into
desuetude, and colleges alone remain.

In our country we have no Universities. Whatever may
be the names by which we choose to call our
institutions of learning, still they are not
Universities. They have neither the libraries and
materials of learning, generally, nor the number of
professors and courses of lectures, nor the large and
free organization which go to make up Universities.
Nor does the connection of Divinity, Law, and Medical
Schools with them give them this character. For law
and medicine a thorough preparatory classical
discipline is not required. In this respect the last
is the most deficient of the two, and great numbers
receive the academical degree of Doctor of Medicine who
have never received an academical education. The
degree of Doctor of Laws is more sparingly bestowed
than any other; and this, as well as Doctor of
Divinity, is never bestowed introductory to the
entrance upon professional life. The schools of
Theology approach more nearly to the University
character than any other, since a collegial discipline
is generally required preparatory to an entrance
therein.

The course of study in our colleges, copying from the
English, was, at their first institution, fixed at four
years. The number of studies then was far more limited
than at present, and the scholarship was consequently
more thorough and exact. There was less attempted, but
what was attempted was more perfectly mastered, and
hence afforded a better intellectual discipline. With
the vast extension of science, it came to pass that the
course of study was vastly enlarged. Instead of
erecting Universities, we have only pressed into our
four years' course a greater number of studies. The
effect has been disastrous. We have destroyed the
charm of study by hurry and unnatural pressure, and we
have rendered our scholarship vague and superficial.
We have not fed thought by natural supplies of

knowledge.   We have not disciplined mind by guiding it
to a calm and profound activity; but, we have
stimulated acquisition to preternatural exertions, and
have learned, as it were, from an encyclopaedia the
mere names of sciences, without gaining the sciences
themselves.

2. A "Junior College" Plan in Georgia

In 1859, the University of Georgia gave careful consideration to a scheme by William Mitchell, a lawyer and member of the board of trustees, to combine secondary education with the first two years of collegiate study. Too many young boys not sufficiently prepared for the rigors of scholarly study had enrolled in the university. Along with other good reasons this condition prompted the faculty and eventually the governing board to look for alternatives, thus this proposal by Mitchell.

How could the university be reorganized to more clearly separate the preparation of young minds from the pursuit of knowledge? How could the lives of young men be shaped for future leadership, their morals be protected while their intellects were sharpened? A collegiate institute was designed at the University of Georgia to do just that. It proved to be a harbinger of the junior college-senior college structure later put in place by President William Rainey Harper at the University of Chicago.

William L. Mitchell, Programme of an Enlarged Organization of the University of Georgia, Athens, Ga.: Sledge & Chase, printers, 1859, pp. 5-7, 9-12, 14. (This document by Mitchell, chairman of the executive committee of the University of Georgia Board of Trustees, is discussed in detail in T. Diener, "A Junior College Idea at the University of Georgia, 1859," The Georgia Historical Quarterly, Vol. LVI (Spring, 1972), 83-91.)

The Report

--------o--------

In view of the resignation of Dr. Church, [University president] which goes into effect on the first day of next January, and the necessity of presenting the University of Georgia to the people of the State in a manner and with organization calculated to command the confidence of the public; and in order that the Trustees of the College may have time for reflection upon a subject of vast practical importance, and of suggesting amendments thereto, the following Programme of a new and enlarged organization, within the means at present at command of the Board, is respectfully submitted:

I.

To establish an Institute, combining all the instruction given in a well regulated village Academy and the Freshman and Sophomore Classes in College, and having sufficient capacity to board all its pupils from a distance, and observing such constant watchfulness as to secure and protect the morals of its pupils, and advance their education as rapidly and as certainly as their natural endowments and previous training will admit; in a word, so to organize this fundamental future of the whole programme, that the citizen bringing his son or ward here to be trained, will feel that he is as safe or safer than at home, and that his mind will certainly be educated. This is the right of the citizen, and therefore the duty of the Trustees to secure, if practicable. No plan has been suggested that promises so well.

The effort to advance the age of admission into the Freshman Class, is deemed impracticable in the present state of College education in the United States; and it seems to be generally conceded, that boys, at the tender age of fourteen or fifteen, are unfit to be left to themselves, as they are in great measure, under the present College regimen in the United States; and that the foundation of failure, if not of ruin, is laid in the Freshman and Sophomore years of College life--a result that might be anticipated if we had no experience on the subject. And hence, the scheme submitted, contemplates the abolishing of the Freshman and Sophomore classes, and having them instructed in the Institute herein contemplated, and there to remain and be watched over night and day, till fully prepared for the Junior Class, which each pupil of the Institute should be allowed to enter without examination by the College Faculty, upon the certificate of the Faculty of the Institute. -- The Institute should be conducted upon the self-sustaining principle, which it is believed can be done from the start, and that soon it would yield a surplus, after amply paying its Faculty. -- A suitable location within the corporate limits of Athens, and yet sufficiently isolated, can be procured. It has been suggested that the Institute might be properly ranked as a Gymnasium.

II.

To establish a College proper, with only Junior and Senior Classes, each of one year's duration as at present, with the same curriculum as now prescribed, except that these Classes might be relieved of a few studies that more properly belong to the University Schools hereafter to be mentioned; and that more time might thus be given to the seven liberal Arts and Sciences which are regarded as the true training studies for the youthful mind; as, for example, the Law of Nations might very properly be turned over to the Law School; the Professorship of Agriculture taken out of the College proper, and made to con-constitute [sic] one of the University Schools. Thus the students of the College proper, would be advanced in age and education so far as to realise the responsibilities of their position, and be very suitable subjects for that species of government existing in the Colleges of the United States, and have their characters sufficiently formed to insure well-grounded hopes of their success in study, and the maintenance of good morals. For efficient instruction in the College proper, there would be needed the President of the University and four professors. The President, however, should not be confined to the business of instruction. As the head of the Board of Trustees, his energies should be given to the general advancement of all the departments of the Institution; to intercourse with the public; to the entertainment of visitors; in a word, to all the external relations of the Institution--keeping it before the public, and promoting its interests by all the means naturally suggested to one who undertakes the office of a labor of love--and none other is fit for a post so high, so honorable and so useful.

III.

To establish University Schools, each independent of the other, and also of the College proper, so far as such schools can be made self-sustaining; and under this division of the Programme may be suggested--
(1.) The Medical College of Georgia. . . .
(2.) A Law School. . . .

(3.) An Agricultural School. . . .

(4.) A School of Civil Engineering and applied Mathematics. . . .

For the establishment of all these highly important and useful departments of a University, we have abundant means with our present income. If as we believe, the system should prove efficient in its workings, and an increasing patronage, State appropriations or individual liberality, shall enable us to do so, we can enlarge its usefulness by the addition of a Commercial School for the instruction of our young men in the great principles and history of Trade, the channels of Foreign Commerce, and the duties of Merchants. And finally any other Schools for instruction in any Branch of Uuseful [sic] Knowledge that will sustain themselves.

*****

V.

The Honors to be established for the foregoing enlargement of our Institution, may be designated as follows:

(1.) A certificate of the successful prosecution of all the studies in the Institute, signed by its Faculty, to enable the holder to admission into the Junior Class of the College proper, without examination.

(2.) A diploma of Bachelor of Arts, to each student who passes successfully through the College proper, signed by the Faculty.

(3.) The Degree of Master of Arts to all graduates of this or other Colleges of three years standing, and of good moral character, or to such graduates as have passed a year in the University Schools, and maintained good morals.

(4.) The Degree of Bachelor of Law. . . .

(5.) The Degree of Doctor of Medicine. . . .

(6.) The Degree of Doctor of Philosophy to such Students in the University Schools as shall spend two years therein, and become proficient in at least three of the Schools.

(7.) The Degree of Doctor of Divinity. . . .

(8.) The Degree of Doctor of Laws. . . .

*****

The proper grounds and buildings for the Institute, will cost not exceeding the sum of $20,000. So that it will be seen that, with the means now at command, we can put into operation, independent of State aid, a scheme far beyond anything yet attempted at the South--

a scheme which promises to elevate the professions of
Law and Medicine; to enlarge the boundaries of
knowledge among our people, to develop the vast
physical resources of our State; and above all, to
protect that most critical period of a boy's life,
lying between his fourteenth and eighteenth year. . . .

*****

3. BARNARD ON EDUCATIONAL REFORM

Henry Barnard, first U.S. Commissioner of Education (1867-1870), responded to a request of the Congress for information about education in the District of Columbia and added his suggestions for improvement. Like other American educators, Barnard was fascinated by the European (and especially German) approach to education. He recommended in this special report a new design for District public education which included "superior and special" schools which might embrace the first two years of a collegiate general education and vocational or professional training.

Barnard (b. 1811 in Connecticut; d. 1900) graduated from Yale College at 19, then taught school and studied law. In 1838 he was named chief state school officer of Connecticut (that is, secretary of the state board of common schools) and later held a similar post in Rhode Island. He was a college president and founder and editor of the <u>American Journal of Education</u>, a widely acclaimed periodical issued from 1855 to 1882. Barnard ranks as one of the prominent educators of the United States in the nineteenth century.

*****

Tested by the standard of secondary schools, or the requisitions, for entering the public service of Prussia, the public schools of this District are lamentably deficient. The best scholar of the best grammar school of this city should not, from any preparation got in any such school, enter the lowest

Henry Barnard, Special Report of the [United States] Commissioner of Education on the Condition and Improvement of Public Schools in the District of Columbia, Washington, D.C.: U.S. Government Printing Office, 1871, pp. 135, 137-138.

class of a real school, or of a gymnasium of Berlin, or be admitted to even a preliminary examination as a candidate for the lowest clerkship. And yet the poorest scholar from any of these grammar schools could enter his name as a student of law or medicine in the professional schools of this District.

3. If we enter the domain of superior instruction -- the range of studies covered by the theory of the American college, abroad, generous culture for any profession or occupation in which the intellectual faculties are to come in play, or the other class of subjects, which the advocates of a more direct scientific technical education would introduce, or the university in the European sense -- we pass at once, not only out of the limits, but out of sight of the public schools of the District. These schools, good as many of them are in their elementary studies, neither furnish this instruction nor the preparation to receive it. Instead of a national university, which Washington recommended, and hoped to endow, and for which a site was set apart in the original plan of the city; instead of a polytechnic school, like that of France, or one of a different type, like that of Zurich, we have numerous incorporated institutions established, endowed, and managed in the interests of a religious sect, or of a class, or a single profession; each with a crowded course of studies, an over-tasked body of teachers, and pupils poorly prepared for their work. No comparison can be instituted in respect to public institutions of this grade between this District and the great capitals of Europe.

*****

In view of the facts set forth in the report and the accompanying documents respecting the population and its distribution; the condition of public schools of every grade, and other institutions and means of education; the fragmentary, dissociated and to some extent antagonistic school organizations within the District, and the experience of communities similarly situated with this as to population and resources in our own and other countries, my belief is that a more efficient system should be instituted by Congress, as the only legislative authority competent to deal with this subject, for the whole District, and that in such a system the following features, or others equally efficient, should be secured.

*****

II.--GRADES OF SCHOOLS AND SUBJECTS OF INSTRUCTION.

The course of instruction should be distributed into five great divisions:

FIRST.   *The Primary Schools*, including the institutions now known as *Kindergartens*, and embracing generally children from three to eight years of age, and covering not only institutions strictly public, but others which may place all their arrangements as to school premises and teachers under the supervision and requirements of the Board of Control; so that schools of this grade shall be sufficiently numerous and conveniently located to provide for all children capable of receiving systematic training appropriate to their years, thereby giving assurance that the rudimentary education of the community is properly provided for and begun.   This step alone would, in short time, extinguish the home supply of illiteracy, which is now the disgrace and danger of our free institutions.

SECOND.   *Intermediate Schools*, embracing generally children from eight to fourteen years of age, including in their curriculum all that is now taught well in the public schools of the District, and so far complete in itself, that a pupil who has been in regular attendance up to this age and is obliged to leave school will possess the foundation of a good elementary education, which he can afterwards continue and complete in evening or other supplementary schools and agencies of the District.

THIRD.   *Secondary Schools*, including generally all between the period of twelve and sixteen years of age, should give something like completeness to what is generally understood to be a common school education, or all that is now attempted in the most advanced classes of the schools of the District, and attained in the best English High School, or Union School in our large cities, including at least one living language beside the English.

FOURTH.   *Superior and Special Schools*, embracing a continuation of the studies of the Secondary School, and while giving the facilities of general literacy and scientific culture as far as is now reached in the second year of our best colleges, shall offer special instruction (in classes or divisions instituted for the purpose, after the plan of the best Polytechnic Schools,) preparatory: (1,) for the teaching profession; (2,) for commercial pursuits; (3,) for mechanical trades, as well as for the arts of design; and (4,) for admission to any national

special school, (including every department of the
public service,) and particularly the languages of
countries with which we have close commercial and
diplomatic relations.

FIFTH. *Supplementary   Schools   and   Agencies*, to
provide (1,) an opportunity to supply deficiencies in
elementary education to any adult who has been denied
or neglected opportunities of the same; (2,) a regular
review and continuation of the studies of the second
and third grade of schools; (3,) for special classes of
children and youth who cannot be gathered into any of
the other grades of schools, and for these purposes,
any existing asylums, schools or classes, under certain
general regulations, can be recognized; and, (4,)
literary and scientific lectures, and class
instruction, in which the various public libraries,
scientific collections, and laboratories of the
District shall be utilized for illustration and for
original research.

The aim of the studies and training in the public
schools and other educational institutions should be,
(1,) the health and physical development, as well as
the good manners, sound morals, and correct habits
generally of all the pupils; (2,) a knowledge of the
English language and its literature to the extent of
being able to speak and write the same with accuracy,
facility and force; (3,) begun early, and continued
through the entire course, at least one language beside
the English (the Latin, German, Spanish, or French;)
(4,) mathematics and the natural sciences so far as may
be required to enter the second year of our national
schools at West Point and Annapolis, or of our best
American colleges; (5,) moral, mental, political and
geographical studies, to include a thorough knowledge
of the human mind, the duties of every member of
society to himself, his neighbor, and to God, and his
legal relations to the State and to other countries;
(6,) drawing and music. . . .

*****

4. A PROGRAM FOR THE AMERICAN UNIVERSITY

John William Burgess, faculty member and leader at Columbia College (and, later, University) in New York City, was distressed at the condition of higher education in the United States. He found solace in an imaginative plan for a great American University, envisioning an expanded role for secondary education upon which superior universities could be built. He decried the intrusion of specialized studies into the college curricula and urged their separation. Burgess called upon the American public to add two or three years of education to the high school or academy curriculum. This, then, should adequately prepare students for the work of the university--the discovery of new truth, the increasing of knowledge. The 19th-century college, Burgess argued, tried to pack too much into too few years, tried to be both preparor for and perpetrator of university studies. This did not work. A clear distinction should be made between collegiate and universities studies, he insisted.

Burgess (b. 1844 in Tennessee; d. 1931) graduated from Amherst College, studied law, and after several additional years of study at German universities, became a college teacher. He was energetic and creative. Burgess created and headed the first faculty of political science in the United States and was prominent in the transformation of Columbia College into a modern university.

*****

I would venture to affirm that very few graduates of American Colleges have been able to pursue successfully a course in a German University and attain to a degree, without learning their Greek, or Latin, or modern

---

John W. Burgess, The American University, Boston: Ginn, Heath, & Co., 1884, pp. 4-6, 18-20.

languages, or their elements of natural science, or even their mathematics (though this less frequently), over again. The American College graduate is not the equal of the "Abiturient" of the German Gymnasium in an exact comprehension and facile use of the elements of all knowledge, though he may have more of what is sometimes called "general information." There was a time in our educational history when the Fitting School and the College, taken together, furnished a student with a pretty fair gymnastic preparation for the University, or at least for some courses of the University. At that time a diligent student could, at the end of the College period, read Greek and Latin with a good deal of facility, and by his mathematical training had become something of a logician; but now the overloading of the College course with University studies, causing the breaking up of the same into a variety of special courses before the student has become generally prepared to select or to profit by the selection, and the introduction of University methods into the College by over-ambitious Professors have put an end to that condition of things in the most of our better Colleges. Before the student learns really to read any language he is now dragged into the most minute philological study, which so limits the amount read that the formation of the vocabulary is stopped; before he learns the elements of the different natural sciences he is invited to enter the laboratory of some particular one and encouraged to seek to become a discoverer ere he knows the first principles of what has already been discovered; while a considerable number make good use of the opportunity to escape in large degree the great disciplinary influence of the pure mathematics, and come thus with immature reasoning powers to the work of the University.

I confess that I am unable to divine what is to be ultimately the position of Colleges which cannot become Universities and which will not be Gymnasia. I cannot see what reason they will have to exist. It will be largely a waste of capital to maintain them, and largely a waste of time to attend them. It is so now. It seems to me that when the American public comes to a clear consciousness of its educational needs it will demand a pretty thorough reformation of our system of secondary education, and that this will be, in outline, the direction which it will take; viz.: the addition of two or three years to the courses of the Academies and High Schools, making in these a continuous curriculum of seven to nine years, during which the pupil shall be taught a thorough knowledge of the English language and a good reading knowledge of at least the Greek, Latin, German and French, the pure mathematics to the Calculus, the elements of the natural sciences, and the elements of universal history and general literature; then the establishment of such institutions in every town of any considerable population, and the advance of the successful graduates of these direct to the University. Such institutions will be, as compared with our present Colleges, inexpensive, and within the reach of every considerable community. They will fit the students better and in larger numbers for the University then the Academy and College now taken together do, and they will enable the student to reach the University by his twentieth or twenty-first year, whereas now the double, and, to a great degree, doubled curricula of Academy and College detain him from the University until the completion of his twenty-second or twenty-third year, on the average.

*****

Secondly. The University Curricula.

It is not easy to draw the line between the Gymnasium and the University in regard to the subjects of their curricula. I think we may get at it better through a series of adjustments than by a direct survey. First, then, the entire realm of the Unknown belongs to the University. The primest function of the University is the discovery of *new* truth, the *increase* of knowledge in every direction. The fitting out of Academies and even Colleges with extensive laboratories, cabinets, museums, and libraries is a great waste of substance. These things all belong to the University, to be used, not as curiosities to entertain, but as means to new discoveries. Secondly, all professional science belongs to the University,--Theology, Jurisprudence, Medicine. This is the universal practice, and is so patent and necessary that I need not expend time in attempting to give reasons. So far there is no difficulty. It is, thirdly, then only when we come to draw the line between the Gymnasium and the non-professional curriculum of the University, the Faculty of Philosophy, that we are driven to take closer observation, since, apparently, many of the studies pursued in the latter are but a continuation of the same subjects taught in the former. Shall, then, the University begin in this curriculum where the Gymnasium leaves off, or the Gymnasium leave off where the University begins, no matter where, or is there a natural line of division between them? It seems to me that the latter is or should be the case, and that the difference of purpose between the Gymnasium and the University should dominate in the solution of this question as well as in that of University method. The University curriculum of Philosophy is a collection of *non-professional specializations,* and the student should enter upon it only after he has become prepared, through the variety, quantity, and quality of his discipline and knowledge, to specialize in any and every direction. He should be able to read those ancient and modern languages which contain the chief literature upon the subjects of all knowledge; he should have the drill and the ground-work of the pure mathematics, and of the elements of the natural sciences generally; he should have stored and classified in his memory the names, dates, and principal events of history; and he should be brought under the discipline of logical thought and composition. He must have all of the disciplines and knowledges in an extent and to a degree that he shall be able to pursue with intelligence and success any branch of Philology, or Literature, or History, or Philosophy, or Moral or Political Science, or enter with profit upon the work of the laboratories, observatories, and cabinets of the Natural Sciences. On the other hand, Philology, Literature, Philosophy, Moral, Historical and Political Science, and the studies of the Laboratories, Observatories, and Cabinets, belong to the University, and should be kept jealously apart from the Gymnasium. If they are not, they will never be successfully pursued. Without the completion of the gymnastic curriculum they cannot be appreciated, and if they be injected into it this must be at the cost of displacing something of far more importance to the gymnast. They will prove a quicksand instead of a rock. This, then, is the general line between the curriculum of the Gymnasium and that of the Philosophical Faculty of the University. It cannot be pretended that the adjustment is minute and exhaustive, but a careful and an intelligent application of the general principles of distinction here advanced would, I think, arrive ultimately thereto.

*****

5. DREAM OF A BUSINESSMAN

This editorial in the 1903 Annual of Lewis Institute in Chicago describes how Allen C. Lewis, midwestern merchant, came to found the Institute which carried his name--one of the first junior colleges in the United States. Clearly Lewis was not satisfied with the classical program of studies; it alone was not sufficient for the demands of a newly emerging industrial society. At the same time, he felt technical or vocational training alone was too narrow. Some balance should be struck between classical or general education and vocational education. A good high school and collegiate-type program would prepare students in both areas.

*****

About the year 1870 a wave of discussion on industrial education swept over this country. Out here in the West, as it was then called, the discussion was as widespread as anywhere. Nor were the reasons far to seek so far as Chicago was concerned. What is to-day in the Middle West was then beginning to make known its wants in a mercantile way, and prominent among these wants was a need for machinery suitable for the farmer

---

Lewis Institute, Annual of 1903, Chicago, Ill.: The Institute, 1903, pp. 22-23. (For an extensive review of the programs of study see The First Twenty Years of Lewis Institute, 1896-1916 (mimeograph) (n.d.) written by George Carman, first director of Lewis Institute, and located in the archives of the Illinois Institute of Technology, Chicago, Illinois. Carman, a friend of President William Rainey Harper of the University of Chicago, attempted to build a curriculum to prepare students for immediate employment and advanced study in a university.)

and the manufacturer, and for the machinists and engineers necessary for the production and operation of such devices. It was true that such machinery and experts could be obtained from New York, or Boston, or Philadelphia, but the cost was great, time was constantly being lost, and general dissatisfaction resulted. In the rising young city of Chicago marked interest was displayed in the consideration of this mercantile problem. Newspaper editorials dealt with the question, and business people talked about the matter as one of vital concern. Gradually certain people came to feel that somehow or other a school of technical education was to be established. "Given the engineers, we shall make our own machinery, and thus free ourselves of inconvenient and costly dependence upon a distant base of supplies." This was felt to be true. In those days the founding of schools was not in so great vogue as it is to-day, and the good citizens waited to see who would make the initial move toward founding an institution which had become a positive want. At that time there were but three technical schools of any importance in the country, and they were situated in the Eastern States.

These matters were not lost upon Allen C. Lewis, hardware merchant. It is entirely probably, in the light of subsequent events, that even before his trip to France in search of health Mr. Lewis had, after much discussion and counsel with his brother, John Lewis, formulated the plan of establishing a school of technical education. He was vividly impressed, not only by the need for skilled artisans on the one hand, but also by the--to him--positive need for thorough training in one art for boys and girls on the other hand.

Mr. Lewis spent three years in Holland, Belgium and France. In those lands he observed the bitter struggle for existence, especially in the cities. He observed that the skill to ply a trade, even a small trade, such as the paper-flower industry in Belgium, was the one thing that stood between many a young person and dependence. Particularly was this true of the young women, and particularly did Mr. Lewis deplore the lack of training that leaves young women, in so many instances, utterly without resources. He came to see clearly that to throw upon the world a boy or a girl incapable of doing well some one thing is to give that boy or girl the most unfavorable start possible in the only life they have to live, and it is believed that, when Mr. Lewis returned to Chicago, he had fully determined to set on foot a project that should lead directly to the establishment of a unique school. This school was to train boys and girls for lifework, and to train them so well that failure would be contingent upon lack of personal effort only.

Mr. Lewis felt that such a school must needs have ample funds or it would fail. In accordance with this wise foresight he constrained himself to go slowly. His business was lucrative, and with wife, child and other near relatives gone, he gave himself up to it that he might thereby further his plans for a school, and when he died, in 1876, it was found that very nearly all of his fortune of about $600,000 had been given to found a school, as previously outlined. Mr. Lewis had inserted clauses in his will which required that the money should rest as he had invested it until such time as it had reached a certain value. He felt that it would be useless to build and operate a school with less than, say, $800,000. In 1896 the trustees of the bequest prepared to carry out the plan of Mr. Lewis and found that the sum in hand amounted to nearly three times the amount he left at his death. After some difficulty regarding a site had been met, the southeast corner of Robey and Madison streets was chosen; a serviceable building was erected and George Noble Carman was made director of the Lewis Institute.

In fulfilling the mission planned for it by its founder, the Lewis Institute has come to occupy a unique position among schools. It is essentially broad in its conception, being not an academy merely, nor a technical school, nor a college, but a closely combined union of the three. It receives boys and girls from the grammar school, and, after taking them through the preparatory course, offers either literary or scientific work through two years of college, or the engineering course to the degree of M. E. During the first two years of study, all engineering students are expected to take literary work with the technical. This affords them the opportunity to make a careful decision as to their course of study, and at the same time gives them a less one-sided training than would be possible in a strictly technical school. Besides this, the Lewis arrangement allows the literary student to take up some work not strictly literary, or the technical student to take up some work not strictly technical, in departments far better organized than would be possible in an exclusively literary or technical school.

This close relationship existing between the literary and engineering departments makes possible the association of all the students in the literary societies, musical and athletic organizations, and in the social life generally, a pleasant relationship which is kept up by the alumni association.

PART II.
EARLY JUNIOR COLLEGE DEVELOPMENTS

As our nation moved into the 20th century, more voices articulated desires for greater efficiency in our educational system, a greater preciseness to the roles of the various institutions. Being enamored with the Germanic ideal of a research university, scholars and presidents alike searched vigorously for ways to protect that institution from the tide of allegedly immature and ill-prepared students.

Thus, one of the great innovators in American higher education, William Rainey Harper, first president of the University of Chicago, attacked this issue on several fronts. He attempted to separate the youthful freshmen and sophomores of his university from the more mature juniors and seniors. (Other supporters of this concept, such as President David Starr Jordan of Stanford University, caught this same vision and worked to incorporate these plans into an educational system.) He urged struggling four-year colleges to reduce their responsibilities and become strong two-year institutions, again preparing students to move on to the university. (This idea was later espoused by U.S. Commissioner of Education P.P. Claxton.) He supported and encouraged efforts by high schools throughout the Midwest to take on the task of completing the secondary education of youth-- preparing them for entrance at an advanced stage to the university. (The material in this Part on the six-year high school at Goshen, Indiana, is vivid illustration of Harper's influence.)

In California, however, A.F. Lange saw the junior college as the capstone of a new design for secondary education, the crowning institution in a junior high school through high school through junior college hierarchy--a quite different view than that of Harper.

New information about the junior college came in the form of the Floyd M. McDowell dissertation reprinted as a bulletin of the U.S. government. This first extensive study of junior colleges in the nation provided evidence for understanding their growth, purposes, and programs. McDowell's dissertation and, more directly, the 1920 national conference on junior colleges, sponsored by the U.S. Bureau of Education, were important steps in publicizing the growth of this institution. They also laid the foundation for the founding of the American Association of Junior Colleges.

Interestingly enough, the U.S. Commissioner of Education participated in this 1920 meeting, lauded the emergence of the junior college, but saw its contribution to education exactly opposite to the view of Lange, Leonard V. Koos, and many other academic leaders. Philander Priestly Claxton viewed the junior college as a remedy for some of the ailments of American colleges and urged it be a part of higher education rather than the public school systems.

The account of how the Southern Association of Colleges and Schools (SACS) met the emergence of this new institution shows what difficulty educators had in sorting out the purposes and programs of the junior college and determining its position in the educational galaxy. SACS also promoted, especially through its selection standards, the notion of the junior college as a member of the higher education community. A famous early scholar of the junior college movement, Leonard V. Koos, made a number of assessments of this institution and found it admirably suited for increasing the effectiveness of American education. And finally, another keen observer of junior college programs, W.C. Eells, conducted a detailed analysis of the junior college and urged consideration of this institution as a separate and autonomous unit in higher education. In a thorough review of the arguments, he advocated the junior college not as part of the 6-4-4 plan so prominent in the literature of the day, but as a collegiate two-year institution.

6. WILLIAM RAINEY HARPER AND THE ASSOCIATE DEGREE AT CHICAGO

President Harper was an innovator. He looked carefully for ways to enhance the University of Chicago. He was among the first to implement a separation of students in collegiate studies (freshmen and sophomore classes) from the more advanced university students (juniors and seniors). He had in 1892 divided the undergraduate colleges into the collegiate (lower) and university (upper) divisions; several years later he used the terms "junior college" and "senior college."

Harper maintained that the associate degree was a reward for students who should or did conclude their education at the end of their sophomore or second year beyond the high school; he saw it as an inducement for those who would be inspired to further and professional or university study. Best of all, Harper hoped that high schools and small colleges would wish to offer this "postgraduate" program, thus allowing universities like Chicago to concentrate on their specialized work.

William Rainey Harper (b. 1856 in Ohio; d. 1906) whirled through a relatively brief but all so brilliant career. At the age of 14 he graduated from Muskingum College (Ohio), delivering the commencement address in Hebrew. Five years later he earned the Ph.D. degree in Semitic languages from Yale College. After some years as college teacher he became the first president of the University of Chicago. Scholar, teacher, administrator, author, and editor, he quickly made deep impressions on American higher education.

University Record, V (April 6, 1900-March 29, 1901), Chicago, Ill.: University of Chicago, 1901, pp. 12-13.

The Associate Degree

From the President's Annual Report for the year closing July 1, 1899, I desire to present the following statements concerning the degree of Associate in Arts, Philosophy, and Science which is conferred for the first time this afternoon:

Upon the recommendation of the Faculty of the Junior Colleges and the Senate, and upon the approval of the University Congregation, the Trustees have voted to confer the title or degree of Associate upon those students who finish the work of the Junior Colleges. The questions involved in this action have been under consideration for several years. The action in the Faculty of the Junior Colleges and in the Senate was practically unanimous--the action in the Board of Trustees was entirely unanimous.

From the point of view of the student, the following considerations have had influence in determining this action: (1) The fact, very generally recognized, that no important step is taken at the end of the preparatory course. The work of the Freshman and Sophomore years in most colleges differs little in content and in method from that of the last year of the academy or high school--except that it is somewhat more advanced; but, on the other hand, (2) at the end of the Sophomore year a most important change occurs, according to the organization of the larger number of institutions--for it is at this point that the student is given larger liberty of choice, and at the same time higher methods of instruction are employed. During the last two years of college work the university spirit and the university method prevail. A new era in the work of the student has begun. (3) It is evident that many students continue work in the Junior and Senior years of college life whose best interests would have been served by withdrawal from college. Many continue to the end, not from choice, but rather from compulsion, because of the disgrace which may attend an unfinished course. If it were regarded as respectable to stop at the close of the Sophomore year, many would avail themselves of the opportunity. (4) Many students who might be courageous enough to undertake a two years' college course are not able, for lack of funds or for other reasons, to see their way clear to enter upon a four years' course. Many, still further, feel that if a professional course is to be taken, there is not time for a four years' college course. It is for this reason that, in part, our professional schools are made up so largely of non-college students. If a student who had in view ultimately the medical, or legal, or pedagogical profession could make provisions to finish a course of study at the end of two years, he

would be much more likely to undertake such a course
than the longer four years' course.   (5) On the other
hand, many students who are thus led to take a two
years' course would be induced at the end of that time
to continue to the end of the fourth year, and in this
way many students of the very highest character, at all
events, would be enabled to take the entire college
course, by whom, under the present arrangements, such a
course would be regarded as impracticable.

From the point of view of the schools, the following
points have been considered: (1) Many academies are
able to do, at least in part, the work of the Freshman
and Sophomore years.   The high schools in some states
are ready to do such work, and in at least one state
the university of the state recognizes the work of the
Freshman year when performed in approved high schools.
(2) It cannot be denied that until young men or young
women have shown some maturity of character, it is wise
that they should not be sent very far away from home.
If, now, the academies and high schools could so
perfect their work that Freshman and Sophomore courses
might be offered, many young people would be enabled to
pursue their education at least to this higher point.
(3) A large number of so-called colleges, which have
not sufficient endowment to enable them properly to do
the work of the Junior and Senior years, should limit
their work to that of the Freshman and Sophomore years.
In many cases the officers of these colleges recognize
most keenly that they are not doing justice to the
students in the higher classes.   In reality they are
defrauding the students who pay their fees in lower
classes in order to obtain a meager sum of money with
which to provide an entirely inadequate course of
instruction for the higher class of men.   These
institutions in many cases would be disposed to limit
their work to the lower field if it were made possible
for them to do so.   They find it necessary, however, to
give a degree.   If they could follow the example of a
large institution and give an appropriate recognition
of the work of the lower years, they would be ready to
adopt such an arrangement.   (4) It is a general law of
educational work that in seeking a college, students
rarely go farther away from home than a hundred miles.
Ninety percent of all the students in American colleges
are to be found in colleges which are within a hundred
miles of home.   If a fair proportion of these
institutions were to limit themselves to the work of
the Freshman and Sophomore years, at the end of this
time the students who had finished this work and
desired to continue would be compelled to go away from
home to some distant institution, perhaps a large
university in which library and laboratory facilities
might be found which would make possible the doing of

good work. If, on the one hand, the academies and high schools were elevated, and if, on the other hand, the scope of work done by many colleges were limited, and as a result institutions developed which would do that work thoroughly, there would come to be a recognized distinction between college and university which does not now exist.

In order, therefore to encourage a movement in the direction thus mentioned, the proposed degree has been established. It is believed that the results will be fivefold: (1) Many students will find it convenient to give up college work at the end of the Sophomore year; (2) many students who would not otherwise do so, will undertake at least two years of college work; (3) the professional schools will be able to raise their standards for admission, and in any case many who desire a professional education will take the first two years of the college work; (4) many academies and high schools will be encouraged to develop higher work; (5) many colleges which have not the means to do the work of the Junior and Senior years will be satisfied under this arrangement to do the lower work.

7. PRESIDENT HARPER'S PANACEA FOR SMALL COLLEGES

President William Rainey Harper of the University of Chicago saw the transformation of small struggling four-year colleges into two-year junior colleges as their chance to survive. The work of many colleges was a fraud, he felt, for they could not really sustain a strong and viable academic program for students. It was far better, Harper maintained, if many small colleges limited their work to the first two years of a four-year program.

*****

III. CHANGES AFFECTING THE SMALL COLLEGE WHICH MAY BE
      EXPECTED AND WHICH ARE TO BE DESIRED

          Strengthening of the surviving colleges. --We come now to the consideration of the changes affecting the small colleges which may be expected and are to be desired. First among these will be the strengthening of some. The laws of institutional life are very similar to those of individual life, and in the development of institutions we may confidently believe in "the survival of the fittest." The severe tests, to which the life of many institutions is subjected, serve to purify and to harden these lives. The institution which has survived the trials and tribulations of early years, and which, by this survival, has justified its existence, not only to its constituency, but to the

---

National Education Association, Journal of Proceedings and Addresses of the Thirty-Ninth Meeting Held at Charleston, South Carolina, July 7-13, 1900, Chicago, Ill.: The Association, 1900, pp. 80-84, 86-87.

world at large, deserves to live; and its subsequent
life will be all the stronger and heartier because of
the difficulties thru which it has passed. The purpose
of suffering is, therefore, much the same in the case
of an institution as in the case of an individual.
There will, of course, be fluctuation, and the
institution destined to live and to exert a strong
influence will at times be less strong than at other
times, its clientage less numerous and earnest, its
standard less ideal, and its life less vigorous; but,
here and there, as determined by the needs of spiritual
life, and by the conveniences of practical life, an
institution will gradually grow into strength which, in
the face of even the greatest difficulties and
disasters, will prove invincible.

The small college, as has already been said, is an
expression of the American spirit, and, unless this
spirit is fundamentally changed, there is no reason to
suppose that the time will ever come when, under proper
conditions, there will not be a function and a mission
for the smaller institution. Whatever may be the
development of the university spirit, however strong
the work of professional education shall come to be,
the need of the other kind of institution will continue
to exist and to grow; and if only the means may be
secured for providing the proper facilities, the worth
and standing of such colleges will be increased and the
advantages of such work will be unchallenged.

Reduction of some colleges to academies. --In this
struggle for existence, however, some of the colleges
that have already been organized, and others the
organization of which is in the future, will be
compelled to limit their activity to the sphere of work
known commonly as the academic, or preparatory, field.
It is probable that a careful examination of the
colleges now chartered in the United States would show
that at least 20 to 25 per cent are doing work of a
character only little removed from that of an academy.
This means simply that the term "college" has been
misappropriated by these institutions. Surely an
institution with a library of less than a thousand
volumes, with scientific apparatus and equipment which
has cost less than a thousand dollars, with a single
building which has cost less than forty thousand
dollars, and with an income of less than six to eight
thousand, is not in a position to do college work; and
yet it is probably true that more than one hundred so-
called "colleges" belong to this category. Forty years
ago such a college, if its small faculty had contained
a few strong men, might have justified itself; but
today the situation is changed, and institutions of
this kind are recognized. . .at their true worth.
These, and, in addition, some that in times past have

been more prosperous, will, in the course of educational development, come to occupy a more honest position before the world, and nothing could occur which would be more advantageous to the cause of education.   Strong academies are needed side by side with the *high schools* of the state, just as strong colleges and *universities*, founded by private means, are needed to work side by side with the universities of the state.

While, therefore, 25 per cent of the small colleges now conducted will survive, and be all the stronger for the struggle thru which they have passed, another 25 per cent will yield to the inevitable, and, one by one, take a place in the system of educational work which, while in one sense lower, is in a true sense higher. It is surely a higher thing to do honest and thoro work in a lower field than to fall short of such work in a higher field.

The modification of some to junior colleges.,--Another group of these smaller institutions will come to be known as junior colleges.   I use the words "junior colleges," for lack of a better term, to cover the work of the freshman and sophomore years.   With these may usually be closely associated the work of the preparatory department, or academy.   This period of six years is, I am inclined to think, a period which stands by itself as between the period of elementary education and that of the university.   The work of the freshman and sophomore years is only a continuation of the academy or high-school work.   It is a continuation, not only of the subject-matter studied, but of the methods employed.   It is not until the end of the sophomore year that university methods of instruction may be employed to advantage.   It is not until the end of the sophomore year that the average student has reached an age which enables him to do work with satisfaction, except in accordance with academy methods.   At present this consecutive period of preparation, covering six years, is broken at the end of the fourth year, and the student finds himself adrift.   He has not reached the point when work in any of his preparatory subjects is finished.   He is compelled to continue the same work under new and strange conditions, with new and strange instructors.   Not infrequently the instructors under whom he is placed in the freshman year of college are inferior to those with whom he has been associated in the academy.   A great waste of energy, time, and interest follows this unnatural break in the prosecution of the student's work.   Nature has marked out the great divisions of educational work, and the laws of nature may not be violated without injury.   My firm conviction is that in time this difficulty will be appreciated, and that a large number, perhaps even a majority, of the colleges now attempting to do the four years of preparatory course and the four years of college work will be satisfied to limit their work to the six years which would include the preparatory training and the first two years of college life. The motives to this change will be found in its economy, and in the possibility of doing thorough and satisfactory work, where today such work is impossible.

There are at least two hundred colleges in the United States in which this change would be desirable. These institutions have a preparatory school as well as a college course. The number of students in the preparatory school is perhaps a hundred and fifty. In the freshmen and sophomore classes they have thirty to forty students, and in the junior and senior classes twenty to thirty. The annual income of these institutions is restricted for the most part to the fees of the students, and will average from all sources, let us say, eight to ten thousand dollars. In order to keep up the name of the college, the income is made to cover the expenses of eight years--that is, the preparatory and the collegiate departments. In order to do the work of the junior and senior years of the college, even superficially, where the classes are so small, as much of the total income is spent upon the instruction during these two years as upon that of the five or six years below. It is evident that, even with this disproportionate expenditure, the work of the junior and senior college years can be done only in a superficial way, because the library and laboratory facilities are meager, the range of instruction is very narrow, and a single instructor is often required to teach three or four subjects.

But this is not the most significant fact. When the money paid by the students of the first six years has been used for instruction of a few men who are working in the last two years, in order that the college may continue to be known as a college, there does not remain sufficient income to do justice to the work of the lower years. This is an attempt to do higher work at the cost of the lower. Nor are examples of this kind limited to states in the West and South. More than one instance will be found in the state of New York, while in Pennsylvania and Ohio, Indiana, Illinois, and Michigan, such institutions abound.

The reduction of institutions of this class to the rank of colleges which shall do, in addition to the preparatory work, only the work of the freshman and sophomore years, will accomplish several results.

1.   The money now wasted in doing the higher work superficially could be used to do the lower work more thoroughly.

2.   The pretense of giving a college education would

be given up, and the college could become an honest
institution.

3. The student who was not really fitted by nature
to take the higher work could stop naturally and
honorably at the end of the sophomore year.

4. Many students who might not have the courage to
enter upon a course of four years' study would be
willing to do the two years of work before entering
business or the professional school.

5. Students capable of doing the higher work would
be forced to go away from the small college to the
university. This change would in every case be most
advantageous.

6. Students living near the college whose ambition
it was to go away to college could remain at home until
greater maturity had been reached--a point of the
highest moment in these days of strong temptation.

The substitution of the six-year institution,
including the academic or high-school course, for the
present four-year institution, without preparatory
work, would, at one stroke, touch the greatest evils of
our present situation.

Development of high schools into junior colleges. --
Directly along this line will be another change,
namely, the development of high schools into junior
colleges. Evidence that this change is already taking
place may be found on every hand. The establishment of
hundreds of high schools thru all the states is in
itself a new element in our educational machinery which
has disarranged the former system, but has, at the same
time, greatly advanced the interests of education
itself. The quickening influence of these institutions
is seen, not only in the increased number of those who
continue their work in the college and the university,
nor merely in the fact that a larger number of more
intelligent men and women is thus contributed to the
various communities, but especially in the fact that
the teachers of the schools of a lower grade are vastly
stronger and better prepared for their work.

The suggestion is made from time to time that the
people will not consent to continue the public support
of these high schools. But, as a matter of fact, they
do continue to support them; and, more than this, these
schools are constantly increasing their requirements
for admission, as well as their facilities for
instruction and the number of years of the curriculum.
It has now come to be generally recognized that the
ideal high school must have a curriculum of four years,
and in many sections of the country this has
practically been accomplished in certain schools in
Michigan and in some of our cities. It can be done at
a minimum of cost. Today only 10 percent of those who
finish the high school continue the work in college.

If the high schools were to provide work for two additional years, at least 40 percent of those finishing the first four years would continue to the end of the sophomore year.

With this modification of the high school on the one hand, and with the suggested modification of many of our colleges upon the other, there would come to be a system of colleges, state or non-state, which would meet the demands of the situation today as they are not met.   Many of the normal schools of western states practically occupy this position.

*****

Development of a system in higher educational work. -- All this points to the development of a system in our higher educational work.   The change of certain colleges into junior colleges, and of others into academies,   the association of the colleges of a denomination or a geographical district with each other, and the close association of such colleges with the universities--all this will contribute toward a system of higher education (something which does not now exist in America), the lack of which is sadly felt in every sphere of educational activity.   System means organization, and without organization, with the sharp distinctions and the recognized standards which come with organization, the work, however excellent, lacks that essential element which gives it the highest character and produces the best results.

There are some advantages, perhaps, in lack of system; if so, we have enjoyed these advantages long enough.   The time is ripe for something more definite and regular and tangible,   and the modifications which have been suggested in the policy of secondary and college education will contribute in this direction.

Conclusion. --I may sum up all that I have said in these sentences:

1.   The small college is certain of its existence in the future educational history of the United States.

2.   It must, however, pass thru a serious struggle with many antagonistic elements, and must adjust itself to other similar and, sometimes, stronger agencies.

3.   In the process of this struggle and adjustment some colleges will grow stronger; some will become academies; some, junior colleges; the high schools will be elevated to a still more important position than that which they now occupy; while, all together, high schools, colleges, and universities, will develop greater similarity of standard and greater variety of   type; and, at the same time, they will come into closer and more helpful association one with another. The general result will be the growth of system in the

higher educational work of the United States, where now
no system exists.

4.   The future of the small college will be a great
future; a future greater than its past, because that
future will be better equipped, better organized, and
better adjusted.

8. A Six-Year High School at Goshen, Indiana

This proposal by a board of education in Indiana illustrates the ready willingness of some midwestern secondary school leaders to offer "postgraduate" studies at a local high school. It demonstrates the rapidly growing influence of President William Rainey Harper and the University of Chicago in developing these plans. Harper was especially interested in improving secondary education through a network of cooperation and affiliation established between the University of Chicago and schools and academies in the Midwest, particularly Illinois (including Joliet High School in Joliet, Illinois, often cited as the first public junior college in the United States), Wisconsin, Indiana, Michigan, Iowa, and Missouri.

Victor W.B. Hedgepeth, "The Six-Year High School at Goshen, Indiana," School Review, Vol. XIII (January, 1905), 19-23. Hedgepeth was superintendent in Goshen when he wrote this article. Many pertinent materials offering rich detail of President Harper's plans for secondary-higher education collaboration are found in the Special Collections of the University of Chicago Library. These include Harper's papers from 1891 to 1906.

Analyses of varying accuracy concerning early junior colleges like Goshen (the question of which was the first junior college cannot be easily resolved!) and enrollments, persons, and factors instrumental in their development are found, for example, in the Junior College Journal in such articles as "Thirty Years' Growth," Vol. V (November, 1934), 104-105, "Analysis of Junior-College Growth," Vol. XIX (February, 1949), 311-319, and "A Brief History of the Development of the American Association of Junior Colleges," Vol. 31 (February/March, 1961), 36-40.

The six years' work offered by the Goshen High School is the result of a real demand, rather than an experiment based on any academic discussion as to the advisability of such an extension.

During the past few years a considerable number of the students have returned, in the year following graduation, to do work in the undergraduate courses. These pupils felt the need of a more extended course in school, but many of them were unable to meet the expense necessary to a course in college. Also a number of parents kept their children at home the year following graduation because they thought them too young to be sent away from home. During the year out of school the boys usually found work whose immediate rewards in dollars and cents seemed greater than the remoter rewards of learning; and the girls developed other ambitions. The plan of extending the course was projected to satisfy the cravings of the first class of boys and girls, and to correct the mistaken tendencies of the second.

Since the field for such a movement existed, locally, there remained but three additional things to do: (1) to provide a faculty whose work would be recognized by the colleges; (2) to provide suitable rooms and equipment; (3) to provide the ways and means financially.

In selecting the instructors we apply directly to the colleges for the material required. This enables us to enroll a faculty of the best grade from the best schools. In Goshen, only in rare cases do we have two from the same college. This year in a faculty of eleven we have represented nine colleges and universities.

In room and equipment we have provided the most modern and thoroughly furnished high school we know how to build; that is, for representing, the best we can, the educational ideas peculiar to the Goshen community.

The ways and means for meeting the extra expense incurred in the addition of two years' work to the curriculum, we obtain, partly, by charging an individual tuition fee of $30. With us this is large enough to avoid extra taxes. In other communities, of course, the fee will be more or less. As long as the institution of these extra courses does not operate to raise the tax levy, the most indifferent citizen cannot object, even though the law does not provide for the charging of fees in the public free schools.

Recently, in order that the so-called gap between the grades and the high school might be properly bridged, we have extended the departmental plan to include the seventh and eighth grades. I should say that this extension has done more than to bridge the gap; it appears to have closed it entirely. Now the seventh- and eight-grade pupils have the same mechanical plan as the high school, the same system of administration, reports, etc. Also the departmental plan will enable the introduction, without loss, of algebra, Latin, and botany into the grades below the high school, if advisable.

This attempt at the co-ordinate development of the physical, mental, and manual lines has met with a hearty response from the pupils, as our high school enrolls about 350, as against 1,250 for the grades. Of this number in round numbers 100 are children of parents living without the corporation and who pay for school privileges. This fund enables us to provide the additional two years at the slight charge of $30. Yet, if the fund were sufficient without this fee, we think it advisable to require it, as it is a good thing for the boy to learn that he must begin to pay for things.

Out of this high-school body of 300 or more, we have annually a graduating class of from 30 to 40. Thirty-five per cent of these find their way to college. To be more exact, the total number graduating in 1901, 1902, 1903, was 105. Of these 37 went to college, and 12 returned to the high school to do further undergraduate work. A careful questioning of this year's class of 42 shows that 15 expect to go to college, and 20 expect to avail themselves of the advanced work offered by the high school. Of those who will do additional work in the high school at home, it is safe to say over half will find ways and means to finish the two years' work away from home. It is something to a boy to be able to see a way clear through, rather than to be looking blankly at the wall confronting him.

The high school is now offering the first year of advanced work, and although the announcements were late, five boys and two girls of the class of 1904 have availed themselves of the opportunity.

The following letter was addressed to the leading citizens and patrons, requesting an opinion of the extension movement.

Goshen, Ind., November 5, 1904.

DEAR SIR:---The University of Chicago desires expressions from the leading citizens in approval, or disapproval, of the Goshen six-year high-school plan.

The plan enables parents to keep their children at home an additional year or two at the saving of college expenses and at no loss of time, the colleges recognizing such work as equivalent to the corresponding work done in residence.

The charge of a tuition fee of $30 per year from those pursuing the postgraduate work covers all additional expense without any increase whatever in taxation.
An early reply will oblige.

> VICTOR W.B. HEDGEPETH,

In view of the cordial reception of the proposed plan, both by citizens and pupils, the board of education voted to extend the course two full years; and, desiring to have this work accepted by the University of Chicago, informed President Harper of their plan in a communication of which the following is a copy:

President W.R. Harper, University of Chicago.

DEAR SIR:---We wish to assure you that the institution of the six-year high-school plan in Goshen is permanent, and has the entire support of the board of education, and the hearty approval and patronage of the citizens. We wish to state, further, that we will do all we can toward placing the last two years' work on such a plane as will entitle pupils to college recognition.

> Very truly yours,
>
> JOSEPH H. LESH,
> FRANK KELLY,
> GEORGE B. SLATE,
> Board of Education.

The University was further requested to send to Goshen a special committee of inspection looking toward the acceptance of the graduate work by the University.

After a personal conference with the Dean of Affiliations and inspection of the school by him and two other officers of the University, the following conditions and courses arranged by Dean Miller and Miss Lillian E. Michael, principal, were agreed upon by the board of education and the superintendent as offering a requisite basis for the proper institution of the additional studies:

PROPOSED ARTICLES OF AGREEMENT BETWEEN THE UNIVERSITY OF CHICAGO AND THE GOSHEN HIGH SCHOOL IN ACCORDANCE WITH WHICH THE UNIVERSITY WILL ACCEPT THE WORK OF THE GOSHEN HIGH SCHOOL FOR ADVANCED STANDING

1. Studies and Prerequisites.

Three majors[1] of work in Latin based upon four full years of secondary-school Latin.

Three majors of work in mathematics based upon three full years of secondary-school mathematics.

Three majors of work in English based upon three full years of secondary-school English.

Two majors of work in modern and medieval history based upon one full years' work in ancient history.

Three majors of work in German based upon two full years' work in elementary German.

Three majors of work in chemistry based upon one full years' work in secondary chemistry.

One major of work in physics based upon one full year in secondary physics.

These studies must be pursued strictly as postgraduate studies; that is, only by pupils who have gained the requisite units of credit for admission according to the University requirement. The courses offered must be equivalent in amount and character to the corresponding courses in the University.

2.   Number of studies.---A student may not pursue more than three studies in any given quarter, except that the school requirement in public speaking may be taken in addition to these.

3.   Teachers.

a.   Each teacher giving instruction in collegiate work must be approved by that department of the University in which his work is to be credited.

b.   His work in the undergraduate department should be so decreased that he may give ample attention to his collegiate work.

4.   Tests.

a.   The work shall be visited from time to time by representatives from the departments concerned at the expense of the Goshen High School.

b.   At the end of each quarter's course a final examination shall be prepared by the teacher which shall be sent to the University for the approval of the proper department before it is sent to the pupils.

c.   Examination papers, when written, shall be sent to the University to be read and graded at the expense of the Goshen High School.

5.   Proposed program of two years' postgraduate study of the Goshen High School.

First year, first quarter--Latin, mathematics, English; second quarter--German, mathematics, English; third quarter--Latin, mathematics, German.

Second year, first quarter--chemistry, English,

----

[1] A major is a study pursued for twelve weeks, five days in the week.

German; second quarter--chemistry , Latin, Medieval
history; third quarter--chemistry, physics, modern
history.

Such a course, if properly based on undergraduate
studies under the conditions prescribed, ought to
enable the boy or girl to enter one of the Senior
Colleges on a sound footing, or upon his years of real
living, with fair chances of touching his environment
in many understandable points.

9. Lange on the Purpose of the Junior College

*In this famous 1917 address, Alexis Frederick Lange speaks up
strongly in support of the emerging junior college and sets it
squarely in the domain of secondary (not higher) education.*

*The junior high school, the high school, and the junior college
are all part of one educational fabric--secondary education. The
junior college is the apex, the point of fulfillment of public
school education. It provides a liberal education for those who
cannot attend a college or university, a vocational training for
others.*

*Lange warns against the "siren voices" of the university--a
kind of educational chauvinism typified by the earlier writings of
William Rainey Harper, president of the University of Chicago.
University faculties and leaders want to manipulate this new
institution to serve their own narrow interests, he argues. The
junior college must be free to set its own directions, to be the
capstone of a new system of secondary education in the United
States.*

*Born in Missouri, Lange (b. 1862; d. 1924) studied at the
University of Michigan and in Germany. He joined the University
of California faculty and held several leadership posts there,
including director of the school of education in 1913 and its dean
in 1923.*

When the dwellers in the hill country of Judea first
heard about the infant son of Zacharias and Elizabeth
and what happened before his birth and soon after in

A.F. Lange, "The Junior College--What Manner of Child
Shall This Be?!" School and Society, Vol. VII
(Saturday, February 23, 1918), 211-216. This is the
published version of an address by Lange before the
Junior College Section of the California Teachers'
Association, Los Angeles, December 20, 1917.

the temple they marveled, saying: What manner of child
shall this be?! In doing so some doubtless merely
wondered; some questioned rather than exclaimed; still
others, looking about them and ahead, thinkingly,
longingly, trustfully, had in mind the special destiny
a child so obviously sent of God would fulfill among
his people in the years to come.

The advent of the junior college was neither heralded
nor attended by portents. But those with eyes to see
and ears to hear received it gladly when it came;
received it with faith in its future.   In California,
particularly, the "child grew and waxed strong in
spirit," like John. Here, within seven years, this
sturdy youngster has now reached the borderline of
adolescence. The dweller in California, too, may well,
therefore, wonder or question or prophesy, each
according to his wit and wisdom. To us sponsors and
intimate friends of the junior college, the saying:
what manner of child shall this be, implies a duty-
call. It is a challenge to seek and find the best
educational and vocational guidance, in order that the
junior college may pass unharmed through the
vicissitudes of adolescence, may acquire a life-career
motive thought out and potent and rooted in the public
welfare, and shape itself thereby, and may learn,
without costly blundering, how best to fulfill its
mission among and together with its fellow-agencies for
making American democracy increasingly safe and sound
and sanely self-directive.

In view of such ends we need to be clear, first of
all, as to the essential constitution of the junior
college. The name discloses nothing beyond the fact
that it is largely a bit of scholastic camouflage.
Smith Senior and Smith Junior probably exhibit traits
of kinship, but should we try to infer the nature and
prospects of the younger or the present occupation of
the elder Smith from the family name? Such procedure,
though common enough in mythology and in reaching
conclusions concerning the junior college would put the
childish guess in place of the basic data needed for
the guidance and self-guidance of Smith Junior, data
revealed only by his individuality and actual status.
Named or nameless then, the junior college is by
descent and nature a secondary school. Its legal
existence, as far as California is concerned, was
ushered in by the law of 1907 as an extension of the
high school. Subsequent legislation has made it an
integral part of the public-school system and thereby
has fixed its status as an institution devoted to
secondary education. In accord with this, it is
identical with the high school as to sources of
revenue, organization, administration, and the methods
of teacher preparation and licensing. Nor is the

present position of the junior college a vagary or an
anomaly.   A comparative glance at European school
systems, for example, suffices to show that it
corresponds to the upper reaches of such secondary
schools as the gymnasium or the lycee.   Historically,
we need only to remind ourselves of the fact that while
the American college at its best approached the English
university type in purpose and function, this
resemblance never extended downward to the two years to
which the junior college has fallen heir.   It is this
fact, among others, that inspires the heartfelt wish on
the part of American universities to be relieved of
these two years of essentially secondary schooling.
That the junior college grades do not belong with what
follows is further attested by the transformation the
upper half of the traditional college has undergone
during the last twenty-five years, most obviously in
state institutions.   A senior college no longer exists
except in name and outward form.   The new spirit that
inhabits and controls the old body is that of the
university "made in Germany."   The older aims of
liberalized personality and leading citizenship have
been replaced by the purpose of research and
professional training.   While the university professor
is not expressly forbidden to educate young men and
women, if he knows how, his first and last duty is
toward his subject.   The university student may still
travel paths along which he may learn to "see life
steadily and see it whole" and to add to his stature as
a human being, but the official trails are those of the
university specialist who may or may not be human in
more than one spot.   Now, it is not necessary to
explain here how the annexation of one half of the
American college by the university has come about nor
to prophesy as to the terms of a permanent peace
between conqueror and conquered; however strongly one
may be moved to predict that the typical American
university of the future will not be, as now, an
overdone imitation in an American setting but an un-
hyphenated American creation, embodying in a new unity
of purposes and practices the best the nation has
inherited and borrowed and originated.   Whatever the
causes at work or their final effects, the American
university-in-the-making has absorbed the upper college
provinces and is not at all likely to relinquish them.
Smith Senior's business has changed hands permanently.
    The implications of this change are too evident to be
missed, especially if we include in our field of vision
the coming of the intermediate or junior high school.
This and the high school and the junior college occupy
the domain of secondary education.   Their
interrelations may well receive various forms of
adjustment and their articulations with the elementary

school and with the university will doubtless need time
for adequate development, but even now a new order
exists, that is, a secondary-school system ministering
over a rapidly extending area to the whole of
adolescence. And so the junior college must never be
thought of in terms of the old obsolescent order. In
the new its place is at the top. It is the culmination
and fulfillment of the educational design incorporated
in the intermediate and the high school.

Such fundamental traits and such ties of blood
relationship, *de facto* and *de jure*, leave little doubt
as to the educational needs the junior college must be
expected to meet, little doubt, therefore, as to its
mission in an evolving democracy. Has it appeared
among us merely to lighten the burden of universities
in order that these may become more efficient in their
own proper sphere? Or must we add the economic relief
it affords to prospective university students? Or is
the list of things to do complete if it also keeps such
students at home for two years more of safe-keeping and
guidance? The answer is that the services indicated
are incidental, are by-products, and that in the
interest of the public welfare the junior college needs
must do something far more vitally significant than to
improve the care and culture of the privileged few and
to ameliorate the sad lot of universities.

The junior college, to begin with, would not be true
to its own self if it did not cultivate the
consciousness of organic oneness with high and
intermediate school and did not in consequence play the
leading role in securing unity for the eight grades
concerned, despite "fifty-seven varieties" of local
adaptions, each more or less necessary or desirable.
Energetic promotion, in city and country, of the twin
causes, the junior college and the intermediate school,
is of course presupposed. When every normal pupil
shall be able to find in the seventh grade the nurture
suited to his years and thenceforth shall have at least
the chance to grow in the same way, year by year,
through middle and late adolescence, then the now
universal criticism of the high school, that it begins
too late and ends too early, will be an anachronism.
Then the concept preparatory school will have its fangs
extracted. Then it will be possible to bring studies
to fruition. Then, even if the student has gone
through the program on the à la carte plan, the junior
college will doubtless enable him to correlate and
generalize and motivate and so convert an example in
fractions after all into an aimful, dynamic
personality.

As intimated, the call to realize a progressively
efficient secondary-school system means also one that
is accessible to a steadily increasing number. If the

traditional high school offers only a truncated
education even to those whose formal schooling will
continue, what of the majority, whose school days end
with high-school education? Is it not certain that in
thousands of cases there is no continuation and
completion simply because opportunities are out of
reach? I have in mind at the moment primarily those
who would go on with a liberal arts course if they
could. To bring the junior college within reach for
such alone would be no mean contribution to national
preparedness and progress, which depend fully as much
on man-centered training. It has always required
faith, the substance of things hoped for but not seen,
to regard the high school as the people's college.
With the inclusion of the junior college the name
stands for a fact. The junior college has come to
fulfill the high school in every part of the state for
all qualified students. And such a consummation will
mean special as well as regular students. It will mean
extension classes. It will imply such a union of
community experience and college activities that there
will be life without and within, a more abundant life,
on a higher plane. It will imply cooperation with
the university but not preparation for it, in the sense
only too familiar to us, still accustomed as we are to
the vassalage of high schools.
    Probably the greatest and certainly the most original
contribution to be made by the junior college is the
creation of means of training for the vocations
occupying the middle ground between those of the
artisan type and the professions. Until recently our
public-school system has offered opportunities for a
complete education only to university and normal-school
students. Now courses of "finishing" vocational
training are in process of development, the
intermediate school functioning as go-between. The
prospect is that before long intelligently organized
and administered continuation and trade-school
arrangements will exist that will assist the great mass
of those with an elementary education in becoming
efficient workers, as much for the sake of a better
human and civic life as for a better living. But how
about occupations that require a higher foundation of
general education, that presuppose greater maturity for
grasp and mastery, that represent the positions of
commissioned officers in the national peace army? Only
one whose educational thought is without a country can
deny the need of a middle vocational system. Is the
high school meeting it? No. Can it do so? Only in a
poor makeshift fashion. The junior college can, and
the law of service is: he who *can* must *do*. From it
should come the scientific farmer, who knows that
farming is an applied science, a business, a mode of

life, and above all, a matter of cooperative
citizenship. From it should come the trained city
employee, familiar with municipal problems and
competent to "do his bit" under civil service rules and
their spirit. From it should come not only highly
skilled mechanics but also those who besides being that
understand the economic and human aspects of the
industries and have the qualifications for a captaincy
but not for the ruthlessness of the autocracy of
capital. With corresponding ends in view, the junior
college needs to train those choosing to go into
commerce. Our national unpreparedness for peace could
hardly be better illustrated than by the fact that our
commercial centers still cling to the method of trial
and error and seem to be satisfied, as far as our
schools are concerned, with training leading to minor
clerkships. Our children, thoughtful men and women are
agreed, should not be brought up wholly as if they were
orphans in charge of maiden aunts. But is not one
cause of this situation that the girl high-school
graduate finds no vocational trail blazed for her
except that which leads into teaching? Here, once
more, the junior college must accept the challenge to
do better things in better ways, to extend, for
example, the routes suggested by the household art and
science of the high school to their vocational termini.
Of course the young woman would not be shut out from
any of the other vocational departments except by her
aptitudes and preferences.

It is an essential part of the junior-college idea
that each junior college have its own individuality, in
accordance with its environment. Thoughtless
duplicating should be out of the question. Hence the
nature and scope of vocational departments must be
determined primarily by the communities served most
directly. However else we limit our selection, no
courses are justified, save in connection with home
interests, that would compel the junior-college
graduate to fare into a far land for the work he has
been trained to do. In cities with several high
schools it will doubtless be rational to connect a
junior-college department of commerce with a high
school so located as to make cooperation easy with
business concerns, a department for the vocations that
have been developed out of home activities in
connection with the high school best equipped already,
etc., provided the danger can be guarded against of
isolated, exclusive, and hence suicidal specialization.
I am more than skeptical about the educational success
of any junior college with only non-vocational
departments. At the very least it should have what for
want of a better term I have called a department of
civic education, which, while only partly vocational in

the specialized sense, would undertake the training of young men and women for efficient municipal service in the various city departments. It would, of course, not be too remote from the centers of city administration, in order that wholetime students may have a chance to observe and practise and city employees may have within reach opportunities for improvement in the service.

The foregoing conclusions as to the mission of the junior college seem inevitable if we really believe in a safe and progressive democracy and hence in our duty to realize its foundation principle: continuity of educational opportunity; completeness of such opportunity.   The old order must pass because it has not achieved and can not achieve either continuity   or completeness.   Now, while the junior college, like any adolescent, is trying to find itself and its best work in a new order, it will probably need to be protected against some of its friends, notably the university. The same process that has brought about the substitution of the university for the senior college has also made away pretty successfully with the college idea in the work of the two years preceding. "Peaceful penetration" from above has resulted in a protectorate. Men trained solely for the exercise of university functions can not be expected to regard the work of the first half of their institution as anything but introductory.   To them the junior college is not the dome of the secondary-school edifice but merely a university entrance hall or vestibule. Moreover, since educational thinking is usually the last thing a university faculty thinks of--this has been true since the middle ages--the naive assumption obtains and controls that "all's right with the world," as far as the existing conception of freshman and sophomore education is concerned, and, further, that technical preparation for university specialties is just what the junior college at home--and therefore elsewhere--is for.   Under these circumstances it is easy to foresee what is bound to happen if the junior college not connected with a university listens to the siren voices issuing therefrom.   Not only will there be pre-engineering, pre-legal, pre-medical, pre-anything-you-please courses, each directed by a university department, but there are not likely to be any pro-student courses. Worse still, the junior college, being directed by the university, will do unto the intermediate and high school as it is being done by. Shall the new secondary-school system, too, like the old, answer to Plato's definition of a slave, one whose conduct is shaped by another? Here is one alternative. The other is for the junior college to cooperate with the university in the selection of foundation courses for this, that and the other profession, and then to

conduct them strictly without reference to possible
professional superstructures. The aim must lie within
the junior college. The suicidal idea of a deferred
education must remain excluded from the non-vocational
as well as from the vocational departments. As to the
non-vocational type of courses the true test is whether
they are adapted to students who do not look forward to
basing a profession on them. How the junior college
will overcome all such temptations to lose its life,
liberty and happiness, who can tell?

*****

What manner of child shall this be?! Not all of us
will be able to second my counsels in behalf of the
junior college. But all of us, knowing that we school
men and school women are largely responsible for the
making or marring of the junior college, all of us can
be and are united in the purpose to secure from it and
through it the largest and greatest possible
contribution to the common good.

*****

10. A NATIONAL STUDY OF JUNIOR COLLEGES

Floyd Marion McDowell produced in 1918 at the State University of Iowa the first doctoral dissertation descriptive of the junior college movement. His study shows the rapid growth and complex nature of this institution even in the first two decades of the 20th century. McDowell found four types of junior college--the first two years of a four-year undergraduate program at a university, the private junior college usually attached to an academy, the 13th and 14th grades extended by a local public high school, and, finally, the teacher training or normal school. He found rapid growth on the part of the junior college movement and concluded that it seemed assured of "a place in our system of education." His dissertation was reprinted as a bulletin of the then U.S. Bureau of Education. McDowell was dean of Graceland College, a junior college in Lamoni, Iowa, during the time of his study.

*****

The purposes of this investigation were stated in Chapter I, as follows:

1. To make a clear analysis of the forces that have contributed to the origin and development of the junior colleges.

2. To ascertain the facts in regard to the present status of the various types of junior colleges throughout the United States.

F.M. McDowell, The Junior College, U.S. Department of the Interior, Bureau of Education Bulletin 1919, No. 35, Washington, D.C.: U.S. Government Printing Office, 1919, pp. 98-103. McDowell's dissertation was titled "The Junior College: A Study of Its Origin, Development, and Status in the United States."

3.   To make a summary of the present attempts at the accrediting of junior colleges in the various States.

4.   To suggest the possible applications of this information to the problems peculiar to the organization and administration of the junior college.

The conclusions reached may be summarized as follows:

I.   Conclusions in regard to the forces that have contributed to the origin and development of the junior college.

1.   The idea of a junior college in the form of an extended period of secondary education probably comes from Europe.   In its present form, however, the junior college is purely an American product.

2.   The University of Michigan was the first institution in this country to recognize officially the junior college idea.   This was in 1883.   It remained for President Harper, of the University of Chicago, and Dean Lange, of the University of California, to work out almost simultaneously a detailed plan for the organization of junior colleges as a part of our educational system.   Since 1892 these institutions have strongly advocated the junior college.

3.   Universities have supported the junior college because--

(a) The very rapid increase in their enrollment has made it difficult to provide for the needs of the freshman and sophomore classes.

(b) The need of early preparation for professional courses has made it necessary to classify entering students on the basis of their future work.

(c) There is a growing conviction on the part of leading educators that there is a need of a redistribution of work between the secondary school and the university.

4.   The recent tendency of normal schools to become colleges or at least to offer college work has given an impetus to the junior college movement:

(a) Normal school officials claim that they must keep pace with the progress of the public school system by providing collegiate training for prospective teachers.

(b) The recent movement toward standardization of all educational institutions has resulted in the belief that a majority of normal schools had best limit the amount of collegiate instruction offered to two years.

5.   Public high schools in a number of cities have been led to extend their courses to include the first two years of the college course for the following reasons:

(a) There is a widespread demand upon the part of an intelligent public to have the opportunities for securing a higher education brought within reach of all.

(b) There is need of certain vocational and completing courses for the large numbers of students who can not or should not go to the university.

(c) Specific local needs in certain cities have resulted in the establishment of junior colleges.

(d) The tendency to raise the entrance requirements of professional schools to include the first two years of college work.

(e) The geographical remoteness of some cities from standard colleges and universities.

(f) The fact that a local college is a financial saving to a community.

6. An increasing number of small denominational colleges have become junior colleges. Various factors have contributed to this change:

(a) With the progress of the standardization movement it has become more and more difficult for the college of limited means to offer more than two years of college work.

(b) Churches have awakened to the folly and danger of establishing in each State a large number of colleges, all endeavoring to cover the same kind and amount of work. The junior college plan will eliminate competition in a large measure and make possible a closely knit together system of church schools.

(c) Officials of small colleges are desireous of having their respective schools become honest institutions by claiming to do only that which they can do well.

(d) The junior college assures a place in our educational system for the large number of colleges for women in the South.

(e) In some sections of the country the junior college has been encouraged as a means of providing additional opportunities for teacher training.

II. Conclusions in regard to the present status of the various types of junior colleges.

1. The junior college movement has made rapid growth during the past 10 years. Sixty-nine junior colleges have been organized since 1907, and more than half of this number since 1915,

2. There may be distinguished four types of junior colleges:

(a) The "junior college" or "lower division" of the college of liberal arts of the university. This organization is found at present in the Universities of Chicago, California, and Washington.

(b) Normal schools accredited for two years of college work. Such institutions have been officially recognized in the following States: Arizona, Indiana, Michigan, Minnesota, North Dakota, Nebraska, Oklahoma, Utah, West Virginia, and Wisconsin.

(c) The public high school extended to include the

first two years of college work.   The names of 39 such
institutions have been reported.   Of this number,   21
are in California.

(d) The small private college which has limited its
work to two years.   The names of 93 such colleges have
been reported.   Of this number, 16 are in Texas, 14 in
Missouri, 9 in Virginia, and 5 in Illinois.

3.   The following facts have been collected in
regard to the sources of support of the last two types
of junior colleges:

(a) The sources of support of the public junior
colleges named in order of importance are: Taxation,
State aid,   and   tuition.   There   is   an   increasing
tendency to regard these institutions as an integral
part of the system of public education and hence as
objects of public support.

(b) The sources of support of private junior
colleges named in order of importance are: Tuition,
church budget, endowment, and offerings and donations.
Fully 75 per cent of the income of these institutions
comes from sources which can not be fixed and assured.
Less than 20 percent comes from a permanent endowment.

4.   The following facts concerning the courses of
study offered in the public and private junior colleges
are of interest:

(a) The traditional freshman and sophomore courses
occupy the bulk of the curriculum of both types of
institutions.

(b) Private junior colleges adhere more closely to
the classical courses than do the public institutions.

(c) Public junior colleges are offering more and a
greater variety of vocational or finishing courses than
the private institutions.   Of the work offered by the
former, 17 per cent may be considered vocational, as
compared with only 9 per cent of that offered by the
latter.   If the courses in education are omitted, the
latter would be reduced to 4.5 per cent.

(d) Sixty per cent of the private junior colleges
reporting offer courses in education, as compared with
only 16 per cent of the public colleges.

5.   A careful study of the training, experience,
and work of th instructors of the public and private
junior colleges yields the following significant facts:

(a) Measured by the academic degrees which they
have secured and by the amount of graduate work which
they have completed, the training of the instructors of
the junior college studied is greatly inferior to the
standard maintained by certain colleges and
universities.   It is also inferior to the standards at
present agreed upon as desirable for the junior
colleges themselves.

(b) The instructors in junior colleges have had
less teaching experience than the instructors of

freshman and sophomore classes in certain standard colleges and universities.

(c) Instructors in junior colleges are required to carry a heavier schedule than are the instructors in certain standard colleges and universities. The number of hours devoted exclusively to freshman and sophomore classes is, however, approximately the same in all classes of institutions considered in this investigation.

(d) The enrollment in the recitation sections in the junior colleges is much less on an average than is that of the first and second year classes in the standard colleges and universities considered.

6. The following facts in regard to the enrollment of public and private junior colleges are significant:

(a) Each of the 74 junior colleges considered in this investigation is operated in connection with an academy or a high school.

(b) The high-school departments of the public junior colleges have an average enrollment of 580 students.

(c) The academies operated in connection with the private junior colleges have an average enrollment of only 80 students.

(d) The enrollment in the private junior colleges increased from 1,771 in 1915 to 2,372 in 1917, or 34 per cent.

(e) The enrollment in public junior colleges increased from 592 to 1,587, or 168 per cent, during the same period.

7. The following facts in regard to the graduates of junior colleges are especially significant:

(a) A majority of the junior colleges grant no degree. A small per cent grant the degree or title of "Associate in Arts."

(b) The number of graduates from public junior colleges increased 211 per cent from 1915 to 1917.

(c) During the same period the number of graduates of private junior colleges increased 21 per cent.

(d) Of the 370 graduates of the public junior colleges for this period of three years, 73 per cent continued their work in a higher institution.

(e) Of the 2,225 graduating from the private junior colleges during this period, 41 per cent continued their work in higher institutions.

III. Conclusions in regard to the various attempts to standardize the junior college.

1.   The junior college had been recognized officially, at least in specific cases, by the following institutions: The State Universities of Arkansas, California, Idaho, Indiana, Illinois, Iowa, Kansas, Michigan, Minnesota, Missouri, Texas, and Washington, together with Leland Stanford University.

2.   The State legislatures of the following States have enacted legislation bearing to a greater or less extent on the junior college movement: California, Idaho, Michigan, Texas, and Wisconsin.

3.   The State departments of education, also, of the following States have recognized the junior college: California, Illinois, Kansas, Texas, Utah, Virginia, and West Virginia.

4.   In addition to the above the following accrediting agencies have attempted to establish desirable standards for junior colleges.   The Kentucky Association of Colleges and Universities, the college section of the State Teachers' Association of Texas, the North Central Association of Schools and Colleges, the board of education of the Methodist Episcopal Church South, and the Association of Colleges and Secondary Schools of the Southern States.

5.   The standards that have been established by these various accrediting agencies approximate uniformity on the following points:

(a) The material equipment necessary for college grade work.

(b) The scope of the work that should be attempted and the requirements for admission and graduation.

(c) The training to be expected of each instructor and the amount of teaching to be required.

(d) The amount of work that a student should be permitted to carry.

(e) The relation of the junior college to the high school or academy with which it is connected.

(f) The general standard that instruction in the junior college must be of college rank.

IV.   Conclusion in regard to the possible applications of these facts to the problems of the junior college.

1.   From the study of the origin and development of the junior college we may conclude that it has appeared in response to certain fundamental needs, and hence that for the present at least it seems assured of a place in our system of education.

2.   From the study of the present status of the junior college we may conclude:

(a) That if the junior colleges are to justify their attempt to offer the first two years of standard college work they must secure better-trained faculties. Fully 50 per cent of the junior colleges studied need to raise their standards in this respect.

(b) That at present the junior colleges, especially the private institutions, do not meet the needs of the comparatively large proportion of their students who do not intend to enter the university upon graduation.   These institutions should offer more and a greater variety of

vocational   or   finishing   courses   of   college
grade.

(c) That public junior colleges should encourage
the movement which seeks to make them a definite part
of the State system of public education.

(d) That private junior colleges should seek to
cooperate with each other and with the State
universities in their respective States to the end that
a better organized and more economical system of higher
education may be established.

(e) That private junior colleges should endeavor to
secure permanent endowment of at least $100,000 for
each institution, and they should at all times limit
the amount of work which they attempt to offer to that
which can be conducted with a maximum efficiency.

3.   From the study of the various attempts to
standardize the junior college we may conclude that the
following minimum standards should be met by any
institution attempting to offer the first two years of
college work.

(a) Requirement for admission--Graduation from an
accredited high school or at least 15 units of credit
in standard secondary school work.

(b) Requirement for graduation--At least 60
semester hours of college credit in advance of the 15
units of secondary work.

(c) Equipment--(1) Library--At least 2,000 volumes
carefully selected with special reference to college
work.   (2) Laboratories--An equipment valued at least
at $1,000 to $1,500 for each science taught.

(d) Teachers--(1) Number--At least five heads of
departments.   (2) Training--At least one year of
graduate work in advance of the bachelor's degree,
with special training in the subject to be taught.
(3) Amount of teaching--No more than 20 periods per
week (60-minute periods).   (4) Character of
instruction--Must in all cases be strictly of college
grade.

(e) The high school or academy operated in
connection with the junior college must be fully
accredited.

(f) Limitations--(1) The institution must prefix
the term "junior" when applying to itself the name
"college."   (2) No junior college should confer a
baccalaureate degree.

II. P. P. CLAXTON AND THE BETTER ORGANIZATION OF HIGHER EDUCATION IN THE UNITED STATES

The U.S. Commissioner of Education, Philander Priestly Claxton, strongly endorsed the junior college as a way to make higher education more efficient. He urged the country to view the junior college as a way of achieving efficiency in its educational system. There are too many weak four-year colleges, he maintained. To achieve a desirable level of economy, many of these institutions ought to refocus their efforts on doing a better job with fewer programs. They do not have the financial resources to be successful. In the name of economy, these colleges should build strong two-year programs.

The following remarks by Commissioner Claxton were made at a national gathering of junior college leaders held in St. Louis in 1920. Out of this conference, sponsored by the U.S. Bureau of Education, came the formation of the American Association of Junior Colleges (later the American Association of Community and Junior Colleges).

Claxton was born in 1862 in Tennessee (d. 1957), studied at the University of Tennessee, Johns Hopkins University, and in Germany. He was federal Commissioner of Education from 1911 to 1921 and later served as president of Austin Peay Normal School (later State University) in Clarksville, Tennessee (1930-1946).

*****

It is quite certain that the burden upon the colleges and universities of the United States will be much larger from this time forth than it has been in the past. The social, civic, political, industrial, commercial, and professional life of the country in the

George F. Zook (ed.), National Conference of Junior Colleges, 1920, Department of the Interior, Bureau of Education Bulletin 1922, No. 19, Washington, D.C.: U.S. Government Printing Office, pp. 21-24.

new era upon which we are entering will require the
services of a much larger number of college men and
women than the old era which passed away with the war,
and will give them more opportunities. Our colleges
and universities must supply the demand for this
country, and, to a very large extent, for other
countries in America and in Europe and Asia. For a
generation at least there can be little danger of
overproduction of college-trained men and women,
provided their education and training are directed
toward present and future needs of service, and are
made to take hold on the life and work of this and the
next generation.

The rapid increase in the number of high-school
students (now more than two million) and the higher
standards of high schools will insure a constantly
increasing supply of young men and women for the
colleges. The increase in wages for the great army of
laborers and the higher prices of farm products will
enable hundreds of thousands of families to send their
sons and daughters to college whose incomes have until
now been too meager to permit them to consider such a
thing as possible.

The salaries of professors and instructors must be
increased to at least double what they were in 1913-14.
New buildings and equipment for classrooms,
laboratories, and for housing students will, at present
prices of material and labor, cost from two to four
times as much as they would have cost in 1913-14.

If the number of college students were no larger than
it was in 1913-14, endowments and appropriations would
need to be fully twice as large as they were then in
order to maintain efficiency. For an increase of 50
percent in the number of students there will be needed
an addition to endowments and incomes fully equal to
the total of those for 1913-14, making the total need
three times as much as the need for that year.

It is already evident that the people are willing to
supply funds through gifts and appropriations in much
larger amounts than formerly. But can we expect an
increase of 200 per cent? Even if we could the time
has now come when it behooves us who have to do with
administration and the formation of policies to study
carefully every reasonable and promising means of
economy--economy not only in money, but in the time and
energy of teachers and students. No doubt there are
many economies worth careful consideration, but I
believe none will yield larger results than can be
obtained through such organizations as will reduce
the number of colleges doing the full four years'
work and at the same time will assure greater
efficiency in the first two college years. This
means, of course, increasing the number of junior

colleges while decreasing the number of senior colleges.

It is partly for this reason that this conference of junior colleges, held at this time, has such significance.

In 1915-16, the Bureau of Education listed 577 colleges and universities. These terms are, as you know, used quite loosely in this country, and in common usage have about the same meaning. Of the 577 colleges, 508 reported their incomes as well as their student enrollments. A large proportion of those that did not report incomes were Catholic institutions, or belonged to or were affiliated with teaching societies which justly count their income largely in service rather than in money.

Since in 1915-16 the colleges had not been much affected by the war, the figures for that year are better for our purposes than would be the figures for later years. If we divide these 508 colleges into nine groups according to incomes, we have the following:

(1) Eight colleges reported incomes ranging from $2,603,489 to $3,915,714, and a student enrollment from 4,889 to 8,510. The average income per student in these groups was approximately $500. (In incomes the private benefactions for endowments are not included.)

(2) Fourteen colleges reported incomes ranging from $1,002,384 to $1,902,005, and student enrollments from 630 (at West Point) to 6,462 (at the University of Michigan). For these 14 colleges the average income per student was approximately $450.

(3) Thirty colleges reported incomes between $500,000 and $1,000,000, and student enrollments from 290 to 3,850. The average income per student for this group was approximately $375.

(4) Fifty-six colleges reported incomes between $250,000 and $500,000, and student enrollments between 105 and 4,138. The average income per student for this group was approximately $335.

(5) Ninety-two colleges reported incomes between $100,000 and $250,000, and student enrollments between 111 and 3,692. The average income per student for this group was approximately $250.

(6) One hundred and two colleges reported incomes between $50,000 and $100,000, and student enrollments between 72 and 1,557. The average income per student for this group was approximately $185--less than half the average for the third group.

(7) One hundred and twenty-two colleges reported incomes between $25,000 and $50,000, and student enrollments between 20 and 861. The average income per student for this group was approximately $145; less than half the average for the fourth group and less than one-third the average for the second group.

(8)   Fifty-four colleges reported incomes between $15,000 and $25,000, and student enrollments between 49 and 388. The average income per student for this group was approximately $120; less than half the average for the fifth group and less than one-fourth the average for the first group.

(9)   Twenty-nine colleges reported incomes ranging from $3,075 to $14,618, and student enrollments ranging from 66 to 345. The average income per student for this group was approximately $75; less than one-half the average for the sixth group; less than one-third the average for the fifth group; less than one-fourth the average for the fourth group; just one-fifth the average for the third group; one sixth the average for the second group; and considerably less than the average cost of high-school instruction.

In most of the largest and richest of these schools, and in some of those in the lower classes both as to incomes and student enrollments, a portion of the income is devoted to graduate work and to research. But in none is the amount thus used large enough to reduce the per capita for undergraduate students by more than a small percentage. Practically all these 508 colleges, reporting incomes ranging from $3,075 to $3,915,714, attempt to do full four years of college work and confer degrees. In some of them all classes are large enough to permit options and specialization on a liberal scale and still give to each section in each subject such a number of students as will keep the cost of instruction within reasonable bounds. In many of the poorer and smaller schools the numbers in the two higher classes are so small as practically to prohibit options and specialization, and to make the sections in some subjects even without division so small as to destroy the interest both of students and of teachers and at the same time make the cost of instruction per pupil comparatively very large.   In many of these colleges nearly half the class sections have less than five students, and a large number of the class sections have only one, two, or three students. In these schools the average cost per student in the higher classes is from 4 to 10 times as much as in the two lower classes. The cost of teaching from 5 to 10 students in the senior class is larger than the cost of teaching from 40 to 50 students in the freshman class. These higher class students are, after all, not well taught, since the colleges are not able to furnish the necessary library and laboratory equipment and to pay sufficient salaries to retain the services of teachers of the best ability.

In some of the larger schools the numbers of students in the freshman and sophomore classes are very large. Several colleges have more than a thousand freshmen,

and some more than two thousand. The freshmen entering
in September are boys and girls who in June were
graduated from the high schools and who had known only
high-school discipline and high-school methods of
teaching and study. In the high schools most of the
teachers are men and women of professional training and
enough experience to give them skill in teaching and
training and directing boys and girls. Coming from
high school to college without any skilled and wise
guidance, through a transition period, many of these
kiddish freshmen, however well meaning, are unable to
adapt themselves to the new conditions and discipline
and go astray sadly. In the freshmen class, and also
to an extent in the sophomore class, students are all
too often taught by young teachers with little or no
experience and who have had no professional training.
Many of these teachers are also without the native
ability and professional skill which will insure final
success. For however rich the colleges may be most of
them still pay the larger salaries to those who give
most of their time to the higher classes and leave the
lower classes to the tender mercies and bunglings of
young, untrained, and inexperienced teachers.
   Here is the opportunity for the junior college and
for a very important economy in college organization.
Practically all the 307 colleges having incomes of less
than $50,000, and a good number of those with incomes
from $50,000 to $100,000 should cease to try to do more
than two or three years of work--preferably only two
years--and should concentrate all their means of money
and men on doing well the work of these two years,
employing as teachers men and women of the best native
ability, the finest culture, and the largest skill that
education and professional training can give; men and
women having the power to inspire and direct as well as
to instruct.
   These colleges could then take in all or most of the
tens of thousands of boys and girls now on the waiting
list of the larger and richer colleges, and offer them
such opportunities for instruction, training, and
interest in college life as would induce them to come
to them for these two years and to bring with them
other tens of thousands who now swell the mobs of
freshmen and sophomores in the larger schools. The
mortality of students in these two years would
become much less than it now is. A much larger
per cent of them would go to the larger and richer
colleges for junior, senior, and graduate work,
thus making up to these schools for the loss in
their freshmen and sophomore classes. The work
done in these higher classes might then be much
better than is now possible. With the better
teachers for the lower classes in the junior colleges

from 25 to 50 per cent more work would be accomplished in these two years than is now accomplished.

Should these poorer and smaller colleges thus limit their field and change the character of their work most of them would soon find themselves with two or three times their present number of students and with incomes three or four times as large as they have now. In addition, they would have the consciousness of serving their country and the world more effectively than they now do or can. Not the least element in this service would be the influence on the work of the lower classes of the larger schools, for as soon as any considerable number of colleges do as is here suggested the larger and richer schools will reorganize their work for the lower classes and among other things will begin to give to the students in these classes teachers as good or better than those in the junior colleges.

Thus with the same amount of money the effectiveness of our schools of higher learning might be increased from 20 to 30 per cent.

In the discussion of the work, organization, and courses of study of the junior colleges, these schools should not be thought of as in any way inferior to schools doing the full four years' work. No schools should lost any of its dignity or worthiness of support by confining its work to the first two college years. On the other hand, both dignity and worthiness will be increased if they will do the work of these two years in a better and a larger way, such as this change should make possible.

12. JUNIOR COLLEGE ACCREDITATION

The work of defining the junior college and judging its value and capabilities to serve students was an issue confronting virtually all accrediting agencies. Here are recorded early efforts by the Association of Colleges and Secondary Schools of the Southern States (now the Southern Association of Colleges and Schools, or SACS) to cope with this novel educational institution.

Unlike California and the West, where public schools played a prominent part in the initial junior college movement, the private academy or college was prevalent in the South. The junior college, as one can see from the first attempts by SACS to define and regulate it, was viewed as a college, not a high school. Its curriculum was primarily classical.

In a few states, most notably Mississippi, one does find public schools extending 13th and 14th grade instruction and that instruction being devoted to vocational interests such as agriculture and home economies. In the main, however, the standard American college with its standard four-year curriculum was the benchmark by which these new institutions were judged by SACS. The junior college was to be just that--a junior or abbreviated version of the four-year college.

Association of Colleges and Secondary Schools of the Southern States, Proceedings of the Thirtieth Annual Meeting, Emory University, Ga.: the Association, 1925, pp.367-369. For an extended review of SACS and its efforts to come to grips with the junior college see Robert W. Day and Barry L. Mellinger, Accreditation of Two-Year Colleges in the South, Atlanta, Ga.: Southern Association of Colleges and Schools, Commission on Colleges, 1973.

c. Junior Colleges

Standard Number 1.   Entrance Requirements.   The requirement for admission shall be the satisfactory completion of a four-year course of not less than fifteen units in a secondary school approved by a recognized accrediting agency.   Any junior college affiliated with recognized senior colleges may be called upon at any time for a record of all the students entering the freshman class, such record to contain the name of each student, his secondary school, method of admission, units offered in each subject, and total units accepted.

Standard Number 2.   Requirements [for] Graduation. The minimum requirement for graduation shall be sixty semester hours of credit.

Standard Number 3.   Degrees.   Junior colleges shall not grant degrees.

Standard Number 4.   Number of College Departments. The number of separate departments maintained shall not be less than five (English, History, Foreign Language, Math., Science) and number of teachers not less than five giving full time to college work.

Standard Number 5.   Training of the Faculty.   The minimum preparation for teachers shall be not less than one year of work satisfactorily completed in a graduate school of recognized standing, it being assumed that the teachers already hold the baccalaureate degree.

Standard Number 6.   Number of Classroom Hours for Teachers.   The average number of credit hours per week for each instructor shall not exceed sixteen.

Standard Number 7.   Number of Students in Classes. The number of students in a class shall not exceed thirty (except for lectures).   It is recommended that the number of students in a   class in a foreign language shall not exceed twenty-five.   The number of students in a laboratory section shall not exceed the number for which desk space and equipment have been provided.

Standard Number 8.   Support.   The minimum annual operating income for the two years of junior college work should be $20,000, of which not less than $10,000 should be derived from stable sources other than students, such as public support or permanent endowment.   Increase in faculty, student body, and scope of instruction should be accompanied by increase of income, from such stable sources.   The financial status of each junior college should be judged in relation to its educational program.

Standard Number 9.   Library.   A working library of not less than 2500 volumes, exclusive of public documents, shall be maintained and a reading room in connection with the library.   A definite annual

income for the support of the library shall be
provided.

Standard Number 10. Laboratories. The laboratories
shall be adequately equipped for individual instruction
in courses offered and an annual income for their up-
keep provided. It is recommended that a school with a
limited income be equipped for good work in one or two
sciences and not attempt work in others.

Standard Number 11.   Separation of College and
Preparatory Classes. Where a junior college and a high
school are maintained together, it is required that the
students be taught in separate classes.

Standard Number 12.   Proportion of Regular College
Students to the Whole Student Body.   At least 75 per
cent of the students in a junior college shall be
pursuing courses leading to graduation.

Standard Number 13. General Statement Concerning
Material Equipment. The location and construction of
the buildings, the lighting, heating, and ventilation
of the rooms, the nature of the laboratories,
corridors, closets, water supply, school furniture,
apparatus, and methods of cleaning shall be such as to
insure hygienic conditions for both students and
teachers.

Standard Number 14. General Statement Concerning
Curriculum and Spirit of Administration. The character
of the curriculum, efficiency of instruction, and
spirit of the institution shall be factors in
determining its standing.

Standard Number 15.   Extra-Curricular Activities.
Athletics, amusements, fraternities, and other extra-
curricular activities shall be properly administered
and shall not occupy an undue place in the life of the
college.

Standard Number 16. Inspection. No college will be
recommended for membership until it has been inspected
and reported upon by an agent or agents regularly
appointed by the Commission. Any college of the
Association shall be open to inspection at any time.

Standard Number 17. Filing of Blank. No institution
shall be placed or retained on the approved list unless
a regular information blank has been filed with the
Commission. The list shall be approved from year to
year by the Commission. The blank shall be filed
triennially, but the Commission may for due cause call
upon any member to file a new report in the meantime.
Failure to file the blank shall be cause for dropping
an institution.

13. KOOS FINDS INCREASING SUPPORT FOR THE JUNIOR COLLEGE MOVEMENT

Leonard V. Koos was an early scholar of both the junior high school and junior college movements. His extensive studies of the two-year college were landmark investigations and served to articulate the practical and theoretical arguments for such an institution.

Koos' studies indicated that the junior college could fulfill a variety of needs in our society. Not only would it provide college-level general or liberal education, it could offer the beginnings of professional education. It should stand for outstanding teaching and individual care for students. It was a means of extending educational opportunity. It gave opportunities for early leadership development. It fostered the reorganization of secondary and collegiate education. It was efficient, avoided waste and duplication in American education, and promoted economy. That was strong support for this new and novel educational creation.

Leonard Vincent Koos (b. 1881 in Illinois, d. 1976) was educated at Oberlin College and the University of Chicago (M.A. degree in 1915, Ph. D. degree in 1916). He taught in rural schools in Illinois and was a professor of education at the universities of Washington, Minnesota, and Chicago. Koos was a prolific writer and longtime scholar-observer of many trends and issues in American education. He served for a time as editor of the Junior College Journal and director of research for the American Association of Junior Colleges.

The materials presented [here]. . . afford ample justification of the junior-college movement. Only an occasional aspect of the many-sided study of the new unit has turned out unfavorable to it, and in most of

Leonard V. Koos, The Junior College Movement, Boston: Ginn and Company, 1925, pp. 313-320.

these exceptions the inadequacy can be ascribed to the
sheer immaturity of the movement.   As it is believed
that this conclusion of justification has been given
adequate support . . . there is no intention to do more
. . . than to direct the attention of the reader . . .
to some of the more prominent of the findings
sustaining the right of the junior college to a place
in our school system.

1.   It has been shown that in the extent of its
offering the average junior college does not fall far
short of the work actually taken by most students
during their first two years in the colleges of liberal
arts.   Although the new unit does not qualify so well
on the requirements of the first two years of work in
preprofessional curricula and in professional curricula
opening with the freshman college year, it does not
appear that sizable units cannot give all the general
and special work needed by any considerable proportion
of the total number of students in higher institutions.

2.   In certain aspects of the instructional situation
the junior college does not yet measure up to other
higher institutions.   This statement applies to the
extent of graduate training that the instructors have
had and to the proportions of instructors adequately
trained for the subjects they are teaching.   In other
respects the comparison is more favorable, as in
experience, in remuneration, and in the extent of
training in education.   Observation of the actual work
of teaching corroborates the conclusion drawn from a
study of training and experience: that, although
instructors in junior colleges seem on the average less
well equipped from the standpoint of subject matter, at
the same time they tend to be superior in instructional
procedure.   The same observation indicated an
approximation to equality in the average level of
student performance in accredited junior colleges and
in other higher institutions, this judgment being
supported by the results of a comparison of average
marks earned in their third year of work in standard
higher institutions by junior-college graduates and by
those who had earned the right to senior-college
standing in an estimable state university.   The
progress of the junior college in these instructional
matters during its brief history is an earnest [sic] of
even more progress and of the ultimate attainment of
satisfactory standards in all respects.   There is no
occasion to doubt that the junior college will achieve
a type of instruction that is much more suited to
students on this level than is much of the classroom
procedure in present-day colleges and universities, in
which there is too much effort to avoid lower-class
teaching responsibilities to get wholesome and
constructive results.

3. The junior college will not only be well suited to serve the needs of those who should or can aspire to higher levels of training, but it is clearly better designed than are our typical higher institutions to provide for those who should not or cannot go on. Its superiority in the solution of this problem rests in the fact that with the first two college years as terminal years in the school containing the junior college, there will be a marked tendency to look out for the interests of this group of students.

This interest in these years as culminal years will result in the development of general curricula as well as special occupational (semi-professional) curricula ending with the close of the junior-college period. It is not to be expected that present-day higher institutions will manifest a constructive interest in curricula of less than four years' duration, because of their logically primary concern with students in curricula four or more years in length. Nor could students be induced to enroll in large numbers for such curricula, because of the loss of caste in aspiring to anything less than the completion of the typical length of curriculum in a given institution.

4. Through proximity and lowered costs the junior college is in a position to make more nearly universal the opportunities of education on this level. This in turn, by removing a large part of the cost in these years, will make it more nearly feasible for many to secure training beyond the junior-college level.

5. Judging from parents' opinions and from the more youthful age of freshmen in junior colleges and in other higher institutions when they reside in the community of location than when they come from outside, the new unit is looked upon by patrons as affording a continuation of home influences during the critical years of social immaturity. No matter what one's opinion may be touching the reality of the moral hazard to students away from home during these first college years, the attitude of parents is a social force to be reckoned with, since it postpones continuance of education and entails a deplorable loss of time. Moreover, few will doubt that there is an actual hazard, especially in institutions with large registrations and staffs inadequate to the purposes of social and moral guidance important for young persons.

6. Not unrelated to this advantage is the greater attention affordable to the individual student in junior-college units. The marked difference as to size of class sections now obtaining between the new institution and the larger colleges and universities is likely in considerable part to disappear as we come to foster and maintain only sizable junior-college units. With a number of junior colleges in each state,

however, there will be few so large as to parallel the
situation that develops the attitude of unconcern
toward the individual students and brings on the
"depersonalization" which long since began to
characterize the institutions affected by the "freshman
flood."

7. Another element of superiority of the junior
college is (and will be more and more) that it gives to
students on this level better opportunities for
laboratory practice in leadership, for there are not
upper-classmen, who in other higher institutions are
usually elected to most positions of student
responsibility.

8. The junior-college movement has the support also
of apparently inevitable forces of reorganization in
higher education. Originating impulses here were the
advancing age of the college entrant, the downward
shift of materials of collegiate instruction, and the
accompanying increase of entrance requirements, all of
which provided the student with approximately two more
years of general training than he formerly received by
the time he had reached any given year-point in his
college career. Upon the heels of these changes have
come others in harmony with them. One was the changing
organization of college curricula, which moved from
complete prescription to almost complete election and
then to the prescription of a major subject which the
student almost always looks upon as occupational
specialization and in the majority of instances makes
use of occupationally subsequently to graduation.
Others are the accommodations that most colleges make
to the desires of students for shortened periods of
nonoccupational training; the trend of enrollment in
higher institutions, which is reducing the proportions
of students in the last two years of colleges of
liberal arts whether these are in separate institutions
or parts of universities, the line of cleavage
appearing in universities between the sophomore and
junior years; etc. Junior-college reorganization is
also sustained by the argument of analogy with French
and German school systems, since the latter include
within the secondary school and the unit underlying it
the whole of the period of general education, the
university giving itself over entirely to
specialization.

9. Finally, the materials presented . . . constitute
a cogent argument for the junior-college movement,
since they show not only a large extent of similarity
and identity of work in the high school and on the
junior-college level in colleges and universities but
also a large amount of actual repetition for the
individual student. To achieve such an organization
and coordination of courses on these two levels as to

economize time and assure proper sequence it is imperative that junior colleges be developed in intimate association with the high-school work below them.

Special purposes of the junior college.
The rather extended list of advantages of the junior college as just epitomized are readily transmutable into its special or distinctive purposes, and will hereafter be so designated. As justified up to this point, these purposes may be restated as follows:

1. To give the first two years of curricula (1) in liberal arts and (2) in preprofessional and professional work (where these professional curricula begin with the first college year).

2. To assure instruction as good as or better than that on the same level in other higher institutions.

3. To provide terminal general education for those who cannot or should not go on to higher levels of training.

4. To develop lines of semiprofessional training.

5. To popularize higher education.

6. To make possible the extension of home influences during immaturity.

7. To afford more attention to the individual student.

8. To improve the opportunities for laboratory practice in leadership.

9. To foster the inevitable reorganization of secondary and higher education.

10. To bring together into a single institution all work essentially similar in order to effect a better organization of courses and obviate wasteful duplication.

It is desirable to point out that one of these purposes is not distinctive in the same degree as are the remainder. Reference is made in particular here to purpose 1. What subtracts from its distinctiveness is the fact that it is now being performed in our traditional types of higher institutions.There are grounds, however, for retaining it as part of the complete list, since, if it cannot be accomplished, there would be no point in the acceptance of attempts at the performance of most of the others.

14. WHAT MANNER OF CHILD SHALL THIS BE? (OR, WHAT'S SO GREAT ABOUT 6-4-4?)

A professor and researcher at Stanford University, Walter C. Eells looked once again at the junior college movement and, in the footsteps of Alexis Lange, searched for an answer to the question of the two-year college's position in the structure of education. The so-called 6-4-4 plan for education was closely examined by Eells . . . and found wanting! Although supported by many writers, the 6-4-4 plan, when examined closely, said Eells, was not the perfect solution to educational problems. (The 6-4-4 was defined as six years of elementary education, followed by four years of junior high or middle school education, followed by four years of secondary and junior college education.) Indeed, the affirmative arguments were often weak, the disadvantages many.

The 6-4-4 plan never became the dominant plan of junior colleges in American education. Eells examined in detail the advantages and disadvantages of the plan, then presented extensive arguments in favor of the junior college as a separate two-year institution, quite apart from primary and secondary education. Is the junior college a part of secondary or collegiate education? Eells opted for its position in collegiate (higher) education.

Walter Crosby Eells (b. 1886 in Washington; d. 1962) received his Ph. D. from Stanford University. He then joined the Stanford faculty in 1927, where he gained national repute as a scholar and writer on junior college matters. Eells edited the <u>Junior College Journal</u> from 1930 to 1945 and served as the first full-time executive secretary of the American Association of Junior Colleges (1938-1945).

Walter Crosby Eells, "What Manner of Child Shall This Be?" Junior College Journal, Vol. I (February, 1931), 309-328. This paper is a condensed version of chapters XXVI and XXVII of Eells' book The Junior College (1931) and a copy of a speech he delivered at the University of California.

Thirteen years ago next month, that honored prophet and leader of the early junior college movement in California, Dr. Alexis F. Lange, dean of the School of Education of the great university at whose doors we are meeting this evening, delivered an address entitled, "The Junior College--What Manner of Child Shall This Be?" It has seemed to me wise today to re-examine the implications of this question in view of the phenomenal development of the junior college movement in the years that have passed. Accordingly I have chosen the same title as Dr. Lange used in 1917. In truth, however, it is no longer applicable, for . . . the junior college, at least in California, has now passed through the stages of childhood and youth to that of early manhood. Probably our question should at least be modernized to read, "What manner of youth shall this be?"

In my judgment the most fundamental problem to consider in endeavoring to answer this question today, and in suggesting the direction of desirable development in the next decade or more, is that of the form of organization of this vigorous and energetic youth and its relation to the other units of the American educational system. In particular, shall it be a two-year or a four-year unit? Is the widely heralded 6-4-4 plan the ultimate *summum bonum* of educational happiness?

In reviewing the literature on the 6-4-4 plan, one is reminded of the classic observation of Mark Twain with reference to the weather, that a great deal has been said about it, but very little seems to have been done about it! Much has been said and written about the 6-4-4 plan, but only a few such institutions have been established. Little has been written about the two-year junior college, but much as been done about it, as indicated by the hundreds of existing colleges of this type. There is danger that the busy, practical school administrator, without time to examine critically the question in its basic aspects, hearing so much of the advantages of the progressive 6-4-4 plan, will come to believe, on account of the mere frequent repetition of the same statements, that there is only one side to the question and that he is distinctly unprogressive if he does not work toward it. There is no difficulty in finding numerous presentations and re-presentations of the advantages claimed for the four-year junior college. Outstanding ones have been made by Harbeson of Pasadena, by Koos, by Zook, by Wood of Stephens, by Proctor, by Eby before this Association at Fort Worth, Texas, two years ago, by Commissioner Cooper in the School Review recently, and by Superintendent Sexson of Pasadena at the Atlantic City meeting of the National Education Association last spring. Search as one may, however, he will not find a single systematic

presentation of the other side of the question.[1]   It
seems, therefore, that there is a distinct place for a
comprehensive discussion of the disadvantages of the 6-
4-4 plan, and of the points in favor of the prevailing
type of institution, in order that the thoughtful
student of junior college problems may weight the
arguments, both pro and con, and draw his own
conclusions.

*****

C. MAIN ARGUMENTS FOR 6-4-4 PLAN
    . . . let us turn now to a consideration of the main
arguments for it as set forth by Commissioner Cooper in
his *School Review*[2] article and by others.
    1.   *The psychological argument* :   "The four-year
junior college is peculiarly fitted to the needs of the
periods of adolescence."
    There are two main theories of psychological
development, the saltatory theory and the gradual
theory.   The former, holding that there are certain
periods when sudden and pronounced mental, physical,
and social changes occur, has been popularized by G.
Stanley Hall and his followers, and has had a profound
influence on educational thought and administrative
practice.   The theory of gradual development, resulting
from thousands of careful scientific measurements by
Thorndike and his followers, seems, however, to be far
better established at the present time and destined to
modify practical school procedure still more.

*****

Doak S. Campbell,   secretary of this Association,   in

---

[1]An exception should perhaps be made in favor of the
brief article by J.B. Lillard, "The 6-3-3-2 versus the
6-4-4 Plan of Organization for the Public Junior
College," School and Society, XXXII (August 23, 1930),
262-64. This was published after the chapter upon
which this paper is based was written.
[2]William John Cooper, "Some Advantages Expected to
Result From Administering Secondary Education in Two
Units of Four Years Each," School Review, XXXVII (May,
1929), 335-46. These and other advantages claimed for
the 6-4-4 plan are fully treated in Chapter XXV of the
author's book, The Junior College.

his Doctor's dissertation, made an attempt to evaluate the whole psychological argument, especially from the junior college standpoint. He examined all available literature dealing with the psychology of adolescence, particularly stressing experimental, quantitative studies. His conclusions, therefore, are worth careful consideration, although time will permit quotation of but a small portion of them:

> So far as the literature discloses there has been no experimentation in this field which bears directly upon the problem of fitting the junior college unit to the period of later adolescence.
>
> Such experimentation as has been reported in this field shows that these periods are not radically different and distinctly separable from those immediately preceding or immediately following, and the consideration of them in this light is responsible for certain erroneous conceptions concerning them.
>
> The conception of the junior college as a completion unit of secondary education, designed to fit the period of later adolescence involves more than the mere mechanical readjustment of administrative machinery.

The psychological argument, then, may be dismissed at the present time as having little if any bearing on the question of the relative merits of the two-year or four-year junior college.

2. *The articulation argument:* "The four-year junior college would eliminate undesirable overlapping of courses (amounting to an average of at least fifteen per cent) between high school and college."

A certain amount of overlapping is not only permissible, but desirable. In teaching freshman mathematics, in college, for example, I found it highly profitable to spend fully fifteen per cent of the time in reviewing high-school mathematics, even though it would be classed as duplication by the criteria employed by Koos. Furthermore, even though the same subject-matter is treated, it may be treated from different standpoints in different schools. Take for example the subject in which Koos found the greatest overlapping, English Literature. As proof of overlapping he found that Shakespears's Sonnets were read in fifteen high schools and twenty-two colleges. It is possible that if a student took a course in Shakespeare in the upper division, he might read the sonnets again. And again in his graduate work. What

lamentable overlapping!   It is possible that he has
studied them from different standpoints each time,
historical, vocabulary, appreciation, and critical.
Possibly, when he gets to teaching English literature
in the junior college he may even overlap some more and
read them again--and not without profit.   Koos'
conclusion that "the actual repetition of materials can
hardly be less than a full fifth of all the work taken
in the high school" has been widely quoted.   Mere
duplication of material, however, is not necessarily to
be condemned.   It may be handled with profit by
different methods and with different levels.
It may be frankly admitted, however, that there is
some undesirable overlapping.   It by no means follows
that such overlapping and duplication of material will
be eliminated because courses are given in one
institution.   We have heard occasional complaints of
overlapping between departments in the same
institution.   I have an impression that overlapping of
courses has also been found to exist even in a single
department--the department of education, for example.
Overlapping, then, is not a matter that is necessarily
related to the question of two- or a four-year
institution.
The elimination of undesirable duplication and closer
articulation is a matter essentially of curriculum
revision and organization.   Superintendent Sexson tells
us how it is actually being accomplished at Pasadena.
He says that:

> There is a committee for each major
> subject of the curriculum, and each
> committee is endeavoring to reorganize the
> curriculum throughout the entire system, in
> such a way as to remove duplication and
> overlapping. . . .A syllabus is finally
> worked out and printed for each subject
> covering all the grades in which it forms a
> part of the curriculum.

This is an excellent description of the technique of
curriculum revision that has been carried out, not only
at Pasadena but at Sacramento during the past two years
under the able leadership of Dr. W.M. Proctor.   There
is this difference, however: Sacramento has an
independent two-year college.   Subject matter
committees have studied each subject throughout the
entire system, from the kindergarten through the junior
college; they have eliminated duplication, coordinated
the whole, published tentative syllabi, almost exactly
as described at Pasadena.   I would not hesitate to
guarantee that Dr. Proctor and his committees have
evolved a curriculum at Sacramento which shows no more

duplication from the grades through the junior college than is found at Pasadena. Curriculum revision and the elimination of undesirable duplication and overlapping are independent of the existence of a two-year or four-year junior college.

3.   *The economy-of-cost argument:*   "The four-year plan will make notable savings in housing, maintenance, and operation."

Unquestionably, one institution can be operated at less expense than two, and in so far as this is true it constitutes a valid argument for a four-year institution which is particularly potent with the taxpayer.   The fancied saving may be somewhat overestimated, however, and there may be other factors that more than offset any financial gain.   It is easy to make general statements of economy. What facts can be found with regard to this feature?   There are two aspects to be considered, (a) saving in capital outlay, buildings, and grounds, and (b) saving in maintenance and operating costs.   These will be considered separately.

a) *Savings in capital outlay.*--Regarding this feature, Harbeson says:

> Three secondary schools, the junior high school, the senior high school, and the junior college, all housed in separate plants constitute not only poor educational organization, but an intolerable waste of public funds, as well.

It must be remembered that the same total school population must be provided for under either form of organization, with sufficient classrooms in either case.   If there are two buildings instead of three, they must be larger ones.   There should be some saving in construction of auditorium, laboratories, and other special features, however.   But it should be remembered that the majority of two-year junior colleges are and for some time to come can be housed with the high school, using one wing or one floor of the existing high school building, with common use of auditorium, cafeteria, gymnasium, athletic fields, and other relative expensive special features and equipment.

Even in the most expensive case, however, where three complete plants are build instead of two, the savings for two plants only would be much less than 33 per cent, since the same school population must be accommodated in either case.   Let us make a liberal estimate, and assume a net saving of 15 to 20 per cent of capital outlay in favor of the 6-4-4 plan. With the life of a building estimated at twenty to thirty years, this would mean a net annual saving of 1/2 to 1 per cent of the total building cost. On a half-million-dollar plant, the annual saving on capital outlay would amount to $2,500 to $5,000 per year--worth saving, of course, but scarcely an "intolerable waste," especially if any educational advantage can be shown as a compensating feature.

   b) *Saving in maintenance.* --From most careful available studies of junior college expenses, it is seen that instructional salaries constitute 67 per cent of the total cost, while all instructional costs are 80 per cent of the total. There can be little, if any, saving in instructional salaries. The same number of classes, with minor exceptions, will have to be maintained in the four-year unit as in the two separate ones. There will be some saving in library and laboratory costs, although maintenance costs in them vary to a considerable extent on a per capita basis-- the chief saving will be found in the general items of operation, maintenance, and fixed charges. Heat, light, and janitor service will be somewhat less. There would be a saving in the salary of one administrator, but the larger four-year institution would probably require a vice-principal or similar officer whose salary would offset the saving to a considerable extent. This is only a rough estimate, assuming entirely separate plants, where the greatest possibilities of economy would be found.

   Where the senior high school and junior college are operated in the same plant, as is the case in most institutions, the saving in the adoption of the 6-4-4 plan would be much less. Pasadena furnishes an excellent example where definite facts can take the place of theory and estimates. Superintendent Sexson, in discussing the economies effected through the administrative organization of the Pasadena Junior College, stated:

> Large savings were effected in administrative offices and in the reduced secretarial staff necessary to handle the unit organization. It is difficult to estimate accurately how much of a saving was effected by reason of the new organization, but a conservative figure would be 20 per cent of the total overhead.

Assuming that the total overhead was 20 per cent of the budget, this means that the net savings was 20 per cent of 20 per cent or 4 per cent of the entire budget. The budget for 1928-29 amounted to $233,000. Truly a saving of $9,000 in a budget of a quarter of a million is not to be despised, if it is not to be obtained at too great a cost of other features. A saving of 4 per cent is somewhat less than might be anticipated, however, in view of the sweeping claims for economy made for this type of organization. If this were really a determinative feature, it would be still more economical to have a single plant for the entire eight-year secondary period. With the financial saving thus shown to be such a minor feature, the ultimate criterion must be in terms of educational desirability, not of minor financial economy.

4. *Economy-of-time argument*:   "The superior student can finish the course in three years instead of four."

This is undoubtedly true and forms a valid argument for the four-year junior college, at least in theory. It would be interesting to have data from Pasadena showing what percentage of the students actually graduate in three years instead of four, but sufficient time has not yet elapsed to secure such information. It will probably be only a small proportion. The two-year junior college is not a strait-jacket, however, for the same brilliant student who can finish the four-year course in three years has the opportunity to finish the four-semester course in three semesters.

There are two educational philosophies. One holds that *material* is the basic unit, the other that *time* is the basic unit. Should the student scurry through curriculum as fast as possible, or should he remain in school the normal amount of time, and if he is extra capable, spend his time in getting just that much more out of a so-called "enriched curriculum" rather than in hurrying on to join an advanced group to which he may not be socially adjusted? I strongly favor the theory that *time* is the basic unit. I would urge that every student entering junior college should normally remain in for the entire two years, taking only the normal number of units if his ability permits. Should the junior college encourage speed or thoroughness? The economy-of-time argument seems partially true, but not highly important.

5.   *The argument of vocational preparation*:   "The four-year junior college can do a distinctive and unique work in training students for semi-professional occupations."

This argument as stated by Dr. Cooper in his *School Review* article is difficult to understand or to accept. It seems to rest upon a misconception of Dr. Leonard's meaning in the quotation which he uses to prove his case. Dr. Cooper says "Professor Leonard suggested a permanent field for our proposed upper secondary [four-year] unit." A careful reading of Dr. Leonard's entire article, however, originally an address before this Association, shows that he was not thinking at all of the four-year college but of the two-year one. He says, for example:

Let us examine a few occupations within the middle level, choosing from among those adapted to full-time junior college instruction. Pharmacy clearly falls within this level. . . .The typical course for pharmacists covers two years of study. . . . Optometry. . . .nursing. . . .commerce. . . . public service. . . .engineering. . . .the great majority of agricultural pursuits, are really of the middle level, and require only two years of training instead of four or five.

Nothing could be clearer from the entire address than that Dr. Leonard was not suggesting a "permanent field for our proposed upper secondary [four-year] unit." A stronger argument could scarcely be made for the two-year junior college from the vocational or semi-professional standpoint than the one contained in Dr. Leonard's address.

6. *Argument from size:*   "The four-year junior college permits college opportunity in places too small to justify a two-year college."

It is not easy to see the significance of this argument. If one hundred students is too small a number for a separate two-year unit, how will two hundred be much better for a four-year one? Athletically, it may be a little better off, but scholastically, what is the difference? As many small upper division classes will have to be maintained. The additional eleventh and twelfth grade students are not going to increase the size of the thirteenth and fourteenth grade classes appreciably.

7. *Guidance argument:*   "More effective organized guidance is possible in the four-year institution than in the two-year one."

There is some strength to this argument, but even as Koos implies in his statement of it, its logic really leads to a single eight-year unit with a unified guidance policy covering the entire period. Junior college guidance is not a matter so much of advice as it is information, and there is no reason why this cannot be given in different units, and with some benefit through contacts with new personalities and different points of view. In a well-organized guidance program a student's test records, personality ratings, and all pertinent personnel data in a constantly increasing amount accompany him in every transition from the kindergarten through the university.

8. *Argument of analogy with German education:* Some writers point longingly to Germany and the German

organization. The German Gymnasium, however, is a single unit, not two four-year separate institutions. Furthermore, conditions are so very different with the German two-class educational system which has developed under foreign conditions from the American single educational ladder for all classes that the analogy is remote.

A convincing answer to those eager to transplant the German Gymnasium to American soil is found in the experience of the American Lutheran Church. To train educated leaders, Americanized Gymnasia were established in the United States as early as 1839, with the curricula of the German humanistic Gymnasia. The intellectual advancement of the young men was equal to the gains obtained in a high school and the two years of junior college. After extensive study, the general convention of the church in 1920 decided to change all of the schools of this type, nine in number, over into four-year high schools, and two-year classical junior colleges. An indigenous tree does not always flourish when transplanted to foreign soil.

9.   *The compulsory school law argument*: "The legal school-leaving age in most states is sixteen, coinciding with the beginning of the four-year junior college."

It is true that there are thirty-one states with sixteen years as the compulsory school age, but there are ten in which it is seventeen or eighteen years, and the tendency seems to be to raise it rather than to lower it. Further, we have seen in discussing the psychological argument that less than half the students at Pasadena in a single grade were actually sixteen years of age. This argument, therefore, seems to have a maximum efficiency of less than half the students in less than two-thirds of the states!

The inquiry may also be made as to whether it is an unmixed blessing to have the school unit coincide with the compulsory age limit. At the present time there is a strong tendency for a boy who arrives at the age of sixteen at the middle of his high-school course to go on and finish it, possibly taking special trade or commercial work in the last two years, thus securing two years of education beyond the legal requirement. The same boy is much less likely to secure any further education if he "finishes" the lower four-year unit at sixteen. It is much harder to enter a new and strange institution than to continue in an old one.

10. *Argument of superior teachers*:   "The four-year   college   attracts   better   teachers   and administrators."

Harbeson says: "The four-year college is educationally the most efficient form of organization for the upper secondary school system. It provides an organization of such dignity and scope as to attract the best-trained and most experienced staff of teachers and administrators."

I have no desire to argue the question as to whether Pasadena has superior teachers. I am sure that it has. I wish to inquire, however, whether it is the four-year junior college with the accompanying "dignity and scope" or the superior salary and enticing climate of Pasadena that are chiefly determinative. The average salary in California in 1928-29 according to official state reports was higher for both principal and instructors at Pasadena than in the state as a whole. From all reports, very superior teaching is found at Stephens College. Is this due to "dignity and scope"? Possibly so. It is worth noticing, however, that the typical salary of a professor at Stephens is $6,500. Given similar resources, one might be able to secure a moderately high grade of administrators and instructors even in a two-year college, although suffering under the handicap of lack of "dignity and scope"!

D. DISADVANTAGES OF 6-4-4 PLAN

Having thus considered the principal advantages claimed for the 6-4-4 type of organization, I keenly regret that limitations of time prevent me from discussion of a half-dozen distinct disadvantages and dangers, some temporary, incidental to transition--some fundamental and permanent. I can only list these here in entirely inadequate form, without time to elaborate them:

1. The difficulty of intercollegiate athletic competition.

2. Difficulty of adjustment to existing administrative practice.

3. Difficulty of adjustment to varying geographical conditions.

4. Difficulty of too great variety in age of students.

5. Difficulty of adjustment of instruction to different levels.

6. Danger of stopping school at compulsory age limit.

E. ADVANTAGES OF TWO-YEAR PLAN

There will next be considered seven advantages which are characteristic of two-year types of organization for the junior college years.

1. *Ease of adjustment to existing administrative and geographical conditions* .--This very real practical advantage of the two-year junior college can be only touched upon briefly. The flexibility of the two-year institution, its possibility of adjustment to all prevailing types of secondary school organization with a minimum of administrative friction and re-alignment, forms

the strongest practical arguments in favor of the two-year institution.

2.   *Advantages of new contacts*. --The advantages of new contacts on the part of the student are worth considering. There is a general feeling in Europe that students gain considerably by attending a variety of institutions. In America there has been more of a tendency for a student to remain in the same institution for a long period of time. There are some advantages in this, from the standpoint of friendships, interests, and loyalties. On the other hand, there is a tendency toward restricted viewpoints and continuation in a rut. There is value in change as well as in continuity. There has been a marked increase in college migration and flexibility in the United States in the last few years--witness the floating university, the junior year abroad, the transfer from college to university at the end of the junior year. The student undoubtedly gains much in educational outlook and breadth of vision from contact with a variety of instructors and with a different student body. The wealth of new and stimulating contacts in another institution are a very valuable experience for the average student. To have three such experiences, instead of one or two, in the entire range of his "secondary educational" experience is often highly profitable and stimulating.

3.   *Development of leadership*.   --This is an exceedingly important function of college education. It is a truism that the college men and women of today are to be the country's leaders of tomorrow. One of the most important agencies for development of leadership is that of student activities. It is quite obvious, however, that mere membership in student clubs, societies, teams, or other organizations does not in itself develop leadership to any marked extent. Vicarious training for leadership is not likely to be highly successful. It is the holding of responsible offices that is most potent. It is the president, the manager, the captain, the committee chairman who develops real leadership in his group. It is perfectly natural in the four-year institution that the majority of such positions go to the upper classmen. In fact it is inevitable and right. This fact is recognized but rather unsatisfactorily excused by Superintendent Sexson of Pasadena, when he says that

> the students in the eleventh and twelfth grades will be given the opportunity of increased training in leadership when they arrive in the upper division.

But why wait until they arrive in the upper division?

With the high school and junior college as separate
units, the same student has two opportunities for such
training in leadership. In the two-year junior college
he waits but one year, instead of three, for election
to the most responsible offices in student
organizations.

4.   *Transitional advantages*.--Much was written and
said in the earlier years of the century regarding the
"classic gap" between the elementary school and the
high school. The transition was too sudden and abrupt
from one institution to the other. As a result the
junior high school was developed, which, among other
valuable contributions, acted as a transitional
institution and has succeeded very largely in closing
the disastrous gap formerly so noticeable.

Similarly there has been an equally bad gap, in many
cases, between high school and university. The tragic
freshman mortality in many universities has been
pointed out by many writers, amounting in some cases to
50 per cent or more. The junior college, like the
junior high school, has operated to close this
unfortunate gap and make the transition easier from
high-school limitations to university independence.
The development of these two institutions has broken up
what was formerly two hazardous and often disastrous
steps, of unnecessary difficulty, into four much
shorter and easier ones. The steps of the educational
stairway have been shortened and the upward progress of
the student made "safer and saner." Experience has
shown that the jumps from the grade school to the four-
year high school and again from the four-year high
school to the four-year college were too long for
safety and happiness in many cases.

Have we any reason to suppose that transitions from
one unit to the other of the 6-4-4 plan will not be
equally difficult and unhappy? The length of the units
has not been changed; they have merely been shifted two
years. Is it not likely that transition from the upper
four-year unit to upperdivision university freedom may
still be fraught with difficulty and peril?

The tendency of a quarter-century of American
education has been toward breaking up educational
progress into a large number of easier steps with
shorter transitions. The two-year junior college is
exactly in line with this apparently desirable
educational tendency and a part of it.

5.   *Advantage of homogeneity of age.*--Much stress has
been placed on the four-year institution from the
standpoint of adjustment to ages of psychological
maturity. This feature has already been discussed.
Here it is only desired to point out an entirely
non-controversial feature, viz., that age group
with its accompanying physical, social, educational,

and psychological characteristics, whatever they may be, is certainly much more nearly homogeneous in this respect in the two-year college.

6. *Distinctive collegiate atmosphere.* --College atmosphere is elusive and intangible when a definition is attempted, but it is very real and important to achieve, and not difficult to recognize. It probably can be maintained in either a four-year or a two-year junior college, but the effort is less likely to be successful in the former case. It is doubtful whether calling high-school juniors and seniors "college" students is going to make them real college students in the eyes of high-school students, their parents, or the public. The great danger is that the four-year junior college, in which normally a considerable preponderance of the students will be found in the two high-school years, will tend to be more "high-schoolish" in atmosphere than collegiate.

7. *Psychology of the American people.* --For generations it has been the deepest desire of thousands of American parents to give their sons and daughters the benefits of a "college" education. Going to college has been the great American ambition and is rapidly becoming the great American habit. America may not know exactly what the college stands for, it may not recognize the technical distinctions between "secondary" and higher education, but it is very sure that college means something distinctive and worth while. In the popular mind college means an institution following high-school graduation, not merely a glorified and amplified high school. It is difficult enough to get the notion into the public consciousness that the two-year junior college is real college; it will be far more difficult for it to feel that "college" is a centaur-like hybrid--half high school and half college.

Of course the 6-4-4 advocates have a quite simple solution to the situation. Just drop "junior" from the vocabulary entirely. Call the lower four-year unit "high school" and the upper one "college." Then America can go to college, only beginning two years earlier. There are already a bewildering array of institutions that call themselves "colleges," from barber colleges on up. Surely it would do no harm to drop the "junior" college and have still another variety of college. It should be remembered, however, that there are some hundreds of standard four-year colleges in the country, almost all of them definitely built upon a foundation of a four-year high-school course, and that these are not going to perish overnight, nor for a long time to come. There are many reasons why it is desirable and seems likely that the term "junior college" will be a permanent addition to our educational vocabulary.

It is rather significant that President W. F. Doughty of Hillsboro Junior College, the earliest 6-4-4 institution in the country, quite frankly prefers the name "senior school" to "junior college" for the upper four-year unit. Is this not a sincere recognition of the fact that the proposed upper unit after all is not "college"?

F. ARGUMENT FROM HISTORY

An argument from history and experience is never conclusive. There is no assurance that what is, or what has been, necessarily should be. Yet the argument from history is often enlightening, and, combined with other facts and arguments, forms valuable corroborative material. It is of especial significance in the present instance because the two-year junior college, the three-year junior high school, and the 6-4-4 plan are so nearly of common age and geographical propinquity in origin and early development.

Origin of the three movements.--It may not be generally known that the 6-4-4 plan was first proposed in California in 1908, while the junior high school movement was launched here at Berkeley in the same state in 1910, and the first two-year junior college in the state was established at Fresno in 1910. Consider now the following facts:

a) Since the first three-year junior high school was established in Berkeley in 1910 it has spread until in 1929 there were at least 1,818 such institutions. While these constitute but 10 per cent of the high schools of the country, 24 per cent of the ninth-grade enrollment of the country is found in them. In twenty years the junior high school has certainly made a place for itself.

b) Since the first public two-year junior college in California (and second in the country) was established in Fresno in 1910, it has spread until in 1930 there were at least 171 public junior colleges in the country with an enrollment of over 40,000 students. In twenty years the two-year junior college has certainly made a place for itself.

c) Since the 6-4-4 plan was first proposed in California in 1908, almost two decades passed before the first institution of this type was organized in Texas, and by 1930 the number, even including private ones, could be counted on the fingers of the two hands. *Why has not the 6-4-4 plan, in the same twenty years with the many advantages claimed for it, far outstripped the other two in this race in which all three had so nearly an even running start?*

It surely has not been for lack of advocacy on the part of an imposing array of vigorous and powerful friends. It may be entirely right, and the other two plans entirely wrong, but it seems a little strange that, with such a long time to prove itself, actual results of the 6-4-4 plan as yet are so very meager, while in the other two cases they are so strikingly abundant.

*****

There remain to consider certain objections that have been raised to the two-year unit and that have not been sufficiently considered in other connections already. Three such may be mentioned:

1.   *Development of traditions and college spirit.*,-- Various writers have expressed the belief that two years is too short a time to instill the traditions, sense of atmosphere, ideals, habits, attitudes, or whatever else may be essential to the formation of "college spirit." As President Wood of Stephens College has so aptly expressed it, "The minority is continually striving to absorb the majority." Superintendent Sexson would leave no room for doubt in his categorical statement: "It is impossible to develop a very dynamic school spirit in a two-year institution....The ideal situation is to have a school organization of four years in length." Yet both statements may be questioned. Is it true, that a two-year institution cannot develop school spirit? One essential for school spirit is a feeling of freedom and independence on the part of the students, and a feeling of unity in a common purpose. This is more likely to be found in a two-year institution with a separate plant and school consciousness, than in one where lower division students with separate clubs, diverse study hall regulations and other necessary disciplinary restrictions tend to break up the unity of feeling and experience.

*****

2.   *Ambitions to become four-year degree-granting colleges*.--There is some danger here, but to recognize it is to guard against it. This has been done by law in many states where extension upward is forbidden.

*****

How great is the real extent of this danger? Dr. Campbell, secretary of this Association, has tried to trace the fate of all junior colleges in the country which have died, merged with other schools, or expanded into four-year senior colleges. He was able to discover exactly eleven, since the beginning of the movement, which have become four-year senior colleges,

an average of much less than one a year.   In the same
period several times this number of four-year senior
colleges have decapitated themselves to become junior
colleges.   The balance is decidedly on the credit side
of the junior college ledger!

    3.   *Junior college as a segment of true education.* --
Various authors call attention to the two-year junior
college as a "mere segment" of true education, and
stress the extra "breaks" in the educational program
introduced by the two-year institution.   This seems to
be merely a matter of words.

*****

    It is fortunate that we do not all agree on
educational policies.   Educational progress results
from difference of opinion, from clash of viewpoints.
It would be a drab, monotonous, uninteresting world if
we all saw alike.   There seems to be no immediate
danger that the junior college world will be drab,
monotonous, uninteresting!   Many writers have set forth
the advantages as they see them in favor of the 6-4-4
type of organization.   I have tried to present the
situation from the standpoint of the two-year type of
junior college.   It cannot be denied that the latter is
the prevailing type of organization at the present
time.   Therefore the burden of proof rests upon the
four-year advocates to justify a change.   After a
careful study of all the arguments on both sides of the
question, I feel that that burden is a considerable
one.   Ultimately, of course, the entire matter will be
decided by experience and experiment, not by theory.
For this reason it is to be hoped that other
institutions will try the Pasadena plan, as two other
California communities are beginning to do--Compton and
Ventura.   But they should be recognized as frankly
experimental.   The verdict is "not proven."   What the
ultimate verdict of history will be, only time can
tell.

*****

PART III.
FROM JUNIOR TO COMMUNITY COLLEGE

By 1920 the junior college movement had gained sufficient stature to encourage a national meeting and launch a national support organization, the American Association of Junior Colleges. In the 1930's scholars and practitioners warmed to the debate on the forms and functions of the junior college. How closely should the college be attached to the high school? Is this a creation of secondary education or higher education? Whom shall it serve? What shall it offer?

The 1930's and 1940's saw the emergence of increasing numbers and variations of the junior college., Circumstances were right. The junior college grew with increasing strength and vigor in the educational and social climate of this country. The dire economic conditions of the 1930's in the United States prompted the erection of "emergency" junior colleges in a number of states. A unique quality of the developing junior college was its focus on meeting individual community needs. But commentators such as Doak Campbell saw this as an aspiration, a dream yet unfulfilled.

After World War II, President Harry Truman's interest in education was sufficient to spur formation of a Commission on Higher Education, a group which recommended highly the public two-year community college. President Truman's personal interest is illustrated here by a letter he wrote in 1950 asking for guidance in suggesting federal assistance to community colleges, a likely follow-up to the recommendations of his President's Commission on Higher Education. The Commission spoke out boldly and decisively on behalf of community colleges.

These events, incidentally, were the first appearance of a substantial interest of the federal government in this type of educational institution. The states, of course, had primary responsibility for education at all levels. The Truman Commission's recommendations, however, were forerunners of the sizable federal support for junior and community colleges provided in the 1960's and 1970's. So was the speech by Representative Dixon of Utah in the House of Representatives in 1957.

So strong had the sentiment grown for the junior and community college that by the time President Dwight D. Eisenhower's Committee on Education Beyond the High School reported (a decade after the Truman Commission had completed its work), the staff of the U.S. Office of Education could be very critical of that Committee's lukewarm support for (and lack of understanding of) a community-oriented, comprehensive, low-cost, easily accessible two-year college.

Most of the materials in Part III are from or about the federal domain of government. This is by design. It is not to imply that locally (or state) controlled and supported junior community colleges were being replaced by national institutions; it does not imply federal domination of the two-year college movement. The boom period of junior community college growth in the 1960's and early 1970's was taking place in the various states and, within them, in scores and indeed hundreds of local communities. The selection of these documents is made for the purpose of highlighting the emerging federal role (one of support and advocacy) and the national attention being focused on the junior college as a valued instrument of national policy. Legislation such as the Higher Education Act of 1965 even provided for the specific earmarking of monies for two-year institutions (in Title III, the Developing Colleges Title, for example) to insure their participation in federal support programs for education.[1]

[1]*The volume by Michael Brick, Forum and Focus for the Junior College Movement, New York: Bureau of Publications, Teachers College, Columbia University, 1964, is of special value in interpreting the development of the junior college movement from the 1920's to the 1960's and highlighting the work of the movement's national, nongovernmental advocate, the American Association of Junior Colleges, later the American Association of Community and Junior Colleges.*

15. COPING WITH ECONOMIC DEPRESSION: A FEDERAL RESPONSE

During the economic depression of the 1930's junior colleges were used to help alleviate severe unemployment problems. Federal monies were made available to several states--principally Michigan, Ohio, New Jersey, Connecticut, Kansas, and Texas--to develop local colleges. These institutions, called by a variety of names, were certainly amoung the first two-year institutions to attempt to be what later would be called "community colleges."

Proposed largely to serve unemployed high school graduates (and unemployed college teachers!), these institutions did attempt to provide educational opportunity at low cost, were easily accessible to students, provided instruction at the collegiate level, facilitated the transfer of students into four-year institutions, experimented with curriculum and instructional forms, and offered opportunities for personal development with courses in art, crafts, and dramatics. Little is known of these temporary, federally-supported junior colleges; they do provide an early glimpse of the characteristics of the now common community-based community college.

Walter J. Greenleaf was a specialist in higher education with the U.S. Office of Education, Washington, D.C.

During 1934, several states recognized the need of providing education, and particularly higher education, for the graduates of high schools who were unable to find employment, and who, because of limited finances, were unable to attend college although qualified. At the same time, they recognized the need of putting to work those teachers and professors who were in the ranks of the unemployed. As reward for their efforts,

---

Walter J. Greenleaf, "Junior Colleges," U.S. Office of Education Bulletin 1936, No. 3, Washington, D.C.: U.S. Government Printing Office, 1936, pp. 25-28.

funds from the F.E.R.A. (Federal Emergency Relief
Administration) were made available to develop
emergency junior college centers where several thousand
students were enrolled. Certain cooperating
universities agreed to accept transfers from these
junior colleges and to give full credit for work done
in them.

Generally speaking, these emergency junior colleges
are makeshift institutions occupying high-school
buildings or donated rooms after hours--that is in the
late afternoon or evening when the buildings are not
otherwise in use. They are granted the use of the
school facilities such as desks, libraries, cafeterias,
and equipment. Teachers are selected from needy
unemployed instructors and professors on a basis of
ability and training. The emergency junior college
movement is not a general one, but is localized in a
few states.

MICHIGAN.--In Michigan these institutions are known
as "freshman colleges" or "community colleges", and 100
have already been established (1934-35) with
enrollments of more than 6,000 students. They aim to
take educational opportunity on a college level to the
thousands of high-school graduates throughout Michigan
whose finances are so limited that it is impossible for
them to attend resident colleges. The State has been
divided into seven zones each supervised by a public
institution--either University of Michigan, Wayne
University, Michigan State College, or one of the four
State teachers colleges. Entrance requirements for the
freshman colleges in each zone are the same as now
prevail in the liberal arts college in the sponsoring
institution. The scope of the programs is determined
by the needs of local students and facilities
available. The subjects taught generally correspond to
those offered to first-year students--English, French,
Spanish, German, history, geography, mathematics,
political science, chemistry, zoology, geology, and
mechanical drawing, together with non-credit courses
which include economics, journalism, art, dramatics,
music, current literature, speech, designing,
accounting, and sociology. The curriculum provided is
intended to meet the needs of the persons enrolled,
especially as concerns citizenship, health, morale, and
a keen awareness of the political, economic, and social
conditions of the world today. The usual length of
freshman college work is 34 weeks and the colleges
close in June when the sponsoring institutions close.

In organizing a new local center, the superintendent
of schools takes the initiative when 40 or more
qualified students who are financially unable to attend
college in residence, desire freshman college work.
Few freshman colleges are organized in cities where

private or public junior colleges are established. Teachers are recruited from the lists of persons qualified on the basis of need and of educational qualifications.

Early in the discussion of these units, local college presidents, particularly in the denominational colleges, were skeptical. Of late, however, the college people recognize that the sophomore class of 1935 will have more than the usual number of students from which to draw. The University of Michigan is already planning for these transfers; the erection of a barracks on the campus is proposed to accommodate these recruits at the rate of $12 per month for board and room, total expenses not to exceed $250 for the college year.

In Michigan it is felt that benefits which arise from these newly created units include interesting many people in the remote parts of the State in the higher educational institutions of the State, and educating the professors of these institutions in situations in the outlying portions of Michigan. The future of the whole movement, however, cannot be predicted.

OHIO.--"Emergency Junior College Centers" in 30 cities and towns were established in Ohio within the year 1934-35. It is reported that more than a thousand boys and girls with median age of 19 years were in attendance. The instructors are college graduates with 1 year of graduate work to their credit. The curricula are on a par with the average freshman studies offered in standard liberal arts colleges. Several Ohio colleges are cooperating with these centers by furnishing syllabi, examinations, and other aids. They have agreed to accept with full credit the work of students successful in completing the emergency college courses.

To establish a new unit the superintendent of schools at a center must make formal application according to regulations set up by the Emergency Schools Administration. The board of education must agree to furnish light, heat, and janitor service if the application is granted.

Another Ohio movement is the emergency junior radio college which was set up in January 1934 at the Ohio State University as a part of the Ohio emergency schools program. Courses of instruction on college level, broadcast by members of the university faculty may be received at nearly every point in Ohio during daylight hours. Radio students make out registration cards, and may take final examinations if they desire. Mimeographed lesson material is distributed free upon request and few textbooks are required. Many counties provide county radio teachers to organize local classes for discussion groups. In 1934-35 the following courses were offered on a regular radio schedule. Psychology, homemaking, French, English, philosophy, education, art appreciation, and engineering. Of the 1,737 students enrolled last year, two-thirds of whom were high-school graduates, 55 passed the course requirements at the first quarter.

NEW JERSEY.--The emergency colleges in New Jersey are for the most part county junior colleges located in six centers--Morristown, Newark, Perth Amboy, Paterson, Roselle, and Long Branch. As a rule the senior high school building in each of these cities is made available for junior-college students from about 4 to 9 p.m. when the high school is not in session and other local facilities are also made available. At Morristown the school library is used, the school cafeteria provides a hot supper at night, and the Y.M.C.A. and Y.W.C.A. cooperate in the physical education program. The junior college at Morristown emphasizes two phases of work: (1) Liberal arts leading to the bachelor's degree, and (2) associate in arts division which is terminal for immediate life needs.

CONNECTICUT.--A new system of "Federal colleges", several of which were established during the autumn of 1934, has been tried out in Connecticut. Each of several communities, including New Haven, Hartford, Meriden, Bristol, Winsted, and Farmington, adopted temporary policies to fit local situations. It was hoped that patterns would emerge from these experiments so that extension of the system to other parts of the State would be feasible. The college at New Haven proved to be the largest and best equipped of the group; 50 people were employed and 40 rooms were made available through Yale University, the Y.M.C.A. and the Y.W.C.A. to provide quarters for more than 700 students. Some tried departing from the traditions of the older universities, and others carried on in their own ways, either holding to the traditional methods or to "progressive" tendencies. Combined enrollments (1934-35) of these Federal colleges were about 1,400. If these colleges prove successful, extension of the system to other cities may be possible.

KANSAS.--Thirteen freshman-college projects under the direct sponsorship of the University of Kansas are in operation (1936) in Kansas. These centers are located at Leavenworth, Atchison, Houlton, Horton, Norton, Olathe, Marysville, Phillipsburg, Atwood, Stockton, St. Francis, Plainville, and Colby. Local high-school buildings are being used for classes which are organized by the University Extension Division. Sixty classes are being given for university credit, and a dozen other classes in art, handicraft, commerce, and dramatics not for university credit are offered.   Thirty-two teachers in all are employed to give instruction in these classes.

TEXAS.--Of the 15 Texas freshman college centers which will open in 1936, five will probably be located in Dallas, Houston, San Antonio, Fort Worth, and Lubbock.   Other centers will be opened and financed when the Federal Emergency Education project is approved.   These will go under the supervision of the college sponsoring them and certifying the credits of students.   Classes may be established in any city or town for a minimum of 10 eligible students who are from 16 to 25 years of age and members of relief families. It is expected that these centers will give freshman training without cost to approximately 750 boys and girls who are on relief, who have finished high school, and who have not enrolled in any college this year.

16. AFTER SIXTEEN YEARS: A PROGRESS REPORT

Reviewing the period 1920 to 1936, a leader in the junior college movement, Doak Sheridan Campbell, tells of its spectacular growth . . . yet cautions of unmet problems. Campbell acknowledged the rapid increase in the number of two-year institutions and an accompanying rise in prestige. Accrediting agencies had to adopt standards by which to judge these colleges--and they were judged as colleges, not high schools.

Their work had been largely devoted to a traditional college program, preparing students for transfer to senior institutions. This approach, Campbell surmised, may be too narrow. After 16 years of growth, junior colleges should look at expanding their programs and services. After careful review, significant social and educational problems may be identified which can be addressed by junior colleges.

Doak S. Campbell (b. 1888 in Arkansas; d. 1973) spent his early professional years as a teacher, principal, and college president. In 1922 he became the part-time executive secretary of the American Association of Junior Colleges. He resigned this nonpaying post in 1938, being appointed dean of the graduate school at George Peabody College in Nashville, Tennessee. He later served as president of Florida State University (1941-1957).

Sixteen years ago the first conference on junior colleges met in the city of St. Louis. The meeting was called by Dr. George F. Zook, then specialist in higher education in the United States Bureau of Education. The purpose of the conference was to provide for "a full and frank discussion of their mutual interests and problems." In his introductory remarks Dr. Zook said, among other things, "....it is becoming increasingly

Doak S. Campbell, "Editorial,"Junior College Journal, Vol. VII (December, 1936), 109-111.

apparent that universities and colleges alike are
beginning to regard the junior college as an
institution of great possible usefulness in the field
of higher education."

At the time of this initial conference there were
probably 175 institutions in the whole country that
might be designated as junior colleges. Their programs
were diverse. There were many types of administrative
organizations. Their status was in many cases
uncertain. In many quarters the junior college had
never been heard of. It was looked upon by some as a
sort of last stand for the weak four-year college
before passing completely off the scene. It was dubbed
a "glorified high school."

Only 34 individuals were reported in attendance
at the first conference. In the group were
representatives of 22 junior colleges in 13 states and
the District of Columbia. Of the 22 junior colleges
represented at the conference six have been closed and
two have been expanded to four-year institutions.

The past sixteen years have seen many significant
changes. The growth in the number of institutions has
been phenomenal. In 1936 there are approximately 520
junior colleges, an increase of 200 per cent during the
sixteen-year period. Comparatively few junior colleges
have been discontinued, only slightly more than 10 per
cent of those that have been established. A large
majority of those that have closed were institutions
that had previously operated as small four-year
colleges under private or church control. Fewer than
10 per cent of the junior colleges established have
been reorganized on a four-year basis.

During these sixteen years the junior college gained
recognition among the various accrediting agencies. In
1920 only one regional body, the North Central
Association of Colleges and Secondary Schools, had
adopted standards for junior colleges. Great
difficulty was experienced by junior colleges in
transferring their graduates to higher institutions.
In 1936 all the regional associations have published
and have provided means of administering standards for
junior colleges. The records of junior college
transfer students have been such that a majority of the
higher institutions throughout the country accept
junior college graduates on the basis of their
transcripts.

Due to numerous influences the junior colleges of
1920 confined their work largely to the traditional
freshman and sophomore courses found in the four-year
colleges. Their work was almost wholly preparatory.
Despite the fact that other important functions had
been clearly stated for the junior college, these
functions were not reflected in the curriculum.

Vocational curricula and general curricula were rarely
offered.   So much emphasis was being put upon
quantitative standards for accreditation at that time
that few junior colleges dared to offer courses that
differed from the traditional practice.

During recent years there has been some trend toward
a broader curriculum.   One is compelled to say,
however, that the curriculum has not developed in
proportion to the number of institutions.   This may be
due in part to the increasing number of various types
of educational services required by young people of
junior college age.   In recent years numerous other
agencies have been called upon to render services which
the junior college might reasonably be expected to
provide.   The studies of the American Youth Commission
will, no doubt, reveal many other problems that have
direct implications for the junior college curriculum
that are not now apparent.   It seems to this writer
that the challenge is clear to junior colleges to re-
canvass their own possibilities as revealed in the
needs of young people in their service area and to
revise their own curriculums in terms of what they
discover.   If the next sixteen years are to be as
significant for the junior college movement as the
sixteen years since the first junior college
conference, this is imperative.

17. PRESIDENT TRUMAN'S INTEREST

By the 1950's even the President of the United States was aware of the junior colleges in this country and interested in a variation called "community college."

The White House

Washington

January 23, 1950

My Dear Mr. Ewing:

In the Budget Message for 1951, I am recommending that the Congress authorize a limited Federal program to assist capable youth who could not otherwise do so to pursue their desired fields of study at the institutions of their choice.

At this time the Federal role in such a program, in addition to financial aids to individuals, should also include careful study and appraisal of the various emerging types of educational institutions and of their present and potential value as parts of the educational system in the community. I am particularly interested in knowing more about efforts to reduce geographic and economic barriers to the development of individual talents through extended educational opportunities which seem to be reflected in many states and localities by so-called "community colleges." It is

Letter written by President Harry Truman, Accession No. 63-A-23, Box 169, "Office of Education--Higher Education Division," Record Group 12, U.S. Federal Records Center, Alexandria, Virginia.

apparent that various patterns are being followed and
that an important educational development is being
undertaken through trial, adaptation, and democratic
experimentation.

I request that you make, in the course of the next
six months, a comprehensive study of the community
college and report to me your findings and
recommendations as to whether the Federal Government
can contribute to the objective of equalizing
educational opportunity by assisting in the development
of these colleges and, if so, the most practicable
means for providing such assistance.

It will be appreciated if you will keep the Director
of the Bureau of the Budget informed about the progress
of this study.

Sincerely yours,

[Harry Truman]

Honorable Oscar R. Ewing
Administrator
Federal Security Agency
Washington 25, D.C.

18. THE PRESIDENT'S COMMISSION ON HIGHER EDUCATION – EXPANSION OF EDUCATIONAL OPPORTUNITY

Established by President Harry Truman, this Commission, viewing post-World War II options in education, saw the community college as a very important facility for increasing educational opportunity. This report, one of the more famous federal documents on American education, looked optimistically to the community college to help higher education expand programs and services to a widening array of citizens.

Diverse human needs must be met by diverse educational institutions and programs. The publicly and locally controlled, multi-purpose, community-based two year college should be the primary model of the new community college. The community college should break away from its almost total fascination with preparing students for transfer to senior colleges. It should develop a series of two-year or terminal programs, preparing students for lives of citizenship and work. The erection of this new community college is a desirable goal for American education.

George F. Zook (b. 1885 in Kansas; d. 1951), a longtime friend of the junior college movement, both with the U.S. Bureau of Education and, later, as president of the American Council on Education, chaired this Commission. Zook and many members of the Commission were advocates of strong but varied institutions of higher education, all working to strengthen democracy and opportunity in the United States.

Education Adjusted to Needs

To make sure of its own health and strength a democratic society must provide free and equal access to education for its youth, and at the same time it

U.S., President's Commission on Higher Education, Vol. I, "Establishing the Goals," Washington, D.C.: U.S. Government Printing Office, 1947, pp. 67-70.

must recognize their differences in capacity and purpose. Higher education in America should include a variety of institutional forms and educational programs, so that at whatever point any student leaves school, he will be fitted, within the limits of his mental capacity and educational level, for an abundant and productive life as a person, as a worker, and as a citizen.

THE COMMUNITY COLLEGE

As one means of achieving the expansion of educational opportunity and the diversification of educational offerings it considers necessary, this Commission recommends that the number of community colleges be increased and that their activities be multiplied.

Community colleges in the future may be either publicly or privately controlled and supported, but most of them, obviously, will be under public auspices. They will be mainly local or regional in scope and should be locally controlled, though they should be carefully planned to fit into a comprehensive State-wide system of higher education. They will derive much of their support from the local community, supplemented by aid from State funds.

Some community colleges may offer a full four years of college work, but most of them probably will stop at the end of the fourteenth grade, the sophomore year of the traditional college. In the latter case they should be closely articulated with the high school.

Whatever form the community college takes, its purpose is educational service to the entire community, and this purpose requires of it a variety of functions and programs. It will provide college education for the youth of the community certainly, so as to remove geographic and economic barriers to educational opportunity and discover and develop individual talents at low cost and easy access. But in addition, the community college will serve as an active center of adult education. It will attempt to meet the total post-high school needs of its community.

Terminal and Semiprofessional Education

In the past the junior college has most commonly sought to provide within the local community the freshman and sophomore courses of the traditional college curriculum. With notable exceptions, it has concentrated on preparing students for further study in the junior and senior years of liberal arts colleges or professional schools.

But preparatory programs looking to the more advanced

courses of the senior college are not complete and
rounded in themselves, and they usually do not serve
well the purpose of those who must terminate their
schooling at the end of the fourteenth grade. Half the
young people who go to college find themselves unable
to complete the full 4-year course, and for a long time
to come more students will end their formal education
in the junior college years than will prolong it into
the senior college. These 2-year graduates would gain
more from a terminal program planned specifically to
meet their needs than from the first half of a 4-year
curriculum.

For this reason, the Commission recommends that the
community college emphasize programs of terminal
education.

                         *****

If the semiprofessional curriculum is to accomplish
its purpose, however, it must not be crowded with
vocational and technical courses to the exclusion of
general education.   It must aim at developing a
combination of social understanding and technical
competence.   Semiprofessional education should mix a
goodly amount of general education for personal and
social development with technical education that is
intensive, accurate, and comprehensive enough to give
the student command of marketable abilities.

Community Center of Learning

Post-high school education for youth is only one of
the functions to be performed by the community college.
One such college has been known to have a daytime
junior college enrollment of 3,000 but an adult
enrollment in the late afternoon and evening of 25,000.

The community college seeks to become a center of
learning for the entire community, with or without the
restrictions that surround formal course work in
traditional institutions of higher education. It gears
its programs and services to the needs and wishes of
the people it serves, and its offerings may range from
workshops in painting or singing or play writing for
fun to refresher courses in journalism or child
psychology.

If the health of the community can be improved by
teaching restaurant managers something about the
bacteriology of food, the community college sets up
such a course and seeks to enroll as many of those
employed in food service as it can muster. If the
community happens to be a center for travelers from

Latin America, the college provides classes in Spanish for salespeople, waitresses, bellboys, and taxicab drivers.

The potential effects of the community college in keeping intellectual curiosity alive in out-of-school citizens, of stimulating their zest for learning, of improving the quality of their lives as individuals and as citizens are limited only by the vision, the energy, and the ingenuity of the college staff--and by the size of the college budget. But the people will take care of the budget if the staff provides them with vital and worthwhile educational services.

In Relation to the Liberal Arts College

The Commission does not intend to suggest that the expansion of educational opportunity at the freshman-sophomore level should be limited to the community college. Part of the needed expansion can be achieved through existing 4-year colleges, part of it through the lower divisions of the universities.

Some of the established colleges may wish to institute terminal curriculums and contribute to the development of semiprofessional training. Others will prefer to concentrate on general education for students who plan to complete a 4-year course. Still others, especially the liberal arts colleges of universities, may welcome the opportunity to focus their energies on senior college programs.

In any case, the liberal arts college is so well established in the American educational tradition that it need not fear community colleges will weaken its own appeal. It should encourage the development of the community college, not oppose it. Experience indicates that these community institutions awaken intellectual curiosity and ambition in many youth who would not otherwise seek college education at all, and in many cases these students will be stimulated to continue their college careers if the 4-year colleges will meet them halfway with liberal admission policies.

There is little danger of lowered standards in this. We know now that ability to complete successfully the work of the last 2 years of college depends more upon the quality of mind and the mental habits a student brings to his work than upon the nature of the subject matter he has already covered. There is no reason to believe that community colleges, if they are adequately staffed, cannot do as good a job as the lower divisions of 4-year colleges in preparing students for advanced work in liberal and professional education.

While it favors the growth of community colleges, the Commission emphasizes that they must be soundly established with respect to financial support and

student attendance. This calls for careful planning on
a State-wide basis in determining location of the
colleges and the curriculum to be offered. Simply to
create more small, inadequately financed institutions
would only retard the development of a sound program of
post-high school education.

19. THE PRESIDENT'S COMMISSION ON HIGHER EDUCATION – THE NEW COMMUNITY COLLEGE

Community colleges, dedicated to reflecting and meeting the needs of their service areas, were sorely needed in the United States if the goal of increased educational opportunity was to be reached, reported the Commission. What should be the essential features of a community college? One, the college should survey its community regularly so it can adapt its programs to the educational needs of the students. Two, opportunities for alternate periods of work and study (cooperative education) are necessary. Three, vocational education should be balanced with general education so students are equipped to be good workers and good citizens. Four, the junior college should continue its already strong work in general education. Five, the college should develop a strong adult education program.

The Commission urged these new colleges to adopt the name "community" rather than "junior" to emphasize their expanded mission. It also side-stepped beautifully the 6-4-4 controversy (is the junior college a part of secondary or higher education?) by advocating no single plan of organization. Its plea, instead, was for state-wide planning which, depending on the state, could result in extension of the K-12 secondary system or a new segment of higher education being created. The Commission was more concerned with the offering of educational opportunities to youth than in prescribing rigid forms of organization.

The Commission was chaired by George Frederick Zook (b. 1885 in Kansas; d. 1951), former U.S. Commissioner of Education and president from 1934 to 1950 of the influential American Council on Education, Washington, D.C.

U.S., President's Commission on Higher Education, Vol. III, "Organizing Higher Education," Washington, D.C.: U.S. Government Printing Office, 1947, pp. 5-15.

COMMUNITY COLLEGES

Only a few decades ago, high school education in this country was for the few. Now, most of our young people take at least some high school work, and more than half of them graduate from the high school.

Until recently college education was for the very few. Now a fifth of our young people continue their education beyond the high school.

Many young people want less than a full four-year college course. The two-year college--that is the thirteenth and fourteenth years of our educational system--is about as widely needed today as the 4-year high school was a few decades ago. Such a college must fit into the community life as the high school has done.

Hence the President's Commission suggests the name "community college" to be applied to the institution designed to serve chiefly local community education needs. It may have various forms of organization and may have curricula of various lengths. Its dominant feature is its intimate relations to the life of the community it serves.

Volume I of the report of this Commission, entitled "Establishing the Goals," should leave no doubt about the urgent need for expanding and improving the program of the thirteenth and fourteenth years of our educational system. The complex demands of social, civic, and family life call for a lengthened period of general education for a much larger number of young people. The postponement of vocational choices until after high school graduation is wise in the case of increasing proportions of young people, thus calling for post-high-school vocational education for many. Adults in increasing numbers are desiring to continue their education through evening classes and hope to find the opportunities for such education near their homes.

Essential Characteristics of the Community College

Volume I of the report of this Commission, "Establishing the Goals," describes the functions and the needed program of education at the community college level. Volume II, "Equalizing and Expanding Individual Opportunity," presents the expanded program of education at this level as one of the main developments required to make available an educational opportunity for all qualified young people. To achieve these purposes, the organization must provide for at least the following:

First, the community college must make frequent surveys of its community so that it can adapt its program to the educational needs of its full-time students. These needs are both general and vocational. To this end it should have effective relationships not only with the parents of the students, but with cultural, civic, industrial, and labor groups as well. These contacts should often take the form of consultative committees which work with faculty personnel. On the basis of such surveys and consultations its program should constantly evolve and never be allowed to become static.

Second, since the program is expected to serve a cross section of the youth population, it is essential that consideration be given not only to apprentice training but also to cooperative procedures which provide for the older students alternate periods of attendance at college and remunerative work. The limited experience which colleges have had over the past three decades with this cooperative method has tended to confirm the belief that there is much educational value in a student's holding a job during his college days, particularly if that job is related to the courses being studied in college.

Third, the community college must prepare its students to live a rich and satisfying life, part of which involves earning a living. To this end, the total educational effort, general and vocational, of any student must be a well-integrated single program, not two programs. The sharp distinction which certain educators tend to make between general or liberal or cultural education on the one hand and vocational or semiprofessional or professional education on the other hand is not valid. Problems which industrial, agricultural, or commercial workers face today are only in part connected with the skills they use in their jobs. Their attitudes and their relationships with others are also important. Certainly the worker's effectiveness in dealing with family, community, national, and international problems, and his interests in maintaining and participating in wholesome recreation programs are important factors in a satisfying life. Many workers should be prepared for membership on municipal government councils, on school boards, on recreation commissions, and the like. The vocational aspect of one's education must not, therefore, tend to segregate "workers" from "citizens."

Fourth, the community college must meet the needs also of those of its students who will go on to a more extended general education or to specialized and professional study at some other college or university. Without doubt, higher education has given a disproportionate amount of attention to this group in the past, and it is well that a more balanced program to serve the needs of larger numbers is in prospect. On the other hand, it must always be kept in mind that

one of its primary functions is to lay a firm
foundation in general education.

Fifth, the community college must be the center for
the administration of a comprehensive adult education
program.   This is discussed at some length in
"Equalizing and Expanding Individual Opportunity," and
a statement on organization in connection with adult
education is made in Chapter VI of the present volume.
It is of utmost importance that the community college
recognize its obligation to develop such a program.

Organization of the Community College

Three essential factors condition the type of program
needed in the thirteenth and fourteenth years and hence
determine the major aspects of organization:

1.   Since a large proportion of young people will be
expected to continue their education through the
thirteenth and fourteenth years, it should be possible
for many of them to live at home, as they now do to
attend high school.   Hence there must be a large
increase in the number of institutions serving
essentially their local communities.

2.   The senior high school and the first two years of
college, particularly the liberal arts college, are
similar in purpose, and there is much duplication of
content in their courses. The program of the community
college must dovetail closely therefore with the work
of the senior high school.

3.   In most States there are many communities of a
size too small to warrant their maintaining community
colleges.   It is essential, therefore, that the
community colleges--including technical institutes,
university branches, and the like--be planned on a
State-wide basis and administered in such a way as to
avoid expensive duplication and to provide training for
each vocation somewhere.   Such training should be made
available to qualified students regardless of their
place of residence within the State.

The Special Role of the Junior College

In meeting these three major conditions, several
problems of organization are involved.   The first is
the relation of the community college to the present
junior college.

While the regular 4-year colleges and universities
include the thirteenth and fourteenth years of our
educational system, the institution which has been
developed especially to meet the needs of this age
group is the institution now commonly called the
"junior college." Its development has occurred almost
wholly in the last 25 years.

*****

It is assumed, then, that the present junior college is pointing the way to an improved thirteenth- and fourteenth-year program. A change of name is suggested because "junior" no longer covers one of the functions being performed. The name was adopted when the primary and often the sole function of the institution was to offer the first two years of a 4-year college curriculum. Now, however, one of its primary functions is to serve the needs of students who will terminate their full-time college attendance by the end of the fourteenth year or sooner. For them a wide variety of terminal curricula has been developed. Such an institution is not well characterized by the name "junior" college.

Relation of the Community College to a State-wide Educational Program

No common pattern of the relationship of the community college to a State-wide education program can be suggested for all States.

A careful study should be made in each State of the needs for more and better educational facilities at the thirteenth- and fourteenth-year level. The State department of education, the public schools, the institutions of higher education both public and private, and interested laymen should join in making the study in order that the resulting plan shall take into account the total educational resources as well as the total needs of the State.

*****

While no minimum enrollment figure is universally applicable, institutions with fewer than 200 full-time students, or the equivalent in part-time students, in the thirteenth and fourteenth years seldom can operate sufficiently strong programs without excessive cost. Even this number will justify only a partial program, but it may be good as far as it goes. On the other hand, many of the community colleges will have highly specialized terminal curricula in which the enrollment will be small, even though they serve a large region or sometimes, indeed, the whole State.

*****

The Need for More and Better Public Community Colleges, Local and District

As indicated above there are now 180 local

communities, mainly municipal school districts, which
maintain the thirteenth and fourteenth years as a part
of their school systems. Sometimes these local
communities are entire counties. Though frequently
organized separately from the local high school, the
college programs have usually been closely integrated
with the high school programs. They are commonly
administered by the same officers who administer the
rest of the local public schools. They are sometimes
wholly supported by funds raised by the school
district; sometimes by district funds supplemented by
State allotments; sometimes in part by fees paid by
neighboring districts for students resident in these
districts, and sometimes partly or almost wholly by
fees paid by the students who attend.

This Commission recommends that all states which have
not already done so enact permissive legislation under
which communities will be authorized to extend their
public school systems through the fourteenth year.

When such permissive legislation has been passed,
local school authorities in municipalities and counties
which meet the specifications prescribed in the law are
urged to give more careful consideration to
establishing community colleges as a part of their
school systems.

Even if all the local communities in a State having
population and financial resources enough to justify
establishing local community colleges do so, in most
States there will be large areas not served. Thousands
of small town and rural high schools should not attempt
to extend their work beyond the twelfth year. In fact
many of them are too small to maintain efficient
twelve-year school systems. Yet their young people
should have the same opportunity to continue their
education as the youth of the more populous centers.

This Commission recommends that to serve this large
group of small communities a State-wide plan be
developed embracing all communities large and small.

From developments to date it seems likely that two
different plans will evolve for meeting the public
educational needs of the State. One plan will be
better in some States, the other plan in other States.
These are: (a) a State-wide system of community
colleges under the jurisdiction of the State department
of education, or (b) a State-wide system of community
colleges under the jurisdiction of some institution of
higher education, or of an authority representing all
public higher education in the State. In either case
the possible participation of the private and church-
related colleges in the plan should be considered, but
without implying that public funds should be used to
support sectarian education. The first of these two
plans amounts essentially to extending the State public

school system through the fourteenth year. The second
plan contemplates retaining the thirteenth and
fourteenth years as a part of higher education and developing a comprehensive program for those years under
the jurisdiction of the higher education authorities of
the State.   The rapid development of centers as
branches of a State or private university indicates how
strong this "university branch" movement is.
    Under either plan the State would need to be divided
into regions or districts not coterminous in most cases
with any existing school districts. The community
colleges in these districts would have to be planned so
as to serve the needs of the whole State.   A special
board for the control of each district community
college might be set up, or the college might be
controlled by the local school board of the
municipality in which it is located. The system of
regional institutions might be controlled by the State
board of education if a part of the public school
system, or by the State board of regents (or similar
body) if a part of the State system of higher
education. They might be supported at least in part by
a district-wide tax or largely by State funds. In fact
there should be the greatest flexibility in the methods
of control and support in order that the development of
community colleges may fit into the existing pattern in
each State, thus serving to strengthen rather than to
weaken each State's present educational program.

The Place of the Private and the Church-Related Community College

    There are 96 privately controlled nonprofit junior
colleges, 191 church-controlled, 39 proprietary, and 7
controlled by other organizations.   Their enrollments
in 1946-47 totaled 78,150.   Many of these junior
colleges are the upper grades of schools with high
school divisions and sometimes elementary schools as
well.
    The need for an improved and a more widespread
opportunity for at least a 2-year course beyond the
high school is a challenge to church-related and other
private colleges as much as it is to public
institutions. It is quite possible, too, that some of
the present 4-year colleges will find it advantageous
to stress even more than at present the work on the
junior college level. Some may even discontinue their
more expensive senior college work.   This Commission
recommends that both the junior colleges and the 4-year
colleges under private and church auspices have the
fullest opportunity to be related to the movement to
improve the program of the thirteenth and fourteenth
years.

Grades to be Included in the Community Colleges

With respect to length of curricula there is no single pattern applicable to all community colleges. In some States the pattern will no doubt follow the traditional arrangement, and thus the community college will be a 2-year institution above the 12-grade school. This is likely to be the plan followed in States which vest the administrative control of the community colleges in a State board since the State will hesitate to disturb the organization of the local high schools. The development of better counseling programs for students and closer cooperation between the high schools and the community colleges will do much to strengthen the continuity of the student's individual program and to enable the community college to serve its young people's needs efficiently.

Where a school extends its program through the fourteenth year, the senior high school and the first 2 years of college are brought under a single administration and into much closer relationship than formerly. About 40 communities or institutions have combined the last 2 years of the high school and the first 2 years of college into such a 4-year unit. This has naturally been accompanied by the expansion also of the junior high school into a 4-year unit. Thus, some communities (Pasadena, California, is a well-known example) have made a three-unit system--a 6-year elementary school, a 4-year high school (sometimes called junior high school) and a 4-year college (commonly called a junior college although in effect a community college).

No single plan of organization is advocated. What is urged, however, is that the present inefficiency and loss of time involved in the transition of students from high school to college be reduced as far as possible.

Lack of Cooperation Between High Schools and Colleges

High schools and colleges traditionally work separately on their common problems of preparing for and admitting youth to college. This is harmful to students and leads to inevitable irritations between high school and college personnel. High schools resist the "unwarranted pressure" from the college, and the colleges scold about the "miserable preparation" their students are getting in the high school. This separateness in jurisdiction of the colleges from the rest of the State system, while not so serious formerly when only a few attended college, is now becoming a major problem of organization.

The present difficulty grows largely out of the fact that the academic work of the last 2 years of the high

school and that of the first 2 years of the typical
arts college are essentially identical in purpose.
Therefore, to have half of this 4-year period
administered by the high schools, under one system of
controls, and the other half administered by the
colleges, under another system of controls, constantly
raises many serious questions. Only two of these will
be discussed.

First, the present plan is wasteful.--Many of the
same subjects are offered in high schools and in
college. Beginning chemistry, biology, or physics;
solid geometry or trigonometry; ancient, medieval and
modern English, or American history; foreign languages,
ancient or modern, these and many other subjects may be
studied in high school or begun in college. Colleges,
therefore, rightly try to dovetail their requirements
for a given student with what that student had in high
school. But great difficulties arise in doing so.

The question may be raised as to whether coordinating
the thirteenth and fourteenth years more closely with
the eleventh and twelfth really solves the problem of
ill-coordination between the lower school and higher
schools. Does not such an arrangement merely postpone
the problem to the transition from the fourteenth to
the fifteenth year?

In reply it must be recognized that transition from
one institution to another is bound to involve some
difficulty. Coordination cannot be perfect if one
institution is under one authority and the other
institutions under another authority. But for many
students the end of the twelfth year falls in the
middle of a program, while the end of the fourteenth
year falls at the end of one program and the beginning
of another. General studies, as distinguished from
concentration or specialization, commonly terminate at
the end of the fourteenth year. Hence the transition
at that point to a different institution involves much
less of a problem of coordination than at a point 2
years earlier.

*Secondly, the present plan provides very inadequately for those
who terminate their formal schooling at the end of the fourteenth
year.* Liberal arts colleges recognize two purposes--
general broadening of understanding through study in
many academic fields during the first 2 years, or, in a
few institutions, during the entire 4 years; and deeper
understanding through concentration in one field,
during the last 2 years. Thus the distinction between
general and specialized functions is recognized. Even
where this is done most effectively, however, the
programs of the first 2 years are designed generally to
serve much better the students who continue through 4
years than those who drop out at the end of 2 years.
To be sure, an increasing number of 4-year colleges and

universities are introducing terminal programs of less than 4 years in length, but these are yet so few that they serve better to emphasize the problem than to solve it.

While there is wide variation among colleges, no less than one-third and in some institutions as many as two-thirds of the students following 4-year curricula in liberal arts colleges drop out before or at the close of the first 2 years. In engineering schools the percentage is higher. For this large group, few educators contend that the present arrangement is the most desirable. Some of these "drop outs" know at the time they enter college that they will attend no longer than 2 years. Others could be led to see the desirability of a shorter than 4-year terminal program by a suitable system of counseling.

It must be remembered, however, that the number of years embraced in a community college is important only as its [sic] facilitates close integration of the work of the senior high school and the first 2 years of the college. If other means are at hand of assuring essential unity of the program of these 4 years, little importance should be attached to the question of whether the community college is a 2-year or a 4-year institution.

Administration of the State-wide System of Public Community Colleges

A State which decides to develop a State-wide system of public community colleges will be confronted by three major questions respecting their management. First, shall they be under the management of the boards of education of the school districts where they are located, or under special boards created for the purpose, or under a State board presumably either the State Board of Education or the board of regents? Second, how shall they be financed? Shall it be by a special tax spread over the local community or the region served by each one; by assessments upon outlying school districts on a fixed-fee basis per student attending the community college from that district; by the State's bearing essentially the total cost; or by relatively high student fees? Third, how shall the location and the programs of the several colleges be determined so as to assure their serving satisfactorily both the community needs and the needs of the larger area?

There is no single answer to any of these questions. A consideration of the merits of each alternative would involve a lengthy discussion. A few general suggestions, however, are given here.

Control. Complicated machinery of control such as a special board for each community college is to be

avoided where possible. Even though the district
served may be larger than the local school district,
the actual administration of a community college may
safely be left in the hands of the board of education
controlling other schools in the community if some
agency outside, such as the State, is in position to
assure consideration by the local board of the
interests of those students living in outlying
territory not represented on the local board.

Meeting the Cost. It is a sound principle to place
upon each school district the responsibility of meeting
at least a part of the cost of public education of the
residents of that district, wherever they must go for
their schooling. This principle now prevails in most
of the States when students go from one district to
another for high school education. It would seem that
it should prevail also for public community colleges.
But it is to be presumed that the State will contribute
a large share of the cost.

Student fees. This Commission believes that the
public community college should be free as are the
other parts of the public school system. The practice
of charging fees would tend to jeopardize the most
distinctive virtue of the American system of free
public schools, and would in the long run greatly
reduce the value which the nation hopes to derive from
the recommended extension of the public school system.
The principle here enunciated is discussed in other
volumes of this Commission's report entitled
"Establishing the Goals," "Equalizing and Expanding
Individual Opportunity" and "Financing Higher
Education."

*Degree of State responsibility in the management of community
colleges.* Without regard to the plan of management or
the measures adopted for financing the community
colleges, they must be so organized that they serve the
interests of the whole State as well as the interests
of the communities in which they are located.
Therefore, what each college includes in its curricula
must be subject to State approval. Similarly, policies
under which students from any section of the State have
an equal chance to enter institutions having curricula
found in only some of the colleges must be adopted by
the State. Plans for transportation and for housing
and feeding students who need these services must be
made by, or at least approved by, the State. Some
State agency therefore must have adequate authority and
supervisory machinery to handle such matters.

20. A CONGRESSMAN SPEAKS OUT FOR JUNIOR COLLEGES

The Congressional Record reports a speech by Henry A. Dixon, representative from Utah, noting an American Association of Junior Colleges annual meeting in Salt Lake City and extolling the virtues of junior colleges in the United States. This is the first lengthy statement in the Congress about the two-year colleges in this country. Dixon was also a junior college administrator and former member of the Commission on Higher Education appointed by President Harry Truman. This statement illustrates the increasing enthusiasm for public two-year colleges in the post World War II era and the increasing national attention given to them.

THE JUNIOR COLLEGES CAN HELP SOLVE PROBLEMS OF HIGHER EDUCATION

Mr. DIXON. Mr. Speaker, I ask unanimous consent to address the House for 1 minute and to revise and extend my remarks.

The SPEAKER. Is there objection to the request of the gentleman from Utah?

There was no objection.

Mr. DIXON. Mr. Speaker, this week the American Association of Junior Colleges meets in annual convention in Salt Lake City. This national meeting is of vital interest to Members of Congress because--

First. A tidal wave of youth will reach college before provision is made for them unless the Nation works at full speed ahead on its planning and preparations.

U.S., Congressional Record--House, 85th Congress, 1st session, (Vol. 103, part 3), March 4, 1957, pp. 3032-3033.

Second.   Dr. Elvis Stahr, executive secretary of President Eisenhower's Committee on Education Beyond the High School will be one of the featured speakers.

Third.   His committee has already issued a preliminary report in which it asks Congress to appropriate $2,500,000 to the States for formulating a comprehensive program of higher education.

I intend to introduce a bill later on to carry out this recommendation.

Fourth.   The findings of the convention of the American Association of Junior Colleges are also significant to us because the President's Committee points to the junior college as one of the most important and economical ways to solve the difficult college problem.

Utah is honored to be host to this great organization, 600 colleges strong, and extends congratulations to its president, James M. Ewing; its executive secretary, Jesse B. Bogue; its other officers, directors, and membership.

Much interest is centered around the Salt Lake City convention because our country turns to the junior--community--college to accommodate a sizable portion of the influx of students soon to reach college.

It is none too early now for Members of Congress to formulate plans to take care of the incoming college population.   Even if we start now, I fear it might be a case of too little and too late as it appears to be with regard to aid for the elementary and secondary schools.

The situation brings to my mind the fable of "The Fox and the Wild Boar," in which the fox came upon the wild boar sharpening his teeth on a rock.   "What are you doing that for?" asked the fox.   "Because when the hounds are after me it's too late," said the wild boar.

The tidal wave of students is now beginning to flood the high schools and will soon reach our colleges. Twice as many youth will graduate from high school in 1969 as did this past year.   This assures us that by 1970 there will be twice as many people attending school on the college level.   If building construction progresses at its present rate of $750 million every year until 1970, there will be room for only 4.3 million of the 6 million applying for admission.

What then are we going to do about it?   President Eisenhower has already made a beginning by appointing a Presidential Committee on Education Beyond the High School.   Its executive secretary, Dr. Elvis Stahr, will be one of the featured speakers at the Salt Lake City convention this week.   Last November the Committee released a preliminary report.   It recommends at the outset that Congress appropriate $2 1/2 million to be distributed among the States to encourage and assist every State to develop a State program designed to meet its college problems. The first thing that Congress can do about it is to appropriate this money.

The President's Committee takes the position that equality of educational opportunity beyond the high school is the goal to be reached and that four important developments are necessary before institutions of high learning are able to achieve that goal. These developments are.

Quantity: There must be a sufficient number of institutions and faculty persons to provide for all qualified students.

Quality: The quality of opportunity offered must be good.

Variety: There must be a variety of educational institutions under a diversity of auspices to offer many choices to individuals of various abilities and talents who differ in interests, aspirations, and beliefs.

Accessibility: There must be facilities for education which are accessible to all students if equality of opportunity is truly to be realized.

Now how can these goals of quantity, quality, variety and accessibility be realized?

More than 20 years' experience as an administrator in a junior college has satisfied me that at least part of the answer may be found in an expanded junior college movement. In fact, the Truman Commission on Higher Education, of which I was a member, stated boldly that the bulk of the increased college enrollment during the next decade should be absorbed by the community--junior--college.

The junior college is usually a 2-year local institution--community or regional--catering to a wide diversity of student population. It has an extremely practical bent. It goes into all of the homes of all of the people who do all of the work of the community and helps them to do their work better and live more happily in those homes. Its mother is the high school and its father is the university. The father wants junior to walk in his footsteps but junior is already making some significant footsteps of his own. For example, junior is less bound by tradition, less regimented by standard university curricular requirements and far more free to do those things most needed to meet the needs of his own students and the needs of his own community.

The junior college takes the position that there is nothing sacred about the word "four," so fixed by senior institutions as the minimum number of years required for a bachelor's degree. It points out that there are many skilled and semiprofessional occupations for which youth or adults might prepare in 1 or 2 years.   Consequently, the junior college gives a certificate of completion to students finishing a 2-year terminal curriculum and a title of associate of arts or associate of sciences for students transferring into the university upon completion of the first 2 years of the traditional university program.

Those completing the terminal--non-transfer--program are encouraged to pursue adult classes in night school. Approximately 55 percent of the junior college graduates are graduated from the terminal programs and go into industry or into semiprofessional work while 45 percent transfer into the junior year of the university.

THE JUNIOR COLLEGE IS SENSITIVE TO COMMUNITY NEEDS

The junior college has an adaptive mechanism within the structure of its organization which makes its program extremely sensitive to community needs.   In setting up a terminal vocational program it usually takes steps as follows: first, it makes an occupational survey to determine positions available in the particular occupation being considered; second, it organizes an advisory committee of people engaged in the occupation; third, it develops the course of study with the help of the advisory committee; fourth, it installs the program; fifth, it places the graduates upon completion of their school program; and sixth, it supervises and assists those graduates to succeed on the job.

Now let me give you three illustrations out of my own experience to show the adaptability of a local college which is free as far as its terminal program is concerned, from the uniformity and regimentation of the university standards.

During the darkest days of the depression when the Weber Junior College graduates could not find work, the occupational survey of the Ogden, Utah, area showed that the 3 railroads centering at Ogden could use 25 station agents.   While hundreds of men applied, no qualified men were available.   Weber Junior College organized an advisory committee of 3 union station agents and 2 railroad administrators, set up a course for station agents, hired the best agent the railroads had as a teacher, and in 12 months turned out 25 good operators, all of whom the committee placed in positions.   Such a course would not be eligible for credit or be considered academically respectable by a university.

Four years ago our survey showed that the hospitals in the Ogden area were short of nurses because the 3- and 4-year programs of the university were not turning out nurses fast enough.   We formed an advisory committee consisting of the president of the county medical association, the head nurses of our two hospitals, the director of nursing at the State university, the State president of the nursing organization and the State supervisor of nursing registration.

The committee heard of the nursing education research at Columbia University encouraged by our esteemed Congressman FRANCES P. BOLTON--which revealed that by placing the nursing program under the college itself and by using the hospitals as a training laboratory, nurses could qualify for registration in 2 years instead of a minimum of 3 or 4 years. Furthermore, it was pointed out that by permitting the girls to live at home instead of living in the nursing home at the hospitals, the hospitals would be freed of the expense of the nursing home, could use it for other purposes, and the girls' school life would be far more attractive.

We announced and offered the 2-year nursing program. Immediately we had more applicants than student stations because living at the nursing home proved to be the chief barrier to girls entering nursing. Fully a year's time was saved by eliminating routine hospital services which the hospitals required the girls to perform long after the educational values of these services had passed. All of the first 2-year graduates except one passed the State examination last year and I am told ranked as high as the nurses with 3 years' training in the old program.

One of the features of the American Association of Junior College Convention now in session at Salt Lake City is a trip to Ogden so the administrators can see the Weber Junior College 2-year nursing program firsthand and appraise its outcomes.

Wealth is created by money, materials, and men, but the greatest of these is men. The dispersal of industry legislation passed by Congress last summer holds out great promise to communities under 200,000 population if conditions are right. One requirement is a high-class competent labor force. The proven ability of Weber Junior College to turn out good technicians was one of the important considerations leading recently to the selection of Ogden as the site of the large Marquardt Ram jet-engine plant.

THE JUNIOR COLLEGE MEETS THE COMMITTEE'S TEST OF VARIETY

This 2-year school caters to a widely diversified school population. Students who want to go on to a 4-year degree can find the standard first 2 years at the junior college and then transfer to the university.

Those desiring a trade or semiprofessional preparation
can complete a well-rounded 2-year course consisting of
both vocational and general education which is more
broadening and far richer in social and civic values
than the narrower work of a strictly trade or area
vocational school.   And those who want a more narrow
intensively vocational program of shorter duration can
find that as well and in a better setting.

The junior college caters to people of all ages.   Its
adult and night school program is meeting with unusual
success.

The junior college is also adapted to varying
capacities and abilities.   It takes an intelligence
quotient of about 115 to get a C or passing grade in
the universities.   Two-thirds of our youth have not an
intelligence quotient that high, yet a large percentage
can find their niche in the variety of offerings of the
junior college.   Only about one-third can complete a 4-
year program at the university while more than one-half
can complete a 2-year program at either the junior or
senior institution.   This is one of the reasons why
one-half of the students in the senior colleges
discontinue their work on or before the end of the
sophomore year.

The junior college is admirably adapted to help the
student discover his interests, aptitudes, and
abilities.   Many students are what President Arthur
Adams, of the American Council on Education calls late
bloomers.

*****

Many of our most outstanding scholars are discovered
in the terminal programs of the junior colleges, and
encouraged to go on into the senior schools.   These
valuable young people might otherwise never have been
discovered.

The smaller school of the junior college variety can
give better individualized instruction than the huge
university.   Our industrial age is so accustomed to the
goals of speed, mass production and uniformity of
product that it tends to impose those goals on the
college to the detriment of the individual enrolled.
The school should resemble a clinic, where each patient
is treated in accordance with his own needs, more than
it should resemble a huge factory.

THE JUNIOR COLLEGE MEETS WELL THE COMMITTEE'S TEST OF
QUALITY

Several rather reliable followup studies have been
made of the success of junior college transfer students
at the university.

Grace V. Bird, associate director, relations with schools at University of California, arrived at the following conclusions:

Junior college transfers make records approximately the same as those made by transfers from 4-year colleges and by native students. There is clear evidence that junior colleges are salvaging a large number of students for success in advanced studies who would otherwise have missed them entirely.

THE JUNIOR COLLEGE MEETS THE COMMITTEE'S TEST OF ACCESSIBILITY

The community college makes college available to more people. Coleman Griffith, in his book The Junior College in Illinois, found that only 19.7 percent of high-school graduates went on to college when there was no free junior college in their community as against 53.5 percent when a junior college was present. In the latter case, also, 46.7 percent of the graduates of lower economic status were found to be attending the junior college.

George Meany, president of the AFL-CIO, has stated that the American worker could not afford in many cases to send a child on for 4 years of education, but a 2-year program could be afforded.

The Truman Commission found that the financial barrier was the greatest barrier in the way of equal education opportunity to all American youth and that the costs to the student are going up rapidly. The Commission refers to a study of one State which shows that only 1 out of 3 of the highest 10 percent of the high-school graduates ever entered college.

W. Hugh Stickler made one of the most reliable studies of comparative student costs in public senior colleges, private senior colleges, public junior colleges, and private junior colleges. In these costs he included tuition, fees, room rent, board, books, supplies, clothing, transportation, and miscellaneous expenses. His results are as follows:

	Cost per year
Public senior colleges	$1,304.00
Private senior colleges	1,531.00
Private junior colleges	1,062.00
Public junior colleges	735.00

It costs the student nearly twice as much each year to attend school at a public senior college as it does a public junior college.

THE JUNIOR COLLEGE MEETS THE TEST OF QUANTITY AND ECONOMY

The junior college is more economical. Senator CLIFFORD CASE of New Jersey, who, incidentally, is an alumnus and trustee of Rutgers University, in a recent news release describing the advantages of community college, stated:

Clearly, the community-college plan produces the most for the tax dollar. It avoids the expensive costs of building dormitories and of long-distance transportation. It gives the student a chance to live at home, to find part-time work among his friends and neighbors, and perhaps to combine education and work.

It is to be hoped that the States will, in their planning with the $2 1/2 million--which I hope our legislation in Congress will give them--give careful study toward establishing a coordinated system of public education beyond the high school which will include the junior college as an integral part of that public-school system and give this segment its fair share of dignity, emphasis, and financial support. Not long ago the completion of the eighth grade constituted in people's minds the end of public-school education. The goal was then raised to the completion of high school. And now nothing short of the completion of the junior college is the goal.

21. A PRESIDENTIAL COMMITTEE REPORTS

Under President Dwight D. Eisenhower another federal task force (chaired by Devereux C. Josephs, chairman of the board of the New York Life Insurance Company; vice chair was David D. Henry, president of the University of Illinois) reviewed conditions in higher education and again support was urged for two-year colleges--although perhaps not as fervently as by the "Truman Commission" a decade earlier. The Committee identified the characteristics of a comprehensive community college. It also urged great caution in establishing too many new two-year colleges, especially institutions without adequate economic support. The tentative tone of the Committee's report is not surprising; most of its 35 members and its professional staff represented universities and businesses. Few strong voices for community colleges were included.

"Two-Year" Higher Institutions

The expansion of the "2-year college" has been one of the most notable developments in post-high school education in twentieth century America.

The phenomenal growth of these institutions, which includes junior colleges, both private and public, community colleges, technical institutes, and 2-year off-campus centers of 4-year colleges and universities, is testimony to their ability to meet diverse student needs.

U.S., President's Committee on Education Beyond the High School, Second Report to the President, Washington, D.C.: U.S. Government Printing Office, 1957, pp. 64-65, 72-73.

From 8 in 1900, these institutions grew to 596 in 1955 with enrollments increasing from 100 students to 700,000 in the same period.

The program of the comprehensive community college includes: (a) The first 2 years of a full collegiate program; (b) many kinds of students for general educational integrated with vocational-technical training for the subprofessional occupations; (c) many kinds of short courses required for upgrading employed persons and for retraining employees because of changes in business and industrial developments; and (d) adult or continuing education programs and courses of the kinds desired by the community. There are indications that adults are more likely to take advantage of opportunities for continuing education if those are offered in a collegiate rather than a secondary school setting.

In many areas the community college has also become a center for social and cultural life, providing opportunities in the creative and performing arts as well as a meeting place for various community groups and individuals seeking to enrich their lives through learning.

These institutions extend further educational opportunities to youth and adults near their homes, thereby reducing the cost to students and frequently to the taxpayers. The cost of constructing a community college where boarding facilities are not required is less than the cost of constructing a residential college. In many cases, at least part of the facilities are available in the local high school on a temporary basis. The program offerings may cover a wide diversity of courses of study and training especially geared to the needs of local occupations in agriculture, business, and industry.

In addition, the community college provides a favorable opportunity for students who have not decided on a career to explore more fully their interests and plans.

Studies in California, where the community college has developed most widely, have shown that students transferring to the junior year of senior institutions have done at least as well as students who had originally entered the senior institution as freshmen. This kind of arrangement has given the senior colleges and universities the opportunity to increase their concentration on upper division and graduate work for which they are particularly well equipped.

In New York, the Department of Education estimates that at least 50 percent of their first-year college students in 1970 will be accommodated in community colleges. Evidence from other States also indicates a major role for the 2-year institutions in helping to absorb the greatly increased enrollments of the sixties and seventies.

Community colleges are not designed, however, merely to relieve enrollment pressures on senior institutions. They have a role and an integrity of their own. They are designed to help extend and equalize opportunities to those who are competent and who otherwise would not attend college, and to present a diversity of general and specialized programs to meet the needs of diversified talents and career goals.

Moreover, the widespread availability of community colleges will undoubtedly lead to greater numbers of students applying to senior and graduate institutions for continuation beyond their first two years. It is important, therefore, that planning for community colleges be coordinated with planning for upper division and graduate facilities in the State or area.

The Committee is aware that there are differences of opinion, strongly and honestly held, as to the ideal auspices for the establishment of 2-year institutions. Indeed there are such differences within the Committee itself. At present there is much variety, and it is good that there continue to be. There are undoubted advantages in close liaison with the area university; there are also advantages in local orientation. The Committee generally believes that the best system for combining these advantages will depend upon particular conditions. Experiment and experience will no doubt narrow the sound choices, but State and local studies and decisions should determine the organization, management and financing of such institutions.

RECOMMENDATIONS

(NOTE.----Most of the Committee's recommendations were approved unanimously, the remainder by substantial consensus.)

1. The Committee recommends that, in the overall expansion and diversification of educational opportunities beyond high school in the years ahead, the expansion and support of existing institutions should in general take priority over the establishment of new ones. The larger numbers and larger needs can be cared for more immediately and more economically in this way. Needed expansion and decentralization will be most soundly effected on the principle of "expansion by addition" without subtraction from the services and resources of existing institutions.

2. Recognizing that community colleges are uniquely equipped to meet the particular needs of the individual community and to be responsive to the diverse interests of its citizens, the Committee recommends that communities anticipating substantial growth in student

population consider the 2-year college as a possible solution to some of the problems of providing additional educational opportunities. However, the Committee also urges that this possibility be approached with caution. Careful planning is essential to ensure success for this kind of educational program. There are already many colleges too small to be economical. Community planning must be closely related to State and regional planning in order to avoid the possibility of developing still more small, uneconomic units.   The errors that were made in developing too many small high schools should not be repeated in the development of community colleges.   Any community college program should be financed in such fashion as not to weaken financial support of the community's elementary and secondary schools.   Without sound planning, what might have become a major community asset may become a community disappointment.

22. U.S. OFFICE OF EDUCATION STAFF RESPONDS TO THE 1957 REPORT OF THE PRESIDENT'S COMMITTEE ON EDUCATION BEYOND THE HIGH SCHOOL

The U.S. Office of Education staff felt the Committee was timid in its support of two-year colleges and sharply criticized many of its opinions and conclusions. The Committee, said the staff, does acknowledge the utility of the two-year college. It is aware of its nature and purpose. But the Committee does not stress the advantages of the two-year institution, it ignores one of its main functions, namely guidance and counseling, and its recommendations are laden with qualifications and cautions which dampen any enthusiasm a reader might have for this institution.

This staff report goes on to rebut many of the inaccuracies or tentative statements made by the Committee, furnishing, in its own way, a stirring defense of the emerging community college.

Statements and Recommendations of the President's Committee on Education Beyond the High School

There are many indications in the report of the President's Committee on Education Beyond the High School that it had a clear understanding of the nature of the problems confronting American higher education today.

*****

The President's Committee (on pages 64 and 65 of its report) gives its longest look at the 2-year college idea and to factors in the movement which show the

U.S. Office of Education Staff Paper No. 2, [unpublished, 1957], pp. 23, 25-27, 29-34. Accession No. 63-A-23, Container No. 64, "Miscellaneous Office of Education Files, 1955-59," Record Group 12, U.S. Federal Records Center, Alexandria, Virginia.

great promise of these institutions. In these two pages, the Committee shows a clear understanding of the true nature and scope of the 2-year college and its relationship to the decentralization of the lower-division level of higher education. Here, too, is presented some documentation for the oft-repeated recommendation that the report brings out, namely, that communities and groups of communities that are facing impending shortages of higher educational facilities consider the establishment of 2-year colleges.

Unfortunately, however, the Committee's report has three weaknesses as far as its position with respect to the 2-year college movement is concerned: (1) It fails to relate pointedly the character and scope, and more particularly, the advantages of the 2-year colleges to the problems now before American higher education and to possible approaches to solving these problems; (2) It overlooks entirely one of the most important functions of the 2-year college, namely, that of providing a medium for counseling and guiding young people, channeling them into realistic career choices either for advanced study or for immediate employment after the 2-year college; and (3) The report reflects a basic lack of genuine sympathy, if not enthusiasm, for the 2-year college, couching most of its recommendations in provisos, cautions, and qualifying statements that leave the reader more impressed with the "pitfalls" that may befall action than with ways that present serious problems may be alleviated. Some of the recommendations of the Committee also appear to be highly challengeable and weak in the light of known evidence about the operation and practice in American higher education.

The following illustrates each of these points of weakness in the report: Failure to Relate the 2-Year College Movement Pointedly to the Problems of American Higher Education.

One of the observations made by the Committee that has already been quoted was that "the percentages of able high school graduates not continuing their education beyond high school are especially high among children of nonprofessional parents, minority groups, girls, and rural and low income families." In the discussion that appears in the report, a section is devoted to each of the groups just enumerated.

In no instance in the Committee's discussion is specific reference made to the effectiveness of the 2-year colleges in removing the barriers to advanced education that the groups of Americans just mentioned are facing. Not even in the discussion of the "Isolated Youth" and that of the "Low Income Groups" is specific mention made of the community colleges. Yet, as a matter of fact, it is precisely because they have

been found to be most effective in reaching out to
students and because they are the most economical means
of providing comprehensive programs of post-high-school
education to large numbers of youth that the 2-year
colleges have attained the recognition and advanced
development they now hold.   Studies of costs of going
to college such as that completed by the Florida State
University . . . document the fact that community
colleges are most effective in reducing the economic
barrier to advanced education.

*****

Oversight of the Guidance Function of 2-Year Colleges

The Committee's report makes much of the need for an
improved guidance and counseling machinery in the
Nation in order that less wastage of talent represented
by qualified high-school graduates failing to go on to
college will occur.   For example, it states:
> "The Committee recommends that school
> systems greatly increase their emphasis on
> developing sound guidance and counseling
> programs which will extend meaningful aid to
> all students within their jurisdictions by
> providing properly trained fulltime
> counselors and the necessary informational
> and auxiliary services; that they increase
> their facilities for counseling parents of
> capable graduates, to the end that they
> become better acquainted with the values of
> education beyond the high school for their
> children; and that colleges and universities
> assist in stepping up programs for the
> recruitment and training of counseling
> personnel." (pp. 55-56)

Yet in the discussion of the functions of 2-year
colleges on pages 64 and 65, indeed nowhere in the
report, does the Committee identify the guidance and
counseling function of these institutions.   In
contrast, this function is one that is greatly stressed
in several other notable treatises on American higher
education such as the report of the New York State
Regents already cited and James B. Conant's Education
and Liberty.   The latter sees the 2-year colleges and
their screening and counseling function as the
salvation of the university.

*****

Basic Lack of Enthusiasm Reflected in Phraseology of
Recommendations Pertinent to 2-Year Colleges

Although the Committee repeats its recommendation
that communities and groups of communities faced with
need for expanding facilities for higher education
consider establishing a 2-year college several times,
it presents the recommendation always with a flood of
qualifications. This can be best and most simply
illustrated by the following direct quotations from the
report:

"Communities or groups of neighboring
communities faced with an impending shortage
of higher educational capacity will do well
to consider new 2-year community colleges as
part of the solution. Experience in a number
of areas has demonstrated that, with
carefully planned facilities and programs,
community colleges can be highly effective in
affording readily available opportunities for
excellent education beyond the high school.

"New community colleges, however, should
not be viewed as a panacea for relieving
pressures upon existing 4-year institutions.
On the contrary, they are bound to accelerate
the overall increase in enrollments, the
demand for teachers and the need for funds.
They may absorb substantial freshman and
sophomore burdens but by sending graduates on
to the upper division, where per student
costs run much higher, they may aggravate the
4-year institutions' financial problems.

"Caution must be exercised, too, against
creating new collegiate institutions which
are too small to be economical. The errors
made in creating too many small high schools
in the United States should not be repeated
at the college level.

"The program of the comprehensive community
college includes: (a) the first 2 years of a
full collegiate program; (b) many kinds of
programs, varying in time-requirements,
needed by vast numbers of students for
general education integrated with vocational-
technical training for the subprofessional
occupations; (c) many kinds of short courses
required for upgrading employed persons and
for retraining employees because of technical
developments or displacements; and (d) adult
or continuing education programs and courses
desired by the community.

"Great good for all higher education might
come from the establishment of a few highly

experimental new colleges which could test
out radically new methods of achieving better
learning through better utilization of
faculty and space, unfettered by traditional
campus practices." (pp. 12-13)
....

"2. Recognizing that community colleges are
uniquely equipped to meet the particular
needs of the individual community and to be
responsive to the diverse interests of its
citizens, the Committee recommends that
communities anticipating substantial growth
in student population consider the 2-year
college as a possible solution to some of the
problems of providing additional educational
opportunities. However, the Committee also
urges that this possibility be approached
with caution. Careful planning must be
closely related to State and regional
planning in order to avoid the possibility of
developing too many small, uneconomic units.
The errors that were made in developing too
many small high schools should not be
repeated in the development of community
colleges. Any community college program
should be financed in such a fashion as not
to weaken financial support of the
community's elementary and secondary schools.
Without sound planning, what might have
become a major community asset may become a'
community disappointment." (p. 21)
....

*****

To be sure, the rapid increase in the number of 2-
year colleges that is now a matter of fact in American
higher education is very likely, as the Committee
observes, "to accelerate the overall increase in
enrollments, the demand for teachers, and the need for
funds" (p. 12). The Committee, furthermore, is quite
right in noting that the shortages of college teachers
is a critical bottleneck (p. 5) in American higher
education. Its recommendation that every effort be
extended to ameliorate this grievous problem that
appears on page 6 and in other places is very well
taken.
But the Committee makes the error of "accenting the
negative" (or what it considers as the possible
negative). The basic issues that should be considered
are: Is the acceleration of the overall increase in
enrollments to the ultimate good of the people and the

Nation? Is it really a means of effecting an economy
to the 4-year colleges by leveling the costs of
operation over the 4-year span where now the costs of
the upper division are greatly out of balance with
these for the lower division because student attrition
leads to small class units at the junior and senior
level? Does it give promise of alleviating the
manpower shortages and concomitant problems of the
Nation's economy? Does it give promise of meeting the
demands for further education expressed by high-school
graduates and adults and thus give to the people
continued opportunity and equal chance of success that
is the American way?

Challengeable Recommendations and Observations

The Committee places itself on the defensive by
presenting a number of statements in the report. One
example is seen in the sentence in one of the above
quotations which reads, "They may absorb substantial
freshman and sophomore burdens but by sending graduates
on to the upper division, where per-student costs run
much higher, they may aggravate the 4-year
institutions' financial problem." The fact of the
matter is that one basic reason why per-student costs
for operating upper-division programs in most fields of
study are higher than those for lower-division
instruction is that the class units are smaller at the
upper-divisional level. This is a result of the high
student attrition that is found in most 4-year colleges
and universities. The Committee must bear the burden
of proof that expanding the enrollments at the upper-
division level would increase the costs per student for
instruction at this level.

Other similar statements of questionable tenability
are those which infer that much of the burden of
expanding enrollments at the college level can be
absorbed by the colleges which heretofore, for various
reasons, have not attracted sufficient students to
completely fill their facilities. Repeated reference
is made to this possibility (pages 12 and 72, for
example). If, as the Committee readily admits, these
institutions have not been under pressure to date, it
is highly unrealistic to presume that large numbers of
students will be attracted to them in the future unless
some basic changes in the character of the institutions
are effected. Indeed, in some instances, the character
of the institution that prohibits attraction of large
numbers of students, for example, unfavorable
geographic location, may be quite beyond the
possibility of any corrective action. Even an
extensive scholarship program may not be effective in
this case for history of the G.I. Bill shows that even

when financially aided to go to college, students will
not attend some certain institutions. Unless coercive
measures as to choice of institution were attached to
scholarship and subsistence grants, some colleges would
still be left below their maximum capacity. Even were
some colleges to find that the factors which limit
attraction of students to its halls are within the
realm of feasible corrective action, e.g., narrow
programs of offerings, high tuition rates, limitations
of admission on the basis of sex, religious point of
view, or other basis, it would also likely be found in
many instances that institutional flexibility was
insufficient to effect the changes necessary to attract
more students.

PART IV.
RECURRING
ISSUES

The golden age of junior and community colleges arrived in this era. Those seeds sown late in the 19th century and cultivated as tender seedlings early in this century reached maturity in the 1960's and early 1970's.

The harvest was magnificent: from hundreds of institutions to over a thousand; from thousands of students to millions; from largely liberal arts transfer programs to a widening array of vocational and technical, career-oriented courses and programs; from a focus on the recent high school graduate to a commitment to serve adults of all ages; from attention to individual student needs to a broad view of community and area socio-educational needs; from small, rural, private or locally controlled autonomous institutions to large, urban, public, state, and multi-campus systems. The W.K. Kellogg Foundation allotted $1.6 million in grants to a number of universities to support and promote the development of community college leaders. The junior college had become, in its modern form called the community college, a most impressive agent of post-secondary education in the United States.

The literature reflected this growth. Leland Medsker, The Junior College: Progress and Prospect, New York: McGraw-Hill, 1960, and Burton Clark, The Open Door College: A Case Study, New York: McGraw-Hill, 1960, offer unusually keen perspectives on this new type of college as does the analysis by Clyde Blocker et al., in The Two Year College: A Social Synthesis, Englewood Cliffs, N.J.: Prentice-Hall, 1965.

Other publications took stock of two-year colleges' expansion, contributions, and needs: B. Lamar Johnson, Islands of Innovation, Occasional Report No. 6, UCLA Junior College Leadership Program [Los Angeles, Calif.: University of California, School of Education, 1964], and Johnson's later Islands of Innovation Expanding: Changes in the Community College, Beverly Hills, Calif., Glencoe Press, 1969 (both dealing with instruction); James W. Thornton, Jr., The Community Junior College, 2nd ed., New York: John Wiley, 1966 (a comprehensive review); Edmund J. Gleazer, Jr., This Is the Community College, Boston: Houghton Mifflin, 1968 (a statement of support for the movement); and Michael Brick, Forum and Focus for the Junior College Movement, New York: Bureau of Publications, Teachers College, Columbia University, 1964 (a history of the American Association of Junior Colleges).

Faculty, students, the curriculum, and state planning were explored in volumes such as: Arthur Cohen and Florence Brawer, Focus on Learning: Preparing Teachers for the Two-Year College, Los Angeles, Calif.: University of California Junior College Leadership Program, 1968; Cohen and Brawer, Measuring Faculty Performance, Los Angeles, Calif.: University of California Junior College Leadership Program, 1969; K. Patricia Cross, The Junior College Student: A Research Description, Princeton, N.J., Educational Testing Service, 1968; Roger Garrison, Junior College Faculty: Issues and Problems, Washington, D.C.: American Association of Junior Colleges, 1967; John Roueche, Salvage, Redirection, or Custody? ERIC Clearinghouse for Junior Colleges, Monograph No. 1, Washington, D.C.: American Association of Junior Colleges, 1968; Allen Hurlburt, State Master Plans for Community Colleges, ERIC Clearinghouse for Junior Colleges, Monograph No. 8, Washington, D.C.: American Association of Junior Colleges, 1969; James Reynolds, The Comprehensive Community College Curriculum, Berkeley, Calif.: McCutchan, 1969.

Positing future directions for the community college were Arthur Cohen's Dateline '79: Heretical Concepts for the Community College, Beverly Hills, Calif.: Glencoe Press, 1969, and a report by the Carnegie Commission on Higher Education, The Open Door Colleges: Policies for Community Colleges, New York: McGraw-Hill, 1970. An excellent and extensive bibliography, especially of materials written in the 1960's and early 1970's, is found in Charles Monroe, Profile of the Community College, San Francisco, Calif.: Jossey-Bass, 1972 (reprinted in 1975).

The community college became an agent for the promotion of a national policy to expand educational opportunities to all persons. Its aim was to be comprehensive--in course offerings and services to meet a broad spectrum of student and community needs. The report by the American Association for Community and Junior Colleges Assembly, "Educational Opportunity for All," catches the buoyant and optimistic spirit of the time.

Women, minorities, older students, and veterans helped push enrollments to new highs. Joining them, though unnoticed at first, was an increasing number of international students looking more and more frequently for short-term and career-oriented occupational training, not just transfer options. The Wingspread Conference and subsequent report on foreign students in two-year institutions examines this phenomenon and explores its consequences. But, illustrating the adage that "the more things change, the more they stay the same," Willingham's monograph on articulation shows that basic problems such as who pays? how much? who controls? who shall learn what? never disappear. Society simply moves from one answer to another.

Despite the almost magical, solve-it-all aura surrounding the community college, troublesome questions persisted. As the nation entered the decade of the 1980's, the era of dynamic growth hurried to a close. Was the "golden age" to tarnish so quickly? Conservation, retrenchment, and limits to growth became prominent words in the educator's and society's vocabulary. Indeed, could it be that the basic and driving ideology of the junior and community college movement was itself flawed? Some critics charged the movement with fraud--posing as a vehicle for social progress and individual achievement while in fact reinforcing ancient societal cleavages caused by economic and social class differences. Some critics denounced the movement's rhetoric for promising too much to too many; some worried if the mission and vision of the movement were becoming so blurred as to be useless for forming a focus for the future. Had fatigue sapped the movement's strength and vitality?

A cluster of materials by Goodwin, Pincus, and Cross are important in the examination of these vexing questions. They demonstrate that the bold American invention--the junior and community colleges of our land--does bring both hope and opportunity for many. But the movement is not the perfect educational and social panacea touted by some advocates.[1] Even beneficial inventions have unexpected consequences.

---

[1] Other critics of junior and community colleges include Jerome Karabel, "Community Colleges and Social Stratification," Harvard Educational Review, Vol. 42 (November, 1972), 521-562, and Frank G. Jennings, "Junior Colleges in America: The Two-Year Stretch," Change in Higher Education, Vol. 2 (March-April, 1970), 15-25.

23. EXTENDING EDUCATIONAL OPPORTUNITY

This statement issued by an Assembly of the American Association of Community and Junior Colleges (AACJC) proclaims a comprehensive agenda for two-year institutions--a mission to provide expanding educational opportunities for nearly all citizens. It is a concise yet comprehensive overview of what community colleges must do to be effective: become totally dedicated to providing educational opportunity for all, become aware of new student clientele, develop comprehensive goals, strengthen and expand the curricula, provide for community involvement in planning and assessment, develop greater financial support. Each college should become part of a state- and nation-wide agenda for action on behalf of individual and community development.

This first Assembly of AACJC, held in late 1972 in Warrenton, Virginia brought together about 100 junior and community college and higher education leaders. They came from throughout the United States to discuss social issues facing the nation and two-year colleges and the implications of these issues for institutional purposes, policies, programs, and services.

This assembly meets at the end of an important year in postsecondary education, a year of recognition--of the swirl of competing domestic priorities; of basic questions about the value of education, particularly higher education; of changes and adjustments in student populations and student educational choices.

Roger Yarrington (ed.), Educational Opportunity for All: An Agenda for National Action, Washington, D.C.: American Association of Community and Junior Colleges, 1973, pp. 141-151. This 1972 Assembly Report was reviewed and adopted by the participants and represents their general consensus.

This was also the year in which major new legislation
for postsecondary education was passed by the Congress
and approved by the President.   The programs and
concepts therein enacted into law will, when
implemented, have important effects on future students,
programs, and institutional arrangements in the field
of postsecondary education.

Community and junior colleges, as well as other
postsecondary institutions, have been and will be
affected by these changes.

Thus it is an appropriate time for an assembly of
community and junior college educators and other
interested persons to meet and discuss these changes
and their implications for the future.

Our charge in these deliberations has been to develop
an agenda for national action for community and junior
colleges.

What role should these institutions play in
postsecondary education?

Who are their future students likely to be and how
should these students be served?

What community needs can and should these
institutions serve?

What kinds of support--financial, administrative and
moral--are needed to enable community and junior
colleges to meet these commitments?

What kinds of national, state and local policies are
needed to insure that the necessary support will be
provided?

We begin with an affirmation of what we have
conceived to be our mission over the past several
decades--a mission that has put us in the forefront of
the effort to bring the concept of "educational
opportunity for all" ever closer to reality. Community
and junior colleges have tried to provided appropriate
postsecondary educational opportunities to all who seek
this experience.   Thus we are committed to the concept
of comprehensiveness--to a broad spectrum of programs
that will meet the individual needs of the wide range
of students in our communities.   We are committed to
serve our communities in as many ways as are
appropriate from training their citizens for employment
to providing programs geared to the needs of retired
people.   We are committed to seeking out potential
students, discovering their needs, and devising
educational programs to help them, perhaps to overcome
educational or motivational deficiencies, perhaps to
upgrade their competence in a particular skill.

We believe that the larger society is also committed
to these goals; that there is a growing recognition
that in a complex society a year or two of
postsecondary training at this level is approaching
definition as a fundamental right for all who seek it,

that the cost to society of fulfilling this right is far less than the costs which result from an untrained, unemployable population.

Who will the future student be?

The future students in community and junior colleges will not be remarkably different from those who presently attend.   They will represent that broad spectrum of people of all ages whose educational needs can be accurately identified by the college serving a particular area, and whose education and training needs can be identified by the college.   Thus they will vary from college to college and region to region, but it is likely that if programs that meet their needs and interest them are available, students will draw from some of the following groups in increasing numbers:
... high school students who come to the college to earn "credits in escrow";
... holders of BA degrees who are attending community college in order to learn a marketable skill;
... mature citizens and older citizens who desire education for leisure pursuits or to lead meaningful lives after they have retired;
... women of all kinds, including mature women seeking entry into the labor market and young women seeking identity;
... veterans and servicemen preparing for return to civilian life;
... recent high school graduates beginning their college experience.
In summary all people in the community are potential students--veterans, prisoners, all age groups, all ethnic and racial groups, the rich, the poor.   Whether these potential students actually come to the college depends on what the college does to attract them. Today's academic marketplace is a buyer's market: other institutions will be competing with the community and junior colleges for students.   The key will be flexibility and imagination in developing programs for them.   This will require part-time programs, improvement and humanization of the liberal art curricula, and special programs for special groups, such as consumer education, internship and work-experience programs, and specialized training in cooperation with business and industry.

What should be the institution's response?

We recommend that individual community and junior colleges stimulate and help to create independent research and development groups from the community and from the colleges to identify more clearly:

(1)   The probable student clientele in the immediate
future,
(2)   their social/educational/training needs to which
the colleges can realistically respond,
(3)   the degree to which these needs are already
being served by the educational institutions in the
community, and
(4) the educational services in which the community
is deficient and which need to be available to the
citizens in the community.   We need to make a
particular effort to support viable and relevant
research and development for the articulation of
bilingual and bicultural, and disadvantaged and
minority student needs.   Colleges, state educational
agencies, and state legislatures should join in this
effort.

When this assessment of the community's educational
needs is made, community and junior colleges will be
able to make informed judgments about their programs,
which ones should be dropped or continued, and what
additional needs should be served.   They will then be
better able to make efficient use of the resources
available to them.

Further this assessment will enable the college to
take a total look at the community's people, society,
economy, and existing educational services.   While
community and junior colleges are properly committed to
the principle of comprehensiveness, there may be
instances in which they do not have the resources to
serve the total needs of the community, and
circumstances in which needed services are provided by
other educational institutions and need not be
duplicated by the community or junior colleges.

We recommend that the community and junior colleges
take the leadership in serving as catalysts in the
assessment of community educational needs.   The
American Association of Community and Junior Colleges
and its member colleges should support the concept of
cooperative use of resources to provide education to
the students who need it.

In developing their programs, community and junior
colleges should:
... aim for the goal of equipping all their students
for personal fulfillment, immediate gainful employment,
or   for   transferability   to   a   four-year   college
with   the   intent   of   reaching   a   defined   career
goal;
... provide for working students the right to access to
instruction at times and places convenient to them, and
consider increased utilization of the external degree,
life experiences, and similar concepts;
... include personal development and self-realization
programs as an essential responsibility to their

students, using appropriate people in the community
as resources.   Faculty-staff-community-student
relationships should be improved through these
programs;
... give equal status to vocational, transfer, and
general education, student personnel, and community
services;
... consider the development of occupational
educational programs linked to business, industry,
labor, and government a high priority.   Increased
opportunity through work experience and/or cooperative
education should be a major thrust;
... utilize new concepts of education through a
learning center, personalizing, if not individualizing,
the instructional process. Learning modules in varying
forms (as to time and content) and other new techniques
and technologies, will help to accommodate the broad
range of needs among students to be served;
... above all things, and at all times, be flexible and
responsive to change, in a continuing effort to provide
more effective educational services. This requirement
goes beyond mere reaction to changes in societal
demands: we must also serve as initiators of change
and new ideas in our communities. We must provide
leadership to assist communities in determining their
educational priorities as well as to respond to them.
     Curriculum reform: Students in the future will
increasingly attend colleges on the basis of the
services and programs that are offered rather than as a
matter of having no other choice. Colleges must define
and integrate their programs in terms of specific
student and societal needs.   For example: Bilingual
and bicultural programs should be established which
reflect the career goals and life styles of large
numbers of potential students for whom English is a
second language.   Such programs are mandatory if the
community college is to be truly accessible to all
citizens.   Career education as a concept can be the
vehicle through which community and junior colleges
undertake a fundamental reformation of their curricula
to make them more responsive to emerging needs and less
dependent on their tradition of the lower division of
the four-year institution.
     Faculty and staff: Community and junior colleges
cannot achieve the many goals they have set for
themselves without competent faculty, counselors, and
administrators who understand the mission of these
colleges and the nature and variety of students who
attend them. Unfortunately, up to this time very few
of the universities and graduate institutions that
train personnel for community and junior college work
have developed programs that prepare their students for
the actual situations they will encounter.

We recommend that the graduate institutions provide, and that AACJC urge them to provide, more effective and relevant pre-service preparation. Community and junior colleges are prepared to assist in this endeavor.

We also recognize that many existing college personnel need additional training to serve our current students effectively, and that colleges must develop in-service training programs for all their staff: faculty, counselors, administrators, and trustees.

We recommend that high priority be given at the national, state, and local levels for the procurement of funds to enable us to upgrade the skills of our staffs. The leadership role of the college president in realizing this priority cannot be overlooked.

Effectiveness of college operations: We note with regret certain conditions in today's society that work to impede the effectiveness of colleges at all levels in the achievement of their goals.   This is the atmosphere of divisiveness in relationships between faculty and administration, counselors and faculty, students and administration, and so forth. Wherever possible, we will work to develop systems that will overcome these problems. Where they cannot be overcome, we must work to find as many commonalities as possible in our mutual commitment to education, to minimize the effects of these adversary relationships. A helpful approach may be found in a serious attempt to involve all of these groups in college decisionmaking.

One proof of effectiveness is the measurement of results. Many colleges have been remiss in developing the data that are needed to make those measurements and the techniques through which these data can be put to use.   Management information systems to test program and cost effectiveness are very much needed.   A critical annual review of college practices would be very much in order.

We recommend that colleges commit themselves and be given support in the effort to develop management systems for deriving and using responsible data about, for example:

(1) what happens to former students,

(2) how individual programs at the college respond to identified student needs, and

(3) resource allocation.

As nearly as possible, these data should be standardized. Where possible, models for such data collection and use should be widely disseminated to the colleges. The American Association of Community and Junior Colleges, state legislatures, federal agencies, and other organizations, such as the National Center for Higher Education Management Systems, should recognize and cooperate in meeting this need.

What support will be needed?

In view of the common interests and in recognition as well of the contribution of the private junior colleges, it is our hope and expectation that future legislation and fiscal support will continue as it has in the past to recognize these colleges.   Both privately and publicly supported institutions are and should be necessary.

In order to clarify areas of decision-making authority and responsibility, state agencies and multicampus colleges, in cooperation with local colleges and the communities they serve, should develop a taxonomy of decisions specifying, to the extent possible, those areas of authority that will be reserved to the local college to give it adequate freedom to respond to the needs of its own constituency.

State and federal decision-makers must be made aware that if community colleges are to serve the state and national priorities currently identified and those that will emerge, particularly with respect to career education, additional funds must be made available to support increased operating costs as well as to provide the facilities and equipment necessary.

We recommend that state support formulas be revised to give colleges greater freedom to develop more effective ways of teaching their students and to compensate for higher costs of some programs that are essential to the effective accomplishment of community-junior college goals.   In order to do this, proposals for review of support formulas should consider, in addition to the usual formulas based on full-time equivalent students, such factors as incremental costs of laboratory and shop-based occupational programs, non-credit community-service programs, and cooperative educational program operations.   As a locally based educational resource system, a community-junior college should be supported to provide comprehensive services to its clientele in ways that do not fit into the credit structure of college operational accounting. Support formulas should encourage, rather than inhibit, the purposes of these institutions.

We recommend that state and federal student aid programs remove economic barriers to access and to choice of postsecondary education.   We commend the Congress for its actions in instituting the concept of entitlement to postsecondary education through the Basic Opportunity Grants, and urge that these grants and the supplemental Educational Opportunity Grants and College Work-Study grants be fully funded to give meaning to the concept of entitlement.   We further urge that financial-aid grants, rather than loans, be the

prime means of aid to students, especially in the
middle and lower economic categories. We advocate that
education be universally available to all who wish it
through the associate degree level.

We commend the Congress for its support of
comprehensive community and junior colleges and
postsecondary occupational education as evidenced by
Title X of the Higher Education Act of 1965 as amended
by the Education Amendments of 1972. We urge that this
vitally important program receive adequate funding at
the earliest possible opportunity.

An agenda for national action

Colleges must become more aware and work within the
framework of the process by which governmental
decisions are made, at the local, state, and federal
levels. The time has passed when education was a magic
word, and when educators had only to name their goals.
Now they must justify these goals as important among a
welter of competing needs.

We recommend that the individual community or junior
college purposefully involve its community in its
operation, purposes, program development and
evaluation, and future planning. In this way the
community will be encouraged to give the college
maximum support in its endeavors.

We recommend that the colleges within a state (public
and private) make strenuous efforts to work together
for consensus on matters to be presented to the
legislature; that to the extent possible, there should
be full and open discussion among all elements and
educators must define with precision the state and
national goals related to the common concerns of their
constituencies. Strategies for achieving these goals
must be developed along with the requirements for
resources to carry them out. The goals and strategies
must then be communicated with clarity and force
through an integrated network of state and national
associations to insure that political leaders
understand and can respond to the educational needs so
defined.

In planning for the future, community and junior
colleges should encourage open discussion with
legislators and appropriate state agencies. Once
again, this is purposeful involvement in the process of
determining support for the needs both of individual
colleges and the groups of colleges in the state. At
the same time, this will encourage the states to make
maximum utilization of the existing educational
resources within the state, and such inter-
institutional cooperation will reduce the need for the
states to mandate and regulate coordination.

We reaffirm our belief that the pluralistic system of American higher education and its diversity of institutions must be maintained to serve the needs of our nation and its great diversity of students. We urge decision makers at all levels of government to participate in maintaining this diversity. Similarly, we urge the AACJC to reaffirm its commitment to preserving that diversity within its own membership and in its services to members.

In conclusion, while we strongly endorse and support Assembly and Association efforts to secure additional resources for our combined programs, we simultaneously recommend greater responsibility, even accountability, from community and junior colleges now in taking seriously the educational missions to which we are committed.

With these joint efforts proceeding simultaneously, we may, in the coming decade, achieve more fully those goals toward which we have worked for so long.

24. INTERNATIONAL STUDENTS: A NEW PHENOMENON

A new issue, the accommodation of students from other lands, emerged as a major concern for many junior and community colleges. The increasing interdependence of the peoples of the world has become important even for American two-year institutions. Students looking for instruction in technologies, developing countries looking for the rapid training of managers and technicians among their people--all these seized the opportunities offered by America's rich resource in technical education, the two-year college.

The entrance of the international student into the community or junior college created both enrichment possibilities for the institution, the faculty, students, and surrounding community, and unique problems. Questions about admissions standards, language capability, financial resources, advisement and counseling, health care and insurance, and housing are often not easily answered.

This statement reviewed the increasing presence of international students in American two-year colleges, supported this presence, and suggested ways this phenomenon could be dealt with on local, state, and national levels. The positions taken and subsequent recommendations were based on discussions held October 18-20, 1977 at The Johnson Foundation Conference Center, Wingspread, near Racine, Wisconsin by a group of persons broadly representative of United States higher education, government, professional groups, and foreign students. These discussions addressed the diverse implications of sizable foreign student enrollments.

The Foreign Student in the United States Community and Junior Colleges, New York: College Entrance Examination Board, 1978, pp. 75-83.

A NATIONAL COLLOQUIUM ON THE FOREIGN STUDENT IN
UNITED STATES COMMUNITY AND JUNIOR COLLEGES:
A PUBLIC STATEMENT

I.
Purpose of International Education in United States
Community Colleges

People of this nation are confronted daily with
issues that transcend national boundaries.   So
interconnected is the political and economic world that
some understanding of those issues and events that lead
to them and some appreciation for customs and cultures
world-wide appear basic to good citizenship.

Education has a responsibility in preparing citizens
to deal with the issues that confront them.   United
States community colleges,[1] as community-based postsecondary institutions, share significantly in that
responsibility.   They enroll over 4.5 million students
in academic or occupational programs and in continuing
education, with the latter often attracting students
beyond the conventional college age.   More than one-
half of all students beginning a college education do
so in a community college.

For many of these students, the community college is
the only college-level educational experience they will
have.   An international and intercultural dimension to
that experience can make a major contribution to their
exercise of reasonable citizenship.

An international dimension to a community college
program can assume a variety of forms such as courses
focusing on other nations and cultures, travel or study
abroad, faculty exchanges, and enrollment of foreign
students in United States colleges.   All can serve the
basic purpose of educating United States citizens and
of furthering mutual understanding between people of
this nation and those of other nations.

II.
Foreign Student Enrollment in United States
Community Colleges as a Facet of an International
Education Program

An   established   means   of   promoting   international

---

[1]Community college is used to represent United States
two-year community-based institutions, including
community colleges, junior colleges, and technical
institutes.

education is enrollment of foreign students[2] in United States postsecondary educational institutions. Objectives are to provide individual students from throughout the world with the education they want and need, to aid in the development of the foreign students' home countries, to strengthen the educational program for United States students by using the foreign students as resources on other customs and cultures, and to contribute to mutual world understanding.

Some United States community colleges, primarily those in urban areas, have developed foreign student programs to meet these objectives; others have either utilized other forms of international education or have restricted the international dimension of their program. Nationwide, foreign students represent less than 1 percent of total community college enrollment, but a growing worldwide awareness of community colleges and the vitality of their community-based educational programs suggests that foreign student enrollment in community colleges will increase if the colleges are ready and receptive.

The rapid expansion of community college education in the 1960's and early 1970's--from 678 colleges with 600,000 students to 1,230 colleges with 4.5 million students--forced attention to factors associated with growth. New buildings, staffing, curriculum, outreach, and continuing education occupied most colleges' attention without major consideration of the international dimension.

Recent years, however, have brought an increased awareness of the role community colleges might assume in international education. Other nations have sought information on this community-based institution. Larger numbers of foreign students apply for admission to these institutions which pride themselves on teaching skills. A new appreciation of occupational education at the technical or midmanagement level as offered at community colleges is apparent. Continuing education has expanded the international horizons of thousands of citizens. Other thousands travel internationally or study abroad. Business has become aware of the significant economic impact of foreign students' currency. And, finally, the nation was abruptly reminded of international interdependence through events associated with the energy crisis.

Are the community colleges prepared for an expanded role in international education? Policy questions must

---

[2]Foreign student refers to those on F-1 (nonsponsored student) or J-1 (exchange-visitor) visas. In some other contexts, refugees are also included as foreign students.

be addressed. These questions relate to the extent the college and its community accept the concept that the college should provide an international dimension to educational experiences, the emphasis placed on varying directions international education should take, provision for fiscal support for curriculum and services in an international education program, and the commitment to utilize such a program as an educational experience not only for foreign students but also for United States students.

The problems faced by community colleges and the opportunities presented to them in international education through foreign student enrollment were given serious attention in prepared papers and in discussion at a national colloquium held at the Wingspread Conference Center, Racine, Wisconsin, in October, 1977. The conclusions of the colloquium are presented in the following section.

III.
Colloquium Conclusions

After review of the papers presented and discussion of the issues, the National Colloquium on the Foreign Student in United States Community and Junior Colleges concluded (1) that community colleges as community-based institutions are uniquely qualified to make a significant contribution to mutual understanding between United States citizens and people of other countries through educational and cultural exchange, (2) that a strong community college foreign student program can be an important facet of that contribution, and (3) that a most essential element in planning and implementing a strong foreign student program is a commitment by the college--governing board, administration, teaching and support staff, students, and the community--to provide an excellent educational experience that enriches both foreign and United States students. With that commitment, community colleges should assume a larger role in international education and do so with the expertise they have already demonstrated in other educational areas.

The National Colloquium urged attention to the following:
A. Local Considerations
    1. A college should view a foreign student program as a part of total international and intercultural awareness in the curriculum. While the educational needs of foreign students are being met, United States students can profit from the contact with students from other countries.
    2. Staff development is necessary to assure that

faculty and support personnel understand the philosophy of the college, to draw upon foreign students to expand international awareness for all students, and to assist foreign students with special problems. An inventory of staff international experiences could provide a beginning point for staff development. Such development should not be limited to the self-evident language and social science areas, but should also include all staff, particularly teachers of occupational curricula since foreign student enrollees in such curricula are most likely to have impact in their home countries in the shortest time span.

3. Foreign students should be selected so that the students' needs can be met by the institution's capabilities. The traditional open-door admission policy of the community colleges should be modified when applied to a foreign student program because of the heavy consequences of failure for the foreign student. A foreign student admissions plan should include appropriate criteria to establish limits of total enrollment within the institution's capabilities and limits by country or world area to assure broad cultural representation.

4. Basic planning guidelines for a total foreign student program should include:

   a. Preadmissions information. The college should provide potential applicants complete and accurate information regarding the nature of the college and the community, available curricula, and the extent of support services such as housing, health, advisement, and financial support.

   b. Admissions. The college should be certain it has the curriculum capability requested by the applicant. The applicant's credentials should be evaluated for reasonable assurance that the prospective student can succeed in the chosen curriculum.

   c. English ability. The college should evaluate the applicant's English language proficiency by means of standard tests or other measurement criteria and admit only those whose English language competence is adequate or whose language needs can be met by a program at the college.

   d. Financial. The college should either attempt to ascertain whether the applicant has adequate financial resources to cover

the costs of the educational program being
proposed or be prepared to provide that
financial support if admission is granted.
The college should provide the applicant
with a realistic estimate of costs that the
student will face in the United States,
including living expenses during vacation
periods.

e. Health and housing. The college should
provide appropriate assistance to the
student in matters of health and housing.
A sound health program is essential. This
includes, but is not limited to, health
information prior to admission and health
and accident insurance coverage during
attendance. The college should provide
assistance in locating housing including in
some cases, the experience of living with
local families.

f. Advisement and counseling. The college
should provide professional staff to orient
foreign students to the college and the
community, advise them in their curricular
programs, provide them with information on
regulations of the Immigration and
Naturalization Service, and counsel them on
matters of personal concern.

g. Instruction. Faculty interest and support
is critical to the success of a foreign
student program. The college's staff
development opportunities should increase
staff members' international and
intercultural awareness and enhance the
faculty's ability to teach students of
other cultures and to draw upon those
students to benefit the international and
intercultural perspectives of United States
students.

h. Community involvement. The college should
develop means for the student to become
involved with the community and to meet
people of the community in their homes and
at their work. The college can serve the
foreign student as a window to community
life. Developing a course that emphasizes
the community, integrating community
experiences into existing courses, or
providing an adequate program of
cocurricular opportunities should be
considered.

      i. Follow-up.   Evaluation of any foreign student program will involve analysis of the student's progress at the college and after completion. For students trained in an occupation, information on job placement in the home country and in the student's major should be examined when possible. For transfer majors, was transfer possible and what was the progress after transfer? An analysis of the impact of a foreign student program on the college, the community, and the students is basic to program improvement.

B. State Considerations

    1. State community college leaders should provide encouragement, leadership, and training for personnel of community colleges planning for or developing a foreign student program. They should recognize that additional student services are required for successful foreign student programs and that these programs do make a contribution to students who are United States citizens as well as to the foreign students.

    2. States or regions should encourage community colleges to organize cooperatively to meet international education requirements. This might include linkages that would lead to contract programs wherein colleges attempt to fulfill specific international education and training needs.

    3. States or regions should identify model international education programs and encourage visits and examination of these programs by college and community personnel interested in improving the overall effectiveness of international and intercultural awareness efforts.

    4. Within states or regions, educational institutions should review criteria for foreign student transfers and coordinate community college and four-year institution admissions policies to provide successful community college foreign student transfers with a reasonable opportunity for admission to a baccalaureate degree program.

C. National Considerations[3]

1. Agencies of the federal government should more
    fully recognize the significant number of
    foreign students now enrolled in community
    colleges and the potential for increases in
    that enrollment, and particularly the
    capability of the community colleges in
    training middle-level manpower.

2. Overseas personnel of the federal government
    and interested private agencies should
    regularly receive information on community
    colleges and should be able to advise and
    counsel prospective foreign student applicants
    about such colleges.

3. Agencies of the federal government should
    embark on a concentrated and continuing program
    of informing appropriate officials of other
    countries on the nature and mission of the
    community colleges. This might include teams
    of community college representatives to other
    countries and increasing visits by world
    educational leaders to selected community
    colleges in the United States. Encouragement
    of student funding support by other nations
    should be a part of the program.

4. Agencies of the federal government should
    consider the possibility of the community
    colleges having a larger role and more
    significant financial support in providing
    technical assistance and educational and
    cultural exchanges with other nations.

D. Organization, Agency and Foundation Considerations

1. Agencies engaged in promoting international
    education should be encouraged to examine their
    literature and advisement efforts to assure
    that information about community colleges is

---

[3]Agencies of the federal government primarily
concerned with international education and related
exchanges are the Office of Education, Department of
Health, Education, and Welfare; the Bureau of
Educational and Cultural Affairs, Department of State;
the United States Information Agency; and the
Immigration and Naturalization Service, Department of
Justice.

accurately   communicated   to   prospective
applicants.

2. National organization dealing with   foreign
    students in admissions, advisement, English-as-
    a-second-language, community services, home
    country needs, and home country placement
    should recognize the unique capabilities of
    community colleges in educating foreign
    students, and should give increased attention
    and assistance to community colleges attempting
    to start or improve a foreign student program.

3. Foundations seeking to further the national
    purpose of increased mutual understanding of
    people of   this nation and those of other
    nations   through   educational and cultural
    exchange should be   encouraged   to support
    foreign students in community colleges through
    direct financial assistance.

4. An organization with expertise in international
    education should be encouraged to examine and
    report on the acceptability of the community
    college Associate in Arts and the Associate in
    Science degrees in other nations.   If the
    report indicates a need for better
    understanding of the degree and the status it
    denotes, necessary follow-up should be
    intitiated.

5. One or more national   organizations   should be
    identified to serve in the role of   clearing-
    house for information regarding education and
    training programs available in United States
    community colleges and the readiness of those
    colleges to admit foreign students. A study of
    consortium or contract programs should be
    conducted to develop a model for consideration
    by community colleges and by other nations.

6. National   organizations   serving   community
    colleges should consider giving special
    attention in their publications to providing
    information and guidance for community college
    trustees and staff regarding international
    programs.   Presentations on international
    education should be scheduled for conferences
    and conventions, including the American
    Association of Community and Junior Colleges
    national convention.

E. Other Considerations

National Colloquium on the Foreign Student in United States Community and Junior Colleges focused on one aspect of international education, namely the enrollment of foreign students in United States community colleges. However, the development of a broad international perspective in other facets of college operations and in the community entered into the discussions. The final colloquium assembly pointed to the need for each college to assess its status and to consider appropriate programs of international education including curriculum enhancement, international cocurricular activities, community service programs, teacher exchanges with foreign countries, provision for United States students to study abroad, and assistance to other countries in need of and requesting the expertise of United States community college personnel.

IV.
Summary

The National Colloquium on the Foreign Student in United States Community and Junior Colleges was convened to discuss the problems and potential of enrollment of foreign students in the nation's community colleges. Data collected are incomplete but they do show a large enrollment of such students. The colloquium participants expect that enrollment to increase and urged colleges to assure sound programs that will benefit both the foreign students and United States citizens. With such programs and related efforts, the community colleges as responsible participants in international education and intercultural awareness can make a significant contribution to the citizenship education of United States students and to mutual understanding between those students and students from other nations.

25. The College Transfer Issue

One of the first issues facing junior colleges in the late 19th century--the transfer of their students to senior colleges and credit for their studies--persists as a major issue in the late 20th century as well. The movement of students among institutions of higher education continues to vex state systems, consortia of colleges, and individual colleges and universities. Guidance and orientation of students before and after transfer is often quite inadequate, admission and financial procedures are quite diverse, and ways in which credit is transferred (or not transferred!) vary greatly.

The matter of extending educational opportunity in the United States depends in large part on the ability and willingness of junior and senior institutions to work together to develop policies and procedures which will aid and support the transfer of students and credit among colleges and universities in higher education.

Warren W. Willingham holds a Ph.D. degree in experimental psychology and psychometrics from the University of Tennessee. Author of many articles in journals of psychology and education, he has been director of research, senior research psychologist, and director of the California office on access research for the College Entrance Examination Board.

There are three main reasons why the movement of students from junior to senior colleges rivals freshman admissions as the second most important problem in access to higher education. One is its critical

---

Warren W. Willingham, The No. 2 Access Problem: Transfer to the Upper Division, AAHE-ERIC/Higher Education Research Report No. 2, Washington, D.C.: American Association for Higher Education, 1972, pp. 43-49.

relationship to the organization of higher education.
Smooth transfer from 2- to 4-year institutions is a
basic requirement of the hierarchical model in which
community colleges serve to expand educational
opportunity. A second reason is the magnitude of
transfer admissions. Rough estimates indicate that one
transfer student enters a senior institution for every
three freshmen; of these transfers, over half come from
2-year institutions. A third reason is the fact that
transfer admissions includes a number of unique
problems, quite different from freshman admissions.

*****

Curriculum Articulation

One basic problem in curriculum articulation is the
fact that students from one junior college fan out to
several senior institutions that may have different
graduation requirements for the same degree, and the
student may not be able to anticipate the college to
which he will transfer. Another fundamental problem is
the fact that the junior college answers to two
masters: its own unique educational commitment and its
responsibility to prepare transfer students. The
former requires innovation and flexibility; the latter
demands close adherence to an educational plan.

When pairs of institutions agree on parallel courses,
educational continuity is greatly improved; but this
does not solve the problem of students transferring to
diverse senior colleges, nor does it encourage
curricular flexibility at the junior college. Blanket
statewide or regional agreements to accept the
associate degree in recognition of general education
requirements helps to solve both problems in the short
run, but can lead to the educational discontinuity that
now characterizes secondary and higher education.
Students need to be protected against trivial
differences in requirements among institutions, but not
at the expense of continuity in instruction or
preparation for a career.

While it is important to achieve middle-ground
solutions, there is virtually no theory of curriculum
articulation to guide such development. Sound
curriculum planning would profit from better
understanding of general principles concerning such
matters as: the types of agreements that constitute
good articulation, the forms of standardization that
are necessary, the forms of flexibility that are
desirable, the discipline continuity that is required,
the instructional continuity that is beneficial, and
the upper-division extensions of career education that
are needed.

Guidance at the Community College

Adequate counseling of students prior to transfer remains a serious problem hampered by inadequate information at the junior college. Important problems that students encounter in transferring seem traceable to their not being informed early about admission and financial aid procedures. Junior colleges could devote more attention to advising transfers and following their progress. Senior institutions need to become more engaged in this process, particularly by supplying systematic information to junior colleges. Guidance of transfer students would benefit markedly from the development and adoption of a practical guide specifying information and procedures that should be incorporated in an effective transfer guidance program.

Orientation at the Senior College

There is widespread agreement that efforts to orient the transfer student to the 4-year college are often inadequate and ineffective. Single orientation programs for transfers and freshmen are still common and still criticized, but separate transfer orientation is not felt to be a sufficient answer. The clearest need is for comprehensive descriptive materials designed specifically for transfers. An AACRAO [American Association of Collegiate Registrars and Admissions Officers] committee makes the reasonable suggestion of putting the transfer orientation problem in the hands of student faculty committees on individual campuses.

Diverse Admission Procedures

Admission practices vary a great deal among institutions. This variation is important for students to understand because it often reflects basically different conditions for student transfer. In only a few states are condensed summaries of institutional transfer policies and practices readily available to students. This lack of adequate advance information is compounded by the fact that junior college students tend to apply for transfer admission later than do freshmen. Late application often makes it difficult for students to obtain financial aid and attend to personal and academic details of transition that had not been anticipated. Rolling admissions without deadlines seems very well suited for transfers, but junior colleges should encourage students to initiate their applications prior to the last term in the junior college.

Diverse Academic Standards

A drop in students' grades after transfer seems
largely due to a grade differential typically found
between 2- and 4-year colleges. This differential
varies widely among pairs of colleges as does the
transfer attrition rate. Because of these persistent
variations between and within institutions, it is
especially important to collect data on student
performance so that admission requirements are fair and
students can be counseled toward colleges and programs
in which they are likely to succeed. At present too
few 4-year institutions provide student performance
data to junior college advisors.

Credit - The Persistent Question

The matter of transferable credit always raises a
variety of specialized questions. Most senior
institutions now accept D grades, and credit policies
are generally liberalized. But as institutions move to
generous credit allowances and acceptance of formula
plans, the critical question becomes not how much
credit is awarded but how many courses are required for
graduation. There is very little information on this
question. On a related issue, junior colleges have
been slow to grant credit by examination even though
most senior institutions accept such credit. Four-year
colleges have been slow to adopt policies regarding new
grading practices or to offer grandfather rights to
transfers who have been following BA graduation
requirements in effect during their stay in junior
colleges. Senior institutions have also been slow to
develop innovative moves in several states to create 2-
year BA programs on top of community college technical
degrees.

Access/Retention-The Salient Problem

There is amazingly little data on what proportions
and what sorts of students transfer from junior to
senior colleges, even though such information is
critical in evaluating the operation of higher
education systems. There is also no statewide data on
holding power to the BA degree, though considerable
institutional data indicates that attrition of transfer
students is sometimes quite high at individual
colleges. It appears likely that minorities are
underrepresented among transfers but almost no
information is available. Reverse transfer is another
major uncharted aspect of student flow. In the only
state from which data are available, more students
transfer from 4- to 2-year colleges than vice versa.

There have evidently been no published investigations
of reverse transfer despite its substantial
implications for articulation and statewide planning.

The Need for Aid

Inadequate financial aid for transfer students
continues to be one of the most serious problems in
transfer articulation. In a selected sample of senior
institutions only two in five report that
proportionately as many transfers as freshmen receive
financial aid. Communication now appears to be a
principal problem. Many institutions report that
junior college students are not getting the word that
senior college is more expensive than they imagine,
that aid is available, and that applications should be
filed early.

The Need for Space

In the early 1970's, space ceased to be the acute
problem it was 5 years earlier. Enrollments became
stabilized in senior institutions and, in some areas at
least, rapid means were developed to inform students
concerning which institutions have space for transfers.
But in all periods there seems to be the continuing
threat of localized inadequate space for expanding
cadres of transfer students. One response that has
gained considerable attention and favor is the
development of upper-division institutions that admit
only transfers. Twenty-five such institutions are now
operating or planned in six states.

Articulation Procedures

There is wide variation from state to state in the
procedures that have been established to develop and
maintain articulation. These procedures have tended to
develop on an ad hoc basis; they are not yet routinized
in many states, though there is evidence of steady
progress. Institutional studies and personal contact
between 2- and 4-year institutions seem especially
important in order to illuminate the articulation
problems that individual students face. Both personal
contact and research appear limited at most
institutions.

This review of the literature of student transfer
from junior to senior institutions suggests two general
conclusions--one positive and one negative. On the
positive side, it is evident from the Knoell-Medsker
research that the junior college is successfully

training large numbers of transfer students. The students themselves typically judge their junior college programs to be quite good, and, in some respects, better than those of the 4-year institutions. These students are gaining admission and succeeding in increasing numbers. The basic problems of professional standards and institutional integrity have been faced and largely solved to the advantage of all concerned. There are ample signs of increasing flexibility and cooperation between community colleges and 4-year institutions.   Everything considered, the future of transfer articulation can only be described as optimistic.

On the negative side, the future is taking a long time to get here and important transfer problems are too often ignored. Consider some of the problems that have been researched exhaustively with respect to incoming freshmen; access rates, student aspirations, financial aid, minority representation.   There is virtually no research on corresponding problems with respect to transfer students, even though nearly one million students enter community colleges each year, two-thirds of whom intend to transfer.   Furthermore, the degree of adherence by many institutions to the recommended guidelines . . . is indifferent at best. Transfer articulation is indeed the Number 2 access problem--second only to freshman admissions in importance, and definitely second-rate in the attention it receives from educators, researchers, and policymakers.

Additional state and local initiatives seem to be necessary in order to give transfer articulation the attention it requires. The leadership expressed in the work of various state agencies and individual institutions should be generalized and broadened in ways that will alleviate existing problems in all areas and institutions having substantial movement of transfer students.   Those states without an appropriate voluntary or legislated agency to monitor articulation should create one. In particular such agencies should:

* Develop procedural and substantive principles of curriculum articulation to serve as a basis for the establishment and maintenance of agreements that encourage curriculum flexibility and preserve educational continuity.

* Undertake flow studies of access and retention that can serve as one basis for evaluating the operation of the state system of higher education.

* Examine the reciprocal relationship between 2- and 4-year institutions, particularly as it is reflected in reverse transfer of students to the community college.

* Facilitate improved information exchange between junior and senior institutions, particularly that

relating to articulation agreements, institutional practices, and research results.

* Evaluate and selectively promote innovative practices that have a beneficial effect upon transfer articulation.

Many individuals at institutions are actively involved with various aspects of transfer articulation as a frequent or exclusive responsibility. There is, however, sufficient evidence to suggest the need for a focused responsibility on each campus to maintain a broad overview of transfer articulation in the student's behalf. This need might well be filled by a standing faculty committee at each institution that receives or sends a substantial number of transfer students. The existence of highly organized articulation machinery at the state level increases rather than lessens the need for such local representation. Such a committee might:

* Systematically evaluate local policies and practices in relation to the Guidelines of the Joint Committee.

* Periodically review research and developments in the field, starting with such literature as cited in this report.

* Initiate studies of transfer students, particularly investigations of performance, retention, and educational experiences and plans.

* Periodically review practices in critical areas such as administrations, financial aid, and guidance.

* Suggest and facilitate the development of improved programs; e.g., orientation, articulation procedures, relations with junior colleges.

Finally, there are broader problems that still await attention from federal agencies and national organizations. More adequate statistics must be gathered routinely on the admission of transfer students into senior institutions. Representation of minority youth is one critical aspect of this problem that requires special attention. Appropriate national groups should describe models of exemplary institutional practice in such areas as guidance at the junior college and equitable administration of aid in the senior college. Transfer from 2- to 4-year institutions has been developed systematically into a primary mechanism for enhancing educational opportunity. Educational leaders have a special responsibility to see that the mechanism is working.

26. IDEOLOGY: A CRITICAL VIEW

*Who were the "men of the junior and community college movement,"
the prime movers, and what ideals for educational and social
development did they hold? In a lengthy study and report on the
junior college movement and the fundamental ideas which underlay
its development, Gregory Goodwin detects what he feels is a strong
tilt toward social efficiency, vocational training, and
conservatism. Stability has been its aim, not social change.*

*Further, the main thrust of the community and junior college
ideology has been to idealize a technological society, control the
"meaner aspects of human nature," and sort out and protect the
elite from the masses. Although sprinkling their writings with
terms such as "democratic citizenship" and "the people's college,"
the concepts behind these terms reflect a greater interest in
social control than in helping individuals to promote their own
development.*

*Goodwin's views of the junior and community college movement
and its ideologic visionaries run counter to the optimistic
allegiance pledged in most of the literature. His is not a
majority opinion, yet he is not alone as other materials reveal.*

*Illustrative of this debate are two books, issued several years
after Goodwin's analysis, which point up the difference in
perspective in sharp detail. Following very much in the
mainstream of the movement's supportive literature, Mary Lou
Zoglin, a community college trustee herself, published Power and
Politics in the Community College, Palm Springs, Calif.:
ETC Publications, 1976, 166 pp. Zoglin reiterates the*

Gregory L. Goodwin, "A Social Panacea: A History of
the Community-Junior College Ideology," Education
Resources Information Center (ERIC) Document No. ED 093
427, September, 1973, pp. 11-15.

recurring community college theme: these colleges are a prime source of upward mobility for talented (though often lower class) students.

L. Steven Zwerling, on the other hand, a community college faculty member in New York, draws the opposite conclusion. Zwerling, in Second Best: The Crisis of the Community College, New York: McGraw-Hill, 1976, sees the community college as an institution with an "insidious function," that is, to preserve the status quo and obstruct the upward aspirations of the working-class student.

An intriguing review of these two books and their themes is presented by Howard B. London in the Harvard Educational Review, Vol. 48 (No. 1, 1978), 107-111.

Partially supported by a grant from the National Endowment for the Humanities, Gregory L. Goodwin extended his doctoral research conducted at the University of Illinois at Urbana-Champaign and completed the work from which these selections are drawn.

National Spokesmen For the Community-Junior College Movement

*****

In order to identify a   large number of important community-junior college national spokesmen, this study tallied all indexed works relating to two-year colleges in the Readers' Guide (Poole's Guide for pre-1900 listings) and the Education Index.

*****

The names of community-junior college spokesmen which were determined by this publishing criterion were as follows:

Jesse P. Bogue	Leonard V. Koos
Doak S. Campbell	Alexis F. Lange
C. C. Colvert	S. V. Martorana
Walter Crosby Eells	Leland L. Medsker
Edmund J. Gleazer, Jr.	Nicholas Ricciardi
John W. Harbeson	James W. Reynolds
William Rainey Harper	Lewis W. Smith
Robert M. Hutchins	James M. Wood
B. Lamar Johnson	George F. Zook
David Starr Jordan	

The selection proved to be satisfactory in terms of distribution of the spokesmen over the span of years in the study and also in terms of their geographic distribution.   Robert M. Hutchins proved to be more a self-appointed spokesman for the community-junior college movement, and S. V. Martorana proved to be ideologically unfathomable because his writings were

largely limited to descriptions of state legislation
and organizational patterns. Overall, however, I found
the writings of these men to contain ample evidence of
ideological positions. The list was not intended to be
an exhaustive one, but it was meant to be sufficient to
provide substantial insight into the community-junior
college ideology.

The writings of these selected national community-
junior college spokesmen, then, constitute the primary
source material for this study. As the following
chapters reveal, the ideology of the community-junior
college movement as expressed by these leaders formed a
powerful and unifying force. Argument and division
occurred at times, but what stands out the most is the
uniformity of the ideology. Although the rhetoric
changed from one generation to the next, and various
purposes were emphasized or de-emphasized in keeping
with the climate of the times, the basic mission of the
community-junior college as a panacea for social ills
remained consistent. These educational leaders knew
the kind of a world they wanted--a world that would be
orderly, efficient, and productive, and they knew the
type of man they wished to mold--a man with the social
conscience to blend harmoniously into the community and
with the skills to perform his proper role at his
proper level. More than any other level of education,
these leaders looked to the community-junior college as
a social panacea. The elementary schools existed for
the masses and the universities adequately educated the
professional elite. It would be the unique mission of
the community-junior college to train men for "middle
management" or as "foremen for society." If such a
force of men were properly developed, it was argued, it
could reduce possible friction between the educated
elite and the masses. In addition, it could provide
skilled assistants, or "semi-professionals," to relieve
at minimum cost the workload of the talented managers
and professionals of the society. The hierarchy of
society was never questioned; indeed, it was idealized.

Stages of Development

The community-junior college movement has been
consistently concerned with educational and social
efficiency, and it has consistently attempted to
prepare a social class to fill the needs of a
developing industrial society. Yet within these
consistencies there has been four distinct phases with
unique points of emphasis. The initial development of
the junior college idea, and the sporadic
institutionalization of that idea, took place during
the latter part of the nineteenth century and the early
part of the twentieth century. During this period

university leaders headed the movement, and they embraced the junior college as a place where the university might unload its burden of adolescents. The goal was to free the university for the higher pursuit of scientific research. Borrowing heavily from the educational design in Germany, these men saw the advantages of more efficient social stratifications in the United States. It was thought that higher education could only be advanced by stratifying various other educational levels in keeping with divisions in human talent.

The second stage of the community-junior college movement occurred between the two world wars. Leaders emerged who were solely committed to the concept of the community-junior college and who sought independence from the domination of university spokesmen. Still concerned with "social efficiency," these leaders struggled with the problem presented by the fact that the so-called "terminal student" aspired to the traditional baccalaureate degree. Time and again they developed masterly "terminal programs," only to have them rejected by a status conscious educational consumer.

After World War Two a third stage of the community-junior college movement came about. Germany, after two wars, was no longer an awe-inspiring model. The fear of communism created in Americans a desire to unify and seek out enemies, foreign and domestic. Everywhere "citizenship training" and "general education" were promoted to develop national unity and agreement upon common values. Community-junior college advocates did not lose sight of the worker, but they rallied around the loftier goal of preparing loyal citizens.

Most recently the community-junior college movement has shifted once again to a concern for the proper ordering of society, addressing itself specifically to the question of whom is best fit to do what. An increasing emphasis upon technical and vocation education, particularly for the "terminal student," is everywhere apparent. Always a favorite with local boards, this goal has increasingly become the target of federal-aid programs. No longer do the leaders of the community-junior college try to elevate their position with any claim of producing a new and higher class of human talent in society. Instead, their developing goal is one of producing better honed cogs, wherever needed, in the existing industrial society.

As distinct as these four stages in the growth and development of community-junior colleges have been, however, their differences are subordinate to the overriding mission of the movement as a social panacea. Implicit in the evangelical rhetoric of the community-junior college movement is the idea that this booming institution is the best hope for insuring an orderly society and an efficient economy. For all of its claim of innovation and rejuvination [sic], the community-junior college movement stands as a profoundly conservative movement. Its primary objective at all times has been social stability, not social change.

27. THE TERMINAL STUDENT

In this material Gregory Goodwin elaborates on his thesis (begun in the preceding chapter) that the junior and community movement has promised more than its performance has been able to provide. To use Burton Clark's now famous phrase, the "cooling out" function of the junior college has indeed worked well to route the (usually) lower-class student into his or her "proper" niche in society--and "proper" does not include positions in the professions or other echelons of the elite society.

Why is it so many community college students profess a desire to transfer to four-year institutions when in fact so few do transfer? Does the community college serve as a guardian of the gates of high-prestige educational programs and choice careers, shunting to the vocational sidelines many gifted youths and adults? Or can it serve as a talent scout identifying and encouraging students to develop to the full their gifts and talents? What changes need to be made in the community college idealogy for it to better serve its students and the nation?

A new view of students, indeed, of human nature is needed, Goodwin maintains, for the junior college to become the talent scout and human development resource it should become in our society.

Partially supported by a grant from the National Endowment for the Humanities, Gregory L. Goodwin extended his doctoral research at the University of Illinois at Urbana-Champaign and completed the work from which these selections are drawn.

The Problem of the Terminal Student

There has been an ominous consistency in the fact that ever since the 1920's about two-thirds of entering

Gregory L. Goodwin, "A Social Panacea: A History of the Community-Junior College Ideology," Education Resources Information Center (ERIC) Document No. ED 093 427, September, 1973, pp. 262-271.

community-junior college students plan to transfer to
four-year colleges and universities but only about one-
third of the total number actually do. Community-
junior college spokesmen have attributed this
phenomenon to several causes: (1) The high prestige
that society has placed upon professional positions;
(2) The inability of many students "realistically" to
appraise their abilities, and their lack of abilities;
and (3) The tendency of community-junior colleges to
concentrate their resources more on transfer curricula
than vocational-technical curricula. There has never
been any suggestion that community-junior colleges
should try harder to qualify two-thirds of their
students to transfer; on the contrary, the idea of
limited room at the top of the educational and social
ladder has been an underlying assumption behind the
consistent demand for increased terminal education.

The problem of the "terminal student" was seen as a
stimulating challenge in the ideological campaign of
community-junior college national spokesmen in the
1920's and 1930's. We have seen how [Leonard] Koos,
[Walter] Eells, and [Doak] Campbell confidently
expounded during those years that semiprofessional
curricula leading to intermediate jobs, above the
trades but below the professions, would appeal to such
students. When terminal curricula was [sic] developed
and found to be unappealing to most community-junior
college students, the ideology was able to sidestep any
reaction by asserting the need for guidance.   If
students were ignorant of their own capabilities and of
occupational opportunities, it was logically argued,
then they could not be expected to make wise decisions.

Since World War Two, some community-junior colleges
have invested considerable effort and money in
establishing wide-ranging terminal vocational-technical
curricula and large student personnel staffs. Students
in such colleges have received excellent information
about themselves and about available careers, and they
have had a wide selection of course programs to choose
from.   But [Leland] Medsker's 1960 study showed that
none of that seemed to matter; regardless of the type
of college or its resources or programs, the general
tendency persisted that approximately two-thirds of its
entering students aspired to transfer on.[1]

With the publication of Burton R. Clark's The Open
Door College in 1960, a painful awareness of what was
happening to the "non-transferring" transfer student
began to enter the thinking of many community-junior
college leaders. Generally, unsuccessful transfer

---

[1]Leland Medsker, The Junior College: Progress and
Prospect (New York: McGraw-Hill, 1960), p.112.

students did not switch into vocational-technical curricula; those curricula were generally filled by the other one-third of community-junior college students who began there in the first place. The unsuccessful transfer students, it was realized, even though follow-up studies on such students were rare, were in most cases drop-outs. Some community-junior college leaders took consolation in the fact that, as Clark described, such students were "cooled-out" rather than "thrown-out" as they might have been at the university. But such consolation was little help to an ideology based upon the promise that the community-junior college would serve the needs of such students.

Particularly painful was evidence that students dropping out of the community-junior college were doing about as well academically as those who stayed. A 1955 study by Jane Matson, which was widely reported in the community-junior college literature, compared a sample of withdrawing community-junior college students with a sample of persisting students and uncovered no significant differences between the groups regarding academic aptitude or grade point average.[2] If academic performance is not the major factor in sorting out students in the community-junior college, then one is left with disturbing questions about the actual causes of the high dropout rate which most studies indicate is approximately fifty percent. The search for adequate answers to these questions has led researchers into various directions. Investigations of personality differences among students, of institutional shortcomings, and of possible faults in society have all yielded different perspectives.

K. Patricia Cross has studied closely the community-junior college student population. Compared to their counterparts at four-year colleges, Cross found commmunity-junior college students less able academically, less intellectually oriented, and less motivated to seek higher education. She cautioned, however, that "we possess only traditional measures to describe a student who does not fit the tradition."[3]

In particular, Cross has been concerned with that group of students an earlier generation would have called "terminal." Cross' definition of New Students includes ethnic minorities and adults, but primarily they are Caucasions from blue collar families:

[2]Jane E. Matson, "Characteristics of Students Who Withdraw from a Public Junior College" (unpublished Ed.D. dissertation, Stanford University, 1955).

[3]K. Patricia Cross, The Junior College Student: A Research Description (Princeton, New Jersey: Educational Testing Service, 1968), p. 6.

Fundamentally, these New Students to higher education are swept into college by the rising educational aspirations of the citizenry. For the majority, the motivation for college does not arise from anticipation of interest in learning the things they will be learning in college but from the recognition that education is the way to a better job and a better life than that of their parents.[4]

Using data from several studies made in the 1960's, including Project TALENT AND SCOPE[5] Cross reported that:

New students are positively attracted to careers and prefer to learn things that are tangible and useful. They tend not to value the academic model of higher education that is prized by faculty, preferring instead a vocational model that will teach them what they need to know to make a good living.[6]

Cross' conclusion has a familiar ring to it, sounding the call for new programs for New Students:

To date, we have concentrated on making New Students over into the image of traditional education. Our concern has been the creation of access models to education. We have devised all kinds of ways to make New Students eligible to participate in traditional higher education. Remedial courses are designed to remove academic "deficiencies"; counseling removes motivational "deficiencies." However, if the answer to the question Who should go to college? is to be an egalitarian response of "everyone," then educational systems will have to be designed to fit the learning needs of New Students.[7]

When one looks at the individual interests, motivations, and abilities of New Students as Cross does, then it appears only obvious that new programs

---

[4]K. Patricia Cross, Beyond the Open Door: New Students to Higher Education (San Francisco: Jossey-Bass Inc., 1971), p. 15.

[5]Project TALENT surveyed over 60,000 high school seniors in 1960, following up with further questionnaires in 1961 and 1965. SCOPE (School to College: Opportunity for Postsecondary Education) studied a four-state sample of over 30,000 high school seniors in 1966 with follow-up in 1967.

[6]Cross, Beyond the Open Door, p. 159.

[7]Ibid., pp. 4-5.

are needed if higher education, or postsecondary
education, is to accommodate such students. Yet Cross
is quite vague about the nature of the programs needed.
She skillfully avoids traditional answers which signal
pedagogic controversies, such as "vocational education"
or "general education." Specifying three spheres which
encompass the "world's work"--working with (1) people,
(2) ideas, and (3) things, Cross proposes that "each
citizen attains excellence in one sphere and at least
minimal competence in the other two."[8] Cross does not
specify educational programs appropriate to each
sphere, nor does she indicate what criteria of
"excellence" and "minimal competence" should be applied
or how. But if the diverging camps behind general
education versus vocational education . . . could
embrace Cross' categorization and incorporate it into a
redirected ideology, the impact could be significant.
There is little evidence, however, that this is likely
to be the case.

Sociologist Jerry M. Katz has charged that
Cross' type of psychological research wrongly
"diverts attention away from the system and
toward the individual."[9] Katz follows Burton Clark's
example and views the community-junior college as a
social institution functioning in full accord with the
values and needs of society. Like Clark, Katz made a
case study of a California community-junior college.
His goal was to determine which young people in the
community were served by the college and how. Katz
reported that the institution existed of, by and for
the middle class. Sufficient barriers to prevent
participation by lower classes existed, Katz charged,
so that the so called open-door was a misnomer:

> Members of lower socioeconomic groups and
> racial and ethnic minorities, to a great
> degree, not only do not pass through the open
> door, they never approach it. The high
> attrition and low high school graduation
> rates of these groups makes attendance for
> most of them impossible. In the race toward
> equality the lower class is, essentially,
> disqualified before the race begins.[10]

---

[8]Ibid., p. 165
[9]Jerry M. Katz, "The Educational Shibboleth:
Equality of Opportunity in a Democratic Institution,
the Public Junior College" (unpublished Ph.D.
dissertation, University of California at Los Angeles,
1967), p. 15.
[10]Ibid., p. 191.

The community-junior college helps maintain the
stability of the class structure, according to Katz,
"by safeguarding low ability children of the middle
class from downward mobility."[11]   While projecting an
image which combines "apple pie and Horatio Alger,"
Katz concludes that in fact the community-junior
college "is, in every respect, the creature of the
middle class. It serves its master well."[12] From
Katz's perspective, all of the rhetoric about assisting
the "terminal student," by whatever label he is called,
is merely a device to insure a fixed social
stratification to the benefit of the middle class.

Jerome Karabel has expanded upon the sociological
investigations of Clark and Katz.[13] Karabel discounts
the claim that the community-junior college has
extended benefits to middle and lower class, charging
that "educational inflation" has eaten up supposed
gains. Both in educational content and economic value,
Karabel finds that high school diplomas and college
degrees have declined in worth as they become more
available. Despite the tremendous expansion of the
educational system this century, Karabel points out
that only minimal changes have occurred in the system
of social stratification.[14]

Karabel reports that research on student attrition
which controls variables such as socioeconomic status,
aspirations, and ability reveals that student
persistence, as measured by returning for a second
year, seem negatively affected by attending a
community-junior college. Karabel notes that the
commuting situation of most community-junior college
students may be a partial cause for the startling fact
that, other things being equal, a student is less
likely to persist in a community-junior college than in
other institutions of higher education. Basically,
however, Karabel finds that the cause is Clark's
"cooling-out function" working effectively to protect
existing social stratifications.[15]

Writers within the community-junior college movement
have ignored or rebuffed the charges that they are part
of an effort to maintain social stratifications by
cooling-out surplus students. Dorothy Knoell reviewed
the existing research in 1966 and concluded that no
conclusion was yet warranted:

---

[11]Ibid., p. xvi.
[12]Ibid., p. 191.
[13]Jerome Karabel, "Community Colleges and Social
Stratification," Harvard Educational Review, XLII
(November, 1972), 522-562.
[14]Ibid., p. 525.
[15]Ibid., p. 533.

. . . no conclusion should be drawn without
considerably more research on the
accomplishments of the non-transfers in
junior college and afterwards, to find out
whether they became college drop-outs in the
sense of a loss to society, or whether they
were in fact terminal students who gained
useful skills and general education while in
college.[16]

While this matter may be in a state of suspended
judgment, the community-junior college ideology cannot
promote with the same zeal its mission to educate that
class of people between the masses and the
professionals. With its terminal curricula and its
systems of guidance, the community-junior college has
been tested and been found wanting. If the community-
junior college ideology is to maintain a theme of equal
opportunity for all, it will have to completely revise
its belief in "guiding" students into their "proper"
positions in society.

In the 1950's and 1960's . . . the community-junior
college national spokesmen attempted to reaccess [sic]
the nature and needs of the "non-transferring" transfer
student. It will be recalled that B. Lamar Johnson
attempted to persuade California community-junior
college administrators to be "talent scouts" in search
of many different types of student talent and potential
rather than screening agents looking for student
weaknesses and inabilities. This theme has been
promoted also by Edmund J. Gleazer, Jr., the major
spokesman for the community-junior college movement
today. In 1959, Gleazer expanded upon the idea of
different types of intelligence, a novel idea at that
time in the community-junior college ideology:

There is not only the kind of intelligence
which characterizes the mathematician and the
scientist. There is the intelligence of the
artist whose insights cannot be classified or
described by quantitative means. There is
the intelligence of manipulative skill, the
dexterity of supple and nimble fingers guided
by a mind that seems tuned to the rhythm of
sound and the beat of the machine. There is
the social intelligence of the teacher with
keen sensitivity to the frustrations and the

---

[16]Dorothy Knoell, "A Critical Review of Research on
the College Dropout," in The College Dropout and the
Utilization of Talent, ed. by L.A. Pervin, L.E. Peik,
and W. Dalrymple (Princeton University Press, 1966), p.
80.

triumphs of her students. There is the
administrative intelligence of the man who
can bring understanding and agreement out of
the differences of strong minds divided in
opinion. And there is the intelligence of
tenderness and compassion of the nurse who
ministers to humankind in valleys of pain and
discouragement.[17]

In his 1968 treatise on the community college, Gleazer
combines factors such as too much status-consciousness,
individual abilities, social need, and varieties of
intelligence to reinforce the ideal of distributing
students more diversely in educational programs:

The problem begins with an enthusiasm in
our society for the "upper" (white collar)
occupations, emphasizing the professional and
managerial categories and consequently giving
lower status to other occupational
categories. In a nation which encourages
aspiration and puts its faith in economic and
social mobility, there is nothing wrong with
this--if a person can indeed qualify for the
presumably greater responsibilities at the
top of the ladder and if society can use him.
Realistically, however, one must face the
fact of an almost infinite variety of human
talent and a bewildering array of societal
tasks. It is to be hoped that talents and
tasks can be linked up. Among the most
urgent obligations of education is that of
removing the handicaps that interfere with
this process.[18]

For most of its existence, the community-junior
college ideology has divided community-junior college
students into transfer and terminal categories. Even
students who stated that they were transfer students
and who enrolled in transfer curricula were viewed,
theoretically, as terminal students if they were not
somehow predestined to transfer. The rationale
supporting this view has been undermined, however, by
an awareness that the two types of students are not
really as different as believed. Furthermore, the needs
of terminal students which were determined by
community-junior college educators were not the needs
expressed by those students themselves, even after the
students were processed through systems of counseling

---

[17]Edmund J. Gleazer, Jr., "From the Executive
Director's Desk," Junior College Journal, XXIX (March,
1959), 424.
[18]Edmund J. Gleazer, Jr., This Is the Community
College (Boston: Houghton Mifflin, 1968), p. 71

and guidance.   To survive at all, it is obvious
that the community-junior college ideology has to
incorporate a new view of students; indeed, a new view
of human nature.   This will not be easily done, for the
old dichotomy goes deep into the structure of the
ideology and affects all of its parts.   Perhaps the
ideas of Johnson and Gleazer are the beginning of a new
perspective on students, and perhaps the views of human
nature held by Cross and other emerging leaders will
further the change.   At this point in time, however,
most of the ideas and structures in the community-
junior college movement reflect the traditional view
that students, indeed all men, can be ranked and
trained to the competency demanded at their level, a
level determined by their nature and by the needs of
society.

28. VOCATIONAL EDUCATION: CRISIS IN CREDIBILITY?

The claims of vocational education advocates have become very optimistic, pervasive, and alluring. Fred Pincus argues in this article that these claims are also misleading. He finds in community college vocational education a well-orchestrated response to the rising educational expectations of working-class Americans. Yet, a careful examination of the history and growth of vocational education leads him to question seriously its actual benefits to prospective workers.

Fred L. Pincus wrote this article while an assistant professor of sociology at the University of Maryland, Baltimore County Campus, Baltimore, Maryland. His professional interests include the political economy of community colleges and education in the People's Republic of China.

Fred L. Pincus, "The False Promises of Community Colleges: Class Conflict and Vocational Education," Harvard Educational Review, Vol. 50 (No. 3, 1980), 332, 333, 348, 349-350, 352-356. Pincus includes an extensive listing of references at the end of his article (pages 357-361). Only a few vital citations are identified here.

The 1970's brought hard times for young people as the
economic security previously promised by a liberal arts
bachelor's degree was replaced by fierce competition
for a relatively small number of college-level jobs.
Between 1974 and 1977, unemployment rates for college
graduates under 25 years of age ranged from 5 percent
to 8.3 percent. Between one-fourth and one-half of
those graduates who found jobs were "underemployed";
that is, they held jobs that did not require a
college degree.

*****

One alternative [to a 4-year degree] was to encourage
students to enroll in a terminal vocational program of
two years or less. . . . In such programs students
could be taught specialized skills and after graduation
enter one of the middle-level occupations that could
provide them with more job satisfaction and economic
security than most jobs not requiring a degree. In a
tight job market the argument continues, a graduate of
a two-year vocational program might be better off than
a student with a four-year liberal arts degree.
Community colleges offer a college curriculum that
prepares students to transfer to a four-year school and
a terminal vocational curriculum that provides students
with skills needed to enter the labor market. These
two-year colleges screen out students who do not have
the skills to complete a bachelor's degree and,
instead, channel them toward an appropriate vocational
program. Community college teachers and counselors
have the job of convincing students with
"unrealistically" high aspirations to be "realistic";
to enroll in a terminal vocational program or flunk out
with no degree at all - a process referred to as the
"cooling out" function. . . .
Supporters of vocational education see this process
as beneficial to just about everyone. Corporations get
the kind of workers they need; four-year colleges do
not waste resources on students who will drop out;
students get decent jobs; and the political dangers of
an excess of college graduates are avoided.

*****

Do students get the jobs for which they were trained?
The most direct approach to answering this question is
to ask the students to describe their current job and
then determine to what degree it is related to their
field of study. . . . Wilms (1975) learned that only
half of the students actually held jobs for which they
were trained. Students in dental assistance,
secretarial, and cosmetology programs were the most

likely to hold related jobs; students in accounting, programming, and electronics technology were the least likely.

*****

Unemployment Among Former Community College Vocational Students

To evaluate the extent of unemployment among former vocational students, it is necessary to compare their level of unemployment with some estimate of the national rate. The national statistics include only those people actively looking for work, so we also excluded former vocational students who were housewives, in the military, or otherwise unavailable for work. Since we decided to use people 16-24 years of age who were not enrolled in school as the national measure of unemployment, we also excluded those former vocational students who were still enrolled in school.

*****

As the data indicate, unemployment rates among former vocational students are high. The median unemployment rate for vocational graduates not enrolled in school was 9.2 percent. Unemployment for vocational dropouts was generally higher than it was for graduates.

National unemployment rates for 16-to-24-year-olds not enrolled in school were available for 1974-1977. The median unemployment rate for 16-to-24-year-old college graduates was 6.5 percent during those years, significantly lower than unemployment among vocational graduates. Young people with 1 to 3 years of college had a median unemployment rate of 8.8 percent, slightly lower than the rate for vocational graduates. High school graduates had an unemployment rate of 11.3 percent, higher than the rate for vocational graduates. The only available national statistic for postsecondary vocational graduates shows that 7.1 percent were unemployed in 1976 (Dearman & Plisko, 1979), an unemployment rate identical to 16-to-24-year-old college graduates for that year.

Although these data are far from conclusive, they do not fully support the optimistic claims made by vocational education advocates. Clearly, vocational graduates are less likely to be unemployed than those who graduated from high school. In all probability, vocational graduates are more likely to be unemployed than college graduates, though as likely to be unemployed as those with some college. The best that can be said is that vocational graduates are no more likely to be unemployed than college graduates. State-

by-state unemployment data that control for age and
level of education would be a more precise measure of
unemployment among vocational graduates, but these data
are not available. However, considering the amount of
money and effort that the advocates of vocational
education use to convince students that vocational
education will lead to some kind of economic security,
it is their responsibility to prove their case.

Income of Former Vocational Students

*****

The most significant finding of Table 4 is that,
contrary to the claims of vocational schools,
nongraduates tend to have higher incomes than
graduates. . . .
In the Illinois study, which included both part-time
and full-time workers, students who dropped out during
the first year made almost $2,000 more than those who
graduated after one year. Students who had more than
one year of college, but who did not graduate, made
over $1,600 more than those who graduated after two
years. The Virginia study, which included only full-
time workers, asked former students to indicate the
salary of their first job after leaving college and of
their present job. Nongraduates made almost $400 less
than graduates on their initial jobs, but over $600
more on their present jobs.
The Maryland study, which included only full-time
workers employed in the fields for which they were
trained, asked for starting and present salaries and
also differentiated between those who began a new job
after leaving college and those who kept the same job
they held while in college. For those beginning a new
job, graduates were better off than nongraduates in
both starting salaries and present salaries. Graduates
had a $1,000 advantage in their starting salaries but
only a $200 advantage in their present salaries. In
other words, the graduates were losing ground to the
nongraduates. Among those Maryland students who kept
the same job, nongraduates were better off than
graduates in both starting and present salaries. In
fact, the gap in earnings between graduates and
nongraduates increased: the nongraduate advantage was
less than $1,500 in their starting jobs, but over
$2,000 in their present jobs.
In the South Carolina study, which included all
former students regardless of employment status,
graduates held a slim $264 advantage. This is the only
study to show that graduates had higher incomes than
nongraduates. Two other studies show that nongraduates
had the advantage, and a third shows mixed results.

TABLE 4
Annual Incomes of Graduates and Nongraduates of
Community College
Vocational Programs in Four States

State (Year)	Graduates	(n)	Nongraduates	(n)
Virginia				
Initial income[a]	$5,320	(1,505)	$4,934	(2,232)
Latest income[b] (1972)	6,759	(1,571)	7,049	(2,358)
Illinois				
First year[c] (1975)	5,508	(254)	7,452	(779)
Second year[d] (1976)	6,792	(774)	8,436	(439)
Maryland				
Began new Job				
Initial income[a]	7,486	(232)	6,469	(233)
Latest income[b] (1976)	9,636	(271)	9,212	(268)
Kept Same Job				
Initial income[a]	7,717	(45)	9,184	(267)
Latest income[b] (1976)	9,471	(50)	11,528	(330)
South Carolina (1977)	7,656	(706)	7,392	(1,181)

[a] Income of first job after leaving college; since not all students left at the same time, these data refer to salaries in several different years.

[b] Income of most recent job.

[c] Students who graduated or dropped out within one year.

[d] Students who dropped out after one year or who graduated within two years.

What are some possible explanations for these
findings?   First, it has been suggested that
nongraduates tend to be those who already have jobs and
come to college for only one or two courses to upgrade
their skills.   This, however, cannot explain the
Maryland findings that of those who still held the same
job they had while in college, nongraduates were better
off than graduates.   In addition, Table 1 showed that
nongraduates tend to have higher unemployment rates
than graduates.   A second possible explanation is that
students continue in school only if they cannot find a
job; those who find work drop out.   Consequently,
nongraduates often have been working longer than
graduates.   If this is the case, nongraduates would be
expected to have higher salaries due to length of job
tenure.   However, none of the studies provide data that
can answer this question.
The economic benefits of vocational education are at
best modest.   Although most students get jobs in the
fields for which they are trained, a substantial
minority does not.   The employment rate of vocational
graduates is no better than that of college graduates,
and it may be much worse.   It is impossible to make any
clear statements about the relative incomes of
vocational graduates and college graduates.   Among
vocational graduates, women make less than men because
they enroll in programs which prepare them for low-
paid, sex-sterotyped jobs, and, although dropouts from
vocational programs are more likely to be unemployed
than graduates, they tend to have higher incomes if
they do find a job.   The data presented here do not
support the claims of community college advocates that
vocational education is the road to economic security
and social mobility.   The status of middle-level jobs
is often exaggerated; most of these jobs involve only
modest skills, little if any decision-making power, and
few opportunities for advancement.
The leaders of business and government regard
vocational education as an institution for solving
political and economic problems stemming from the
rising aspirations of the working-class and minority
populations who are the main constituencies for
vocational programs.   These data suggest, however, that
terminal vocational education may be part of a tracking
system that reproduces and legitimates the social and
economic inequalities that are endemic in a capitalist
society.   Working-class and minority students are
overrepresented in vocational programs in general, and
in lower-level vocational programs in particular.
Women, who comprise over half of community college
enrollment, have been led to believe that terminal
vocational education can help overcome sex inequalities
in employment, but the data suggest that this

optimistic view is false. Vocational education in community colleges helps reproduce sex inequality as well as class and racial inequality.

So-called meritocratic standards give legitimacy to the tracking function of community colleges and make the resulting class and race inequalities appear inevitable. As the foreword to the HEW-sponsored Study of the Achievement of Our Nation's Students concludes: "The schools go along with society's tendency to route children of privileged families into privileged positions, and to route under-privileged children to under-privileged positions. It is not a plot on anybody's part or a conscious policy of education; it is just the way things work out" (Mayeske, 1973, p. iii).

Most advocates of terminal vocational education would probably agree with this statement. They would probably add that the educational and economic inequalities accompanying vocational education are the best that can be expected, given the nature of American capitalism in the last quarter of the twentieth century. Others understand the community colleges' role as trying to resolve some of the contradictions of American capitalism. For example, a former community college president states: "If historical evidence can be used as a guide to future events, no matter what the shape of the nation's economy, it is certain that the educational opportunities for the unemployed cannot be curtailed. National security and welfare will depend upon how the community colleges can provide a safety valve for the alleviation of the public discontent and revolutionary tendencies" (Monroe, 1972, p. 385).

However, even safety valves have their limits. In recent years, increasing numbers of community college advocates have called for a new sense of realism. For example, Arthur Cohen (1975), Director of ERIC Clearinghouse for Junior College, states: "Admit that college is not for everyone. . . . How much rhetoric is enough? It is one thing to make high sounding promises in order to gain funding that will allow maintenance of certain necessary levels of service. But if the gap between expectations and realities is a mark of discontent, then community college proponents might well ask how much is added to the general state of social anxiety by promoting jobs, higher status, and so on to all matriculants" (p. 63).

The consumerism movement and its emphasis on truth-in-advertising has reinforced this new realism. In addition to raising false hopes which could result in a crisis of credibility, community colleges risk being taken to court by dissatisfied customers, that is, students. . . . A report issued by the Federal Trade Commission (FTC) in December 1978 documented the false claims made by proprietary postsecondary vocational institutions about job availability, placement of graduates, and potential salaries of graduates. The FTC has issued a set of regulations which requires proprietary schools to substantiate their advertising claims or face stiff fines.[11] But the FTC specifically excludes public community colleges and vocational schools from these new regulations, despite evidence that some of these public institutions "have engaged in questionable advertising and enrollment practices" (Federal Trade Commission, 1978, pp. 38-39, see also Fields, 1979). It is probably true that the administrators and governing boards of public institutions do not resort to the blatant claims of profit-making schools, but they do remain interested in promoting vocational education and reducing the oversupply of college graduates. Hence, they tend to portray middle-level jobs in the best possible light in spite of the fact that these jobs lack many of the advantages of college-level jobs. How else could a counselor convince students to enroll in teacher aide programs that lead to jobs which pay half the salary of the teachers they will be helping?

The United States economy places limits on the ability of the leaders of business and government to bring the educational system into complete and permanent correspondence with the needs of the labor markets. . . . The new sense of realism among some vocational education supporters might well reduce the enrollment in vocational programs as students strive for upward mobility through four-year colleges, causing an even greater oversupply of college graduates. On the other hand, if the optimistic marketing campaign of the [U.S.] Office of Education and the Advertising Council succeeds in swelling enrollments in terminal vocational programs, these graduates could become disenchanted when the jobs they receive are something less than what they had been led to expect. In a few years, there might well be an oversupply of middle-level workers to add to the present oversupply of college-level workers (Bellico, 1979). Finally, if the salaries of middle-level workers begin to increase, past trends show these workers will be replaced by machines and will need additional training. Economic recessions and

---

[11]A federal appeals court overturned part of the FTC regulations in December 1978, saying that they were too broad and not clearly enough linked to proven trade school abuses (Fields, 1980).

reductions in municipal services will also result in layoffs. For example, during the New York City fiscal crisis, the number of teachers' aides employed in the public schools dropped from 13,500 in April 1974, to only 9,500 in September 1976. . . .

Capitalism in the United States cannot always deliver what it promises. There are a limited number of decent, well-paid jobs, and most working-class and nonwhite young people are not destined to get them. Vocational education does not and cannot change this. Cohen (1975) discusses some of the dilemmas arising from the egalitarian ideal of open access: "If, as it is alleged, college attendance enhances social standing, then open access, especially if it changes the lines of social stratification, must have a negative effect on certain groups. Who are those groups? What form will their discontent take? Will those who have positions near the top of the heap lose status? If so, how can they be convinced that egalitarianism is desirable?" (pp. 160-161).

Cohen is right when he says that changes in the stratification system "must have a negative effect on certain groups." But it is not simply a case of men giving up jobs to women or whites giving up college seats to Blacks. Business and government leaders - those at the top of the heap - regard postsecondary vocational education as a means of solving the political and economic problems created by the rising expectations of the working class. "If one accepts the existing system of social stratification, there is an almost irresistible logic to the vocational training argument; there are, after all, manpower shortages to be filled and it is true that not everyone can be a member of the elite" (Karabel, 1972, p. 557). Many educators who support postsecondary vocational education probably see the resulting inequalities as the best that can be hoped for.

But things look different to the students destined for the middle-level jobs. More and more working-class and minority students want to use college as a way up the ladder, while the Carnegie Commission, the Advertising Council, and the Department of Health, Education and Welfare, knowing that there is not much room at the top, want to convince them to lower their aspirations and redefine their goals.

It is important that working-class and minority students understand that vocational education in community colleges benefits their employers more than themselves. These students have a right to protest being tracked into low-paid dead-end jobs. They also have reason to question why economic security and meaningful work remain so elusive in the world's richest country.

In viewing vocational education as a way of adjusting students' aspirations to present economic realities, business leaders, the Office of Education, and commissions on higher education endorse vocational education as a means of preventing student unrest. If community college educators want to help working-class and minority students, they should provide them with a historical and political context from which to understand the dismal choices they face. Vocational education students might then begin to raise some fundamental questions about the legitimacy of educational, political, and economic institutions in the United States.

References:

Bellico, R. Higher education: Crisis of expectations. Educational Record, 1979, 60, 93-98.

Cohen, A. M., & Associates. College responses to community demands. San Francisco: Jossey-Bass, 1975.

Dearman, N.B., & Plisko, V.W. The condition of education: 1979 edition. Washington, D.C.: U.S. Government Printing Office, 1979.

Federal Trade Commission. Vocational schools trade regulation rule: Statement basis and purpose. Washington, D.C.: Author, 1978.

Fields, C.M. FTC adopts stiff rules to regulate advertising by vocational institutions. Chronicle of Higher Education, January 8, 1979, p. 16.

Fields, C.M. Strict FTC rules on proprietary schools struck down by federal appeals court. Chronicle of Higher Education, January 7, 1980, pp. 15, 20.

Karabel, J. Community colleges and social stratification. Harvard Educational Review, 1972, 42, 521-562.

Mayeske, G.W. A study of the achievement of our nation's students. Washington, D.C.: U.S. Government Printing Office, 1973.

Monroe, C.R. Profile of the community college. San Francisco: Jossey-Bass, 1972.

Somers, G.G., Sharp, L.M., & Myint, T. The effectiveness of vocational and technical programs. Madison, Wis.: Center for Studies in Vocational and Technical Education, 1971.

Wilms, W.W. Public and proprietary vocational training: A study of effectiveness. Lexington, Mass.: Lexington Books, 1975.

29. WHERE ARE THE VISIONS OF THE FUTURE?

The shock of precarious economic conditions, severe questioning of the American educational establishment and its capabilities to provide both access and quality, a dampening of the seemingly unquenchable spirit of optimism once held by community college boosters--all these and more combined to turn the early 1980's into a time of uncertainty.

Has the community college movement become fatigued? Complacent? Is it living off the energy and drive of days gone by? Is it in danger of losing its uniqueness, its special contributions to American education?

Cross presents a provocative analysis of community college goals. She suggests the movement has reached a hiatus in its growth, that the motivating dreams of yesteryear have lost their compelling energy. New dreams have not yet appeared to serve as guiding stars for the movement, Cross contends.

Kathryn Patricia Cross has been director of research and distinguished research scientist with the Educational Testing Service, Princeton, New Jersey, and research educator for the Center for Research and Development in Higher Education, University of California, Berkeley. She has written widely on higher education students and organizations including the community college.

K. Patricia Cross, "Community Colleges on the Plateau," Journal of Higher Education, Vol. 52 (March/April, 1981), 113-123.

In this article I shall put forth the thesis that the late 1970s and early 1980s represent a plateau between two periods of high energy and a sense of mission in the community colleges. The old ideals that sparked enthusiasm and the sense of common purpose in community colleges have receded, and new ideals have not yet emerged to take their place. Meanwhile, community colleges sit, not altogether comfortably, on a plateau assimilating and consolidating the social changes of the 1950s and 1960s, concerned about what the future holds.

This thesis is suggested by some recent data on community college goals collected by Educational Testing Service in a field test of its new Community College Goals Inventory. . . . In January and February of 1979, the CCGI was administered to eighteen geographically dispersed community colleges ranging north and south from Main to Florida and east to west from Massachusetts to California. Almost fifteen hundred faculty members, administrators, and trustees reacted to statements about the goals of their institution, as they see them now and as they wished they could be. At the same time, almost three thousand full-time and part-time students and a small community group of two hundred citizens expressed their opinions about the goals of their local college. When data for the twenty goals of the CCGI were analyzed, a sobering picture emerged.

Table 1 gives brief titles for the twenty goals assessed by the CCGI. Each goal is measured by four items in the inventory, and respondents are asked to make judgments about how important 'each statement is and how important it should be. Mean scores are computed for each item, and the means are rank-ordered with a rank of 1 indicating that the goal was assigned top priority by the group, whereas a rank of 20 indicates low importance. The top five Should Be goals for each constituent group have been marked with an asterisk.

As indicated by the consistently high rankings for vocational-technical preparation in Table 1, all of the groups agree that community colleges have a major obligation to provide vocational/technical education for students. The vocational-technical goal of CCGI consists of the following four items: (1) to provide opportunities for students to prepare for specific vocational/technical careers, such as accounting, air conditioning and refrigeration, nursing, and so on; (2) to offer educational programs geared to new and emerging career fields; (3) to provide opportunities to update or upgrade present job skills; and (4) to provide retraining opportunities for individuals who wish to qualify for new careers or acquire new job

Table 1
Ranks for Is and Should-Be Goals of Community Colleges

Goals		Faculty N=1064	Administrators N=321	Trustees N=94	Students N=2866	Community N=203
General Education	SB	2.5*	4.0*	3.0*	3.0*	4.0*
	IS	1.0	1.0	2.0	1.0	1.0
Intellect. orient.	SB	2.5*	6.0	4.0*	5.0*	4.0*
	IS	9.0	10.0	8.5	3.0	6.5
Lifelong learning	SB	10.0	8.0	10.0	9.0	8.5
	IS	4.0	7.0	6.0	5.0	3.5
Cultural/aesthetic awareness	SB	19.0	19.5	19.0	20.0	20.0
	IS	19.0	19.0	19.0	20.0	20.0
Personal develop.	SB	7.0	9.5	9.0	4.0*	4.0*
	IS	11.0	13.0	14.0	12.0	12.0
Humanism/altruism	SB	15.0	16.0	15.0	15.0	14.5'
	IS	16.0	18.0	18.0	17.0	17.0
Vocational/tech. preparation	SB	4.0*	1.0*	1.0*	2.0*	1.0*
	IS	2.0	2.0	1.0	2.0	2.0
Developmental/ remedial prep.	SB	5.0*	3.0*	6.5	6.5	6.0
	IS	10.0	12.0	11.0	8.5	14.0
Community services	SB	18.0	17.0	17.0	18.0	17.5
	IS	14.0	15.0	16.0	18.0	18.0
Social criticism	SB	20.0	19.5	20.0	19.0	19.0
	IS	20.0	20.0	20.0	19.0	19.0
Counseling and advising	SB	9.0	7.0	8.0	1.0*	2.0*
	IS	5.0	4.0	7.0	6.5	11.0
Student services	SB	16.0	14.0	14.0	6.5	12.0
	IS	6.0	5.0	12.0	4.0	9.5
Faculty/staff development	SB	6.0	9.5	11.0	12.0	13.0
	IS	13.0	11.0	10.0	14.0	15.0
Intellectual environment	SB	11.0	13.0	12.0	11.0	10.0
	IS	15.0	16.0	14.0	15.0	13.0

232

Table 1 continued

Goals		Faculty N=1064	Administrators N=321	Trustees N=94	Students N=2866	Community N=203
Innovation	SB	13.0	15.0	16.0	16.5	16.0
	IS	17.0	17.0	17.0	16.0	16.0
College community	SB	1.0*	2.0*	2.0*	8.0	7.0
	IS	18.0	14.0	8.5	13.0	9.5
Freedom	SB	17.0	18.0	18.0	16.5	17.5
	IS	8.0	9.0	14.0	8.5	8.0
Accessibility	SB	12.0	11.0	13.0	10.0	14.5
	IS	3.0	3.0	5.0	6.5	6.5
Effective	SB	8.0	5.0*	6.5	14.0	11.0
management	IS	12.0	8.0	4.0	10.0	5.0
Accountability	SB	14.0	12.0	5.0*	13.0	8.5
	IS	7.0	6.0	3.0	11.0	3.5

Source: Ranks derived from the Community Colleges Goals Inventory Preliminary Data Report, Educational Testing Service, 1979.

Note: SB = Should Be; IS = Is.

*High priority SB goals (top 5).

skills.   Data not shown in Table 1 indicate that 84
percent of the combined group of faculty,
administrators, trustees, and staff ranked vocational-
technical preparation high or extremely high in
importance, and 80 percent of the students gave it an
equally solid endorsement.   Moreover, when respondents
were asked to indicate how much importance Is currently
assigned by their college to the vocational/technical
preparation of students, all constituent groups
expressed satisfaction by ranking vocational-technical
preparation among the top two goals currently being
carried out.

The situation is comparable for the set of four CCGI
items that make up the goal of general education, which
includes items regarding "the acquisition of general
knowledge, achievement of some level of basic
competences, preparation of students for further, more
advanced work, and the acquisition of skills and
knowledge to live effectively in society."   Table 1
shows that all constituent groups ranked general
education among their top five Should Be goals, and
that all feel that the goal of general education is
currently given very high priority by their college.

Most community colleges were established as
comprehensive postsecondary institutions, with the
intention of providing education for careers as well as
general education, and that intention is firmly
established in the faculties and curriculum of most
community colleges.   Thus it would be surprising if
there were not high agreement on the importance of
those kingpins of community college education, and it
would be disappointing, to say the least, if those
closest to the community colleges felt that those
missions were not being accomplished.

What is surprising is that a founding principle of
the community colleges, equal access, does not make the
top five Should Be goals of any constituent group. The
CCGI goal that expresses the concern for equal access
is labeled accessibility and is defined as "Maintaining
costs to students at a level that will not deny
attendance because of financial need, offering programs
that accommodate adults in the community, recruiting
students who have been denied, have not valued, or have
not been successful in formal education, and with a
policy of open admissions, developing worthwhile
educational experiences for all those admitted." Many
people, especially those who were most active in the
founding of community colleges, thought opening the
routes of access to college for all those previously
denied a college education was a major commitment of
the community colleges. Now, however, faculty and
administrators, at least, seem to feel that that goal
has been accomplished; they rank accessibility third in

current importance, indicating that their college is presently giving high priority to accessibility. While Table 1 shows that all groups rank accessibility substantially higher in current accomplishments than on Should Be goals, it is important to recognize that the ranks shown in Table 1 show relative priorities.[2] Actually, most people still think that accessibility is an important Should Be goal. Mean absolute scores for the five groups fall between 3.64 and 4.01, where 3 represents "medium" and 4 "high" importance. What these data seem to say is that while the constituent groups of community colleges are not turning their backs on making college more accessible, there is a feeling that present practices with respect to accessibility are acceptable, and other issues now have higher priority.

For the most part, the Should Be goal statements that are pushing the issue of accessibility relatively lower are those concerned with teaching students who have already obtained access. Intellectual orientation and developmental-remedial preparation, for example, are given high Should Be rankings by all of the constituent groups. The intellectual orientation goal of the CCGI includes items concerned with teaching students how to solve problems, synthesize knowledge, think openly about new ideas, and undertake self-directed learning. The goal of developmental/remedial preparation includes "recognizing, assessing, and counseling students with basic skills needs, providing developmental programs that recognize different learning styles and rates, assuring that students in developmental programs achieve appropriate levels of competence, and evaluating basic skills programs."

Those two goals refer not so much to the establishment in the curriculum of subject matter content, such as vocational/technical education and general education, but rather to working with students to inculcate intellectual values and skills. Teaching students intellectual skills and appreciations is an age-old educational goal, and there will probably never be full satisfaction with how much attention is given to it and how well it is done. Faculty, in particular, think teaching students intellectual skills and appreciations is highly important, ranking it among their top three Should Be goals, but they rank it in ninth place when it comes to the attention that is

---

[2]Mean Should Be scores are almost always higher than Is scores, that is, all groups think things could be improved. But when relative rankings are used, an Is rank may stand above a Should Be rank.

currently given to it. Only students appear well
satisfied with the current emphasis on intellectual
orientation.

Developmental/remedial preparation of students is a
recent and special instructional goal for community
colleges, and dissatisfaction with current attention to
it is evident. The discrepancy between what Is and
what Should Be in the realm of developmental/remedial
education is very high for the three groups
representing leadership in community colleges -
faculty, administrators, and trustees. People in the
community are also sensitive to the problem. Indeed,
it seems to stand today as one of the major
dissatisfactions in the community college. Although
the research of the past decade shows no easy answers
to the massive problems of teaching open admissions
students lacking basic academic skills (see Cross [3]
and Maxwell [7]), the recognition of its importance,
combined with the dissatisfactions of community college
leaders with the attention it is currently getting,
should bode well for continued and maybe even renewed
attacks on the problem.

One of the ways to find solutions to either new or
old problems is through innovation and experimentation,
but things do not look very bright for the future of
innovation in the community colleges. When Peterson
[8] carried out his study of the goals of California
colleges, he found a fairly high interest in innovation
in the California colleges, especially among
administrators, but also among faculty. Today, faculty
rank innovation (defined by the CCGI as a climate in
which continuous educational innovation is an accepted
way of life) thirteenth in Should Be goals and
seventeenth in current importance among the twenty
goals of the CCGI. Administrators and trustees offer
no more hope for optimism; they rank innovation among
the lowest five goals in Should Be importance, as well
as in current emphasis. While most people think
innovation should be more important than it is, it is
clearly not a major direction for the immediate future.
A related CCGI scale labeled faculty/staff development
would emphasize exposing faculty to new knowledge to
improve their teaching, but it doesn't fare much better
than innovation. While faculty think it should rank
sixth in importance, they think it does rank
thirteenth, and since administrators and trustees rank
it down in the middle of the list of Should Be goals,
it doesn't appear to have a strong position on the
agenda for the 1980s.

Finally, we should take a look at the remaining goals
given very high (top five) Should Be rankings by any
constituent group. Students are especially interested
in personal development and in counseling and advising,

administrators are interested in effective management,
and trustees are giving accountability a high Should Be
ranking.   These rankings represent what I would call
"special interest" concerns.   Of these, the greatest
dissatisfaction lies in student perceptions of the
attention given to their personal development and to
counseling and advising.   Personal development is
defined by the following four items of the CCGI: (1)
to help students identify their personal goals and
develop means for achieving them; (2) to help students
develop a sense of self-worth, self-confidence, and
self-direction; (3) to help students achieve deeper
levels of self-understanding; and (4) to help students
be open, honest, and trusting in their relationships.
These goals are presumably accomplished, in part,
through counseling and advising, and students are
intensely unhappy with present attention to both
counseling and advising[3] and personal development.   Not
shown here is a discrepancy index, which is derived for
CCGI goals by subtracting mean Is scores from mean
Should Be scores.   For each one of the four student
groups tabulated - full-time transfer and career
students and part-time transfer and career students -
the discrepancy index is higher for personal
development and counseling and advising than for any of
the remaining eighteen.   Students are joined in their
concern by citizens of the community.   Data from other
constituent groups, however, suggest that while
attention to the personal development of students is
not a top priority goal, it should be given more
attention.   Counseling and advising, however, is
already seen as ranking somewhat higher relative to
other goals than it should be.   With colleges trimming
budgets by cutting back on counseling and nonteaching
positions, the future does not look bright for meeting
student desires for some help with decisions beyond the
classroom.
     The special interests of administrators and trustees
meet a similar fate.   Trustees perceive accountability
as among the top five goals for their college, but
faculty and administrators have other priorities; they
rate accountability in the lower half among their
Should Be goals.   Even so, administrators admit that
accountability is "of high importance" (M=3.97); it's
just that other goals seem more important now.
Management, the special interest of administrators,
does not appear to be a critical issue.   Administrators

---

[3]Counseling and advising includes items calling
for career counseling, personal counseling services,
academic advising, and job placement services.

regard it as very important, and they get a fair amount of support from faculty and trustees. Contrary to popular thought, the data from this small sample of citizens of the community suggest that they are more concerned about improving counseling, advising, and attention to the personal development of students than they are with management and accountability.

I have left until last the discussion of the goal that is of paramount importance to the leadership of community colleges - and a cause for immense dissatisfaction. Faculty give college community top priority in their Should Be ratings but rank it near the bottom in current emphasis. The college community goal of the CCGI is defined as "Fostering a climate in which there is faculty and staff commitment to the goals of the college, open and candid communication, open and amiable airing of differences, and mutual trust and respect among faculty, students, and administrators." In one sense, college community is a measure of morale. While faculty, students, administrators, and trustees are firmly convinced of the critical importance of trust, open communication, and commitment, most do not find it on their own campuses.

It is hard to conclude with authority that esprit de corps in the community colleges has deteriorated significantly over the past decade, but from the data available, it appears that mutual trust and respect is less prevalent on community college campuses today than it was in the early 1970s. Data from Project Focus [2] show that ninety community college presidents ranked the goal of encouraging "mutual trust and respect among faculty, students, and administrators" first on Should Be goals and second in accomplishment. Peterson [8] reported that California community college administrators ranked community (defined by the same four items in 1973 as today) as second on Should Be goals and third on Is; faculty ranked it first among Should Be and seventh among Is goals. Thus it appears that morale, mutual trust, and respect are as desirable as ever, but the discrepancy between what people would like to have and what they think they do have on their own campuses has grown in a distressing direction. It is probable, I think, that morale in most institutions of postsecondary education is lower today than it was a decade ago. Declining enrollments and reduced funding are bound to increase internal competition, and retrenchment is quite likely to generate dissention and mistrust.

Almost as interesting as the goals that are important in community colleges today are those that are not. The goals that dominated college campuses in the 1960s are ranked very low in importance as we enter the

1980s. Goals such as freedom (protecting the rights of faculty and students to present and hear controversial ideas and to engage in off-campus political activities); social criticism (helping to bring about change in the society,); and humanism/altruism (respect for diverse cultures, understanding of moral issues, and pursuit of world peace) are ranked very low in priority by every constituent group. The old idea that the academic community should serve as social critic is clearly rejected, with all groups giving it a rank of nineteen or twenty in both Is and Should Be ratings.

These data from the CCGI, while not necessarily representative of the broad scope of community colleges in the United States, seem to reflect so well what people are seeing and feeling in education, and in the broader society, that it is hard not to give considerable attention to the message. To me, the message seems to say that the old ideals of the 1960s that used to excite and inspire, albeit midst frequent controversy, are gone, and new ones have not yet emerged. In the meantime, community colleges are working on rather pragmatic, conventional goals, assimilating the social changes of the idealistic 1960s - a difficult and not always very rewarding task. It will take some clarity of vision and strong leadership to identify the new ideals that can unite and inspire to move community colleges off the plateau.

People can differ about where community colleges should direct their energies and resources for the future. One logical choice is to direct efforts toward the alleviation of high discrepancies between what is and what should be. That choice would have the obvious advantage of capitalizing on some potential momentum for change directed toward what most people think needs improvement. Searching Table 1 for goal statements where Should Be ranks are at least five ranks higher than Is ratings for three out of five constituent groups suggests that community colleges have potential momentum for improvement in three areas - college community, remedial education, and personal development of students. If community college leaders could marshall the latent energy that seems to exist for moving toward student-centered education, that is, helping students become academically competent as well as to grow personally, it is quite possible that the morale and esprit that constitute the college community goal would be natural by-products of working toward commonly accepted goals.

Since community colleges were established as teaching institutions with a concern for correcting past educational inequities, the scenario of working harder toward making community colleges more student-centered would be a reasonable goal. It is even possible that

such directed energies could fire community colleges
with the zeal that once burned bright for equal access.
    There are problems, of course.   When community
colleges were fired with the mission of bringing about
equal access, they had the field to themselves – and
the money and students to implement it.   Other colleges
were not, for the most part, interested in competing
for the clientele served by open admissions colleges.
Community colleges didn't have to prove they could do
the job better than other colleges; they just had to
express a willingness to do the job that society wanted
done.   Now, however, the field is quite crowded with
colleges eager to demonstrate their "student-
centeredness."   While community colleges have more
experience than most other institutions with remedial
education for students lacking basic academic skills,
there is, according to the CCGI, not much confidence on
campus that they know how to do it.   The prospect seems
even worse for establishing a reputation for attending
to the personal development of their largely commuting,
part-time clientele.   Research suggests that student
development is best accomplished in selective, private
residential colleges. [11].
    The other scenario for the future of community
colleges would be to follow a visionary course of
action rather than one dictated by common consensus.
This position probably has the advantage of generating
more missionary spirit than the common consensus model
– if a persuasive leader can convince the diverse
constituencies of community colleges that they have a
new mission.   Many, myself included, believe that a
visionary mission for community colleges lies in the
lifelong learning movement.   (Other people may have
other visions; there is no need for initial consensus
in the visionary scenario.)   No group of colleges is as
well situated as community colleges to serve the
growing army of commuting, part-time adult learners.
Although many colleges would like to capitalize on the
worldwide lifelong learning movement, their locations,
traditions, and faculty are rarely as well suited for
the mission of teaching largely career-oriented
subjects to pragmatic, commuting adult part-time
learners (see Cross [4] for research on the needs and
interests of adult part-time learners).   The comparison
could be made with an earlier era when community
colleges had the field to themselves in filling the
need of society for college access for unserved
segments of the society.   It was clearly an important
mission and no one else was doing it.   Some believe
that there is today a comparable need for providing
locally for the needs of adult part-time learners.
Edmund Gleazer [6] speaks of the "community's college"
with a mission to "involve the citizenry in learning

activities with the expectation that a better community
will result." The mission envisaged by Gleazer for
community colleges in the decade ahead is "to encourage
and facilitate lifelong learning, with community as
process and product."

However, Table 1 reveals that the visionary scenario
of moving community colleges off the plateau toward
lifelong learning has little apparent energy waiting to
be converted to action. The goal of lifelong learning
is perceived by most constituent groups as only
moderately important, and it seems to be getting
relatively more attention than most people think it
should. Community services fares even worse as a
potential rallying goal. Some of the lack of
enthusiasm for community services can probably be
attributed to funding problems. Proposition 13 in
California, for example, did considerable damage to
existing community education programs. It may be that
the constituencies of community colleges simply see the
goal of providing community services as unrealistic for
the 1980s.

These two scenarios for the future of community
colleges are based, it should be remembered, on
aggregated data across a group of colleges. The
analysis, however, is still appropriate for suggesting
future directions for individual colleges. Some
colleges might find the consensus model easier and more
realistic, whereas others might choose to follow the
vision of a dynamic leader. If colleges go their own
way, the community colleges will probably lose the
cohesiveness and zeal that was apparent among the
founders of community colleges who prized the
distinctiveness of the community college mission.
Community colleges would blend into the network of
postsecondary institutions, probably maintaining some
missions common to community colleges, but responding
largely to local goals.

The future of the community colleges cannot be
written yet. Possibly the spirit and cohesiveness
present in the founding of new institutions is a one-
time phenomenon, and community colleges are now
entering a less exuberant phase of maturity,
consolidating the major social reforms of the 1940s and
1950s. Possibly, the head start made by community
colleges into developmental/remedial education can be
parlayed into a position of national leadership on a
problem that is of increasing concern now to a majority
of institutions of higher education. Possibly, the
lifelong learning movement will provide the spark that
will reunite community colleges in a sense of common
mission.

References

1. Astin, A.W. Four Critical Years: Effects of College on Beliefs, Attitudes, and Knowledge. San Francisco: Jossey-Bass, 1977.

2. Bushnell, D.S., and I. Zagaris. Report from Project Focus: Strategies for Change. Washington, D.C.: American Association of Junior College, 1972.

3. Cross, K.P. Accent on Learning: Improving Instruction and Reshaping the Curriculum. San Francisco: Jossey-Bass, 1976.

4. _____ . "Adult Learners: Characteristics, Needs, and Interests." In Lifelong Learning in America, by R.E. Peterson and Associates. San Francisco: Jossey-Bass, 1979.

5. Educational Testing Service. Community College Goals Inventory: Preliminary Comparative Data. Princeton, N.J.: Educational Testing Service Community and Junior College Programs, 1979.

6. Gleazer, E.J. "Community Colleges: The Decade Ahead." Paper presented to the Florida Association of Community Colleges, Miami, Florida, November 1, 1979.

7. Maxwell, M. Improving Student Learning Skills: A Comprehensive Guide to Successful Practices and Programs for Increasing the Performance of Underprepared Students. San Francisco: Jossey-Bass, 1979.

8. Peterson, R.E. Goals for California Higher Education: A Survey of 116 College Communities. Sacramento: California Legislature, 1973.

BIBLIOGRAPHIC ESSAY

The formal literature on the junior and community college movement developed slowly. One of the earliest scholars to review the field and provide detailed analysis was Leonard V. Koos. His studies are reported in The Junior College, Vols. 1 and 2, Minneapolis: University of Minnesota Press, 1924, and The Junior College Movement, Boston: Ginn, 1925. Walter C. Eells added his significant work a few years later: The Junior College, Boston: Houghton Mifflin, 1931. Eells also debated the role of vocational education with two books: Present Status of Junior College Terminal Education and Why Junior College Terminal Education? both published in Washington, D.C.: American Association of Junior Colleges, both in 1941. Jesse P. Bogue contributed his support to the expanding mission of the community college in his The Community College, New York: McGraw-Hill, 1950.

Then came the 1960's. Leland L. Medsker's study of the two-year institution and movement resulted in his widely used volume The Junior College: Progress and Prospect, New York: McGraw-Hill, 1960. Building on the earlier efforts of the U.S. President's Commission on Higher Education, Higher Education for American Democracy, Washington, D.C.: U.S. Government Printing Office, 1947 (6 vols. in 1), the National Education Association issued its statement of strong support for access for all in Universal Opportunity for Education Beyond the High School, Washington, D.C.: Educational Policies Commission, National Education Association, 1964. A perceptive analysis and interpretation of these developing colleges appeared in 1965: Blocker, C.E., Plummer, W.,and Richardson, R.C., Jr., The Two-Year College: A Social Synthesis, Englewood Cliffs,

N.J.: Prentice-Hall. Michael Brick's Forum and Focus for the Junior College Movement, New York: Teachers College Press, 1965, positioned the American Association of Junior Colleges in the mainstream of two-year college development and explored the growth of the movement up to that time. By 1966 the literature was extensive and sufficiently varied that a selective and annotated bibliography of over 100 pages could be produced: Rarig, Emory W., Jr., (ed.), The Community Junior College: An Annotated Bibliography, New York: Teachers College Press. Emerging changes in the community college were described and reviewed by B. Lamar Johnson in Islands of Innovation Expanding: Changes in the Community College, Beverly Hills, Calif: Glencoe Press, 1969.

In the decade of the 1970's a plethora of volumes was published on a wide variety of topics and issues in the community college movement. A brief sampling: Carnegie Commission on Higher Education, The Open-Door College, New York: McGraw-Hill, 1970; Medsker, L., and Tillery, D., Breaking Down the Access Barriers: A Profile of Two Year Colleges, New York: McGraw-Hill, 1971; Monroe, C.R., Profile of the Community College: A Handbook, San Francisco: Jossey-Bass, 1972; Thornton, J.W., Jr., The Community Junior College, 3rd ed., New York: Wiley, 1972; Bushnell, D.S., Organizing for Change: New Priorities for Community Colleges, New York: McGraw-Hill, 1973; Cohen, A.M., and Associates, College Responses to Community Demands: The Community College in Challenging Times, San Francisco: Jossey-Bass, 1975; Zwerling, L.S., Second Best: The Crisis of the Community College, New York: McGraw-Hill, 1976; Rudolph, F., Curriculum: A History of the American Undergraduate Course of Study Since 1636, San Francisco: Jossey-Bass, 1977; London, H.B., The Culture of a Community College, New York: Praeger, 1978; Olivas M.A., The Dilemma of Access: Minorities in Two-Year Colleges, Washington, D.C.: Howard University Press, 1979.

Two books in the 1980's are of special value. Edmund J. Gleazer, Jr., then president of the American Association of Community and Junior Colleges, attempts to depict a future vision of the community college. He examines a concept of nexus, of connection, by which the community college becomes a link among and between a host of community groups and interests and their learning needs (see The Community College: Values, Vision, and Vitality, Washington, D.C.: American Association of Community and Junior Colleges, 1980). The other is a comprehensive review and critique of the community college: Cohen, A.M., and Brawer, F.B., The American Community College, San Francisco: Jossey-Bass, 1982. In addition to a wide-ranging analysis of

students, faculty, governance and administration,
finances, curriculum, instruction, and future mission,
the authors have provided an extensive bibliography of
books, journal articles, and "fugitive" literature such
as dissertations. Further, an annotated bibliography
is supplied of prominent works in the community college
literature and major periodicals and monograph series.
Entries are categorized under five headings:
institutions, people, functions, journals, and
monograph series. This work is a most useful tool to
the student or scholar of the community college
movement.

This essay has focused on significant books. Access
to periodical and other literature about the community
college movement is important, too. One excellent
service is ERIC (Educational Resources Information
Center), an information system in existence since 1966
currently sponsored by the National Institute of
Education within the U.S. Department of Education.
ERIC provides users with ready access to English-
language literature dealing with education. Such aids
as Resources in Education and Current Index to Journals
in Education are found in most libraries; they are of
help to anyone seeking more information about the
community college movement. Copies of ERIC documents
are available from the ERIC Document Reproduction
Service (EDRS), Arlington, Virginia.

ERIC also includes a series of specialized
clearinghouses, each of which provides information and
assistance in locating literature in its assigned
field. The clearinghouse for community college
information is called "Junior Colleges" and is located
at the University of California, Los Angeles,
California. This clearinghouse has produced a variety
of in-depth analyses of community college topics and
issues.

Finally, the publisher Jossey-Bass has a quarterly
series of source books, each of which presents a
collection of essays addressing a single topic related
to community colleges. Each source book presents an
overview of current knowledge on the topics at hand,
theory and practice-based analyses, practical
suggestions for action, and further references.
Information is available from Jossey-Bass, Inc.,
Publishers, 433 California Street, San Francisco,
California 94104.

INDEX

ABOUT THE AUTHOR

THOMAS DIENER is Executive Director of Kentuckiana Metroversity in Louisville, Kentucky. He has contributed numerous articles and papers to journals and symposia in education, administration, and related areas.